The Shetland Bus

The Shetland Bus

David Howarth
Lieutenant-Commander R.N.V.R.

The Shetland Times Ltd.,
Lerwick.
1998.

CONTENTS

LIST OF ILLUSTRATIONS

LIST OF MAPS

FOREWORD

IT IS a pleasure to learn that a new edition of the World War II classic, *The Shetland Bus* by David Howarth, is being published. To a Norwegian this title is synonymous with courage, bravery and the will to fight oppression.

During the war a group of small Norwegian boats manned by Norwegian refugees, normally with a background as fishermen, maintained a route between The Shetland Islands and occupied Norway. Originally established and led by British military authorities, but later as a shared responsibility with the Royal Norwegian Navy, the main task was to land undercover agents and supply the Norwegian resistance movement with weapons and supplies for sabotage actions. Another important task was to bring Norwegian refugees to Shetland.

These operations obviously contributed to the Allied military operations and victory against Germany. At the same time these operations had an important psychological impact on the Norwegian population. *The Shetland Bus* was seen as a way to freedom from occupied Norway. But it also showed that it was possible to fight the occupation army even with small resources. After the war this was an important factor in the will to maintain a strong defence, and the decision to join NATO as a founding member in 1949.

The co-operation between Great Britain and Norway which is so well related in this book, added to the excellent relationship between our two countries during World War II, a relationship which is still so important to both countries.

Kjell Colding
Norwegian Ambassador in London
1998.

PREFACE

DURING THE German occupation of Norway, from 1940 to 1945, every Norwegian knew that small boats were constantly sailing from the Shetland Isles to Norway to land weapons and supplies and to rescue refugees. The Norwegians who stayed in Norway and struggled there against the invaders were fortified by this knowledge, and gave the small boats the familiar name which is used for the title of this book: 'to take the Shetland bus' became a synonym in Norway for escape when danger was overwhelming. This record of adventures of the Norwegian sailors who manned the boats is offered as a tribute from an English colleague to Norwegian seamanship, and as a humble memorial to those who lost their lives.

D. H.
Scalloway 1951

Approximate Pronunciation of some Proper Names

Aalen, Ove	*aw'len, ō've*	Klausen	*Klow'sen*
Ålesund	*aw'-le-soond*		
Andalsnes	*an-dalz-ness*	Larsen, Leif	*lar'sen, līf*
Aursund	*or-soond*	Leröy	*lā-roi*
Averö	*ah'ver-ŭ*	Lerwick	*ler'wik*
		Lofoten	*lo'fōt-en*
Baalsrud, Jan	*bawlz'rood, yan*	Lunna	*lŭn'a*
Berge	*ber'gĕ*		
Björnöy	*byŭr'noi*	Målöy	*mawl'oi*
Blystad, Per	*blees'ta, pār*	Mosjön	*mō-shyŭn*
Brekke, Ivar	*brek'e, ee'vahr*	Naeröy,	*nā'roi,*
Bremnes	*brem-ness*	August	*ow'goost*
Bueland	*boo-ĕ-land*	Nipen, Nils	*nee'pen, neelss*
		Nordsjöen	*nor(d)sh-yŭn*
Edöyfjord	*ā'doi-fyord*		
Eide	*ī'dĕ*	Øklandsvaag	*ŭk-lands-vawg*
Eidsheim	*īdz'him*		
Enoksen	*e'nok-sen*	Reine	*rā-nĕ*
Faeröy	*fā'roi*	Siglaos	*sig-lowss*
Fagerlid	*fahg'-er'lĭ*	Sjö	*shyŭ*
Feie	*fā'yĕ*	Skeia	*skā-ya*
		Smölen	*smŭl-en*
Gjertsen	*yert'sen*	Svinöy	*sveenoi*
Griphölen	*grip-hŭ-len*		
Grotle, Bård	*grot'lĕ, bord,*	Traena	*trāna*
Ole	*o-lĕ*	Tromsö	*trom-sŭ*
		Trondelag	*tron'de-lag*
Hauge, Leif	*howg'ĕ, lif*	Trondheim	*tron-yem*
Hovde	*hov'dĕ*		
		Utvaer	*oot-vār*
Iversen, Kåre	*ee-ver-sen, kawr'-ĕ*		
		Vika	*vee-ka*
Kaarfjord	*Kaw-fyord*	Vinjefjord	*vin-ye-fyord*
Kilpisjarvi	*Kil'pĭsh-yar-vi*	Vita	*vee-ta*

CHAPTER ONE

THE BEGINNING OF A SAGA

SAGA is an old Norse word which originally meant simply a story. But from its association with the kind of story which ancient Norsemen liked to tell, it has come to mean a story of heroism and endeavour, and of adventure at sea.

This story is a modern saga, but it has a strangely ancient setting; for it tells of voyages in small boats, in the dark winters of the far north, from the Shetland Islands to Norway. The seamen who made the journeys were descendants of the Vikings who sailed those same seas, in boats of about the same size, just a thousand years before. The journeys were even made for a similar purpose; for in both the tenth and the twentieth centuries Norwegians who were living in exile, and who believed power in Norway to be in the hands of a usurper, used Shetland as a base for expeditions to the Norwegian coast.

The circumstances which caused the modern journeys to be made arose from the German invasion of Norway in 1940, and their object was to land men and cargo in Norway without the knowledge of the Germans, and to rescue refugees. Nothing but war would have made seamen attempt such dangerous journeys. Some were two thousand miles in length, and lasted three weeks, and all of them, for three years, were made in the depth of the sub-arctic winter, in fishing boats from fifty to seventy feet long, which sailed alone.

The North Sea and the north-east Atlantic were a no-man's-land at that time, deserted by shipping but patrolled by aircraft. Small boats are no match for aircraft, except in calm water, however heavily they are armed, and the fishing boats crossing to Norway or returning were sometimes attacked and sunk in a few minutes, hundreds of miles from a friendly ship or shore. Their crews had no hope of being saved.

But such dangers of war were a commonplace, and these journeys were more memorable for the dangers of wind and sea which were overcome. The journeys were made in winter, because in the summer, so far north, there is continual daylight, and the crews needed darkness to make their secret landings in Norway. In this the journeys differed from the voyages of the Vikings, which were made in summer weather. The seas between Shetland and Norway in the winter are among the stormiest in the world, and it is possible that in all the history of man's seafaring no other series of journeys has been undertaken deliberately in such bad weather and in such small boats. Certainly it is centuries since men sailed in such an empty ocean. In the last four winters of the war the boats on these journeys steamed for ninety thousand miles, and in this vast distance only four strange ships were sighted. To bring such small boats through hurricanes, fogs, extreme cold and continuous darkness, to make landfall on a distant, unlit and guarded coast, sometimes put to severe tests our modern knowledge of the ancient crafts of seamanship. So the record of these voyages is a story of the sea rather than a story of the war.

The work was carried out from a small base in Shetland, of which I had the honour to be second-in-command. My own part in the work of the base was quite unheroic, and I can therefore write of the work as a saga without any lack of modesty. But in writing of events in which one has taken an intimate part, it is hard to avoid making too much of one's personal experiences, opinions and impressions, and if any of my colleagues should read this account of our mutual adventures they will think me too self-centred. I hope they will forgive me and understand that to write impersonally of a matter which absorbed our whole interest for five years of our lives would call for unusual literary skill.

It was in the spring of 1941 that I was first sent to Shetland. I was a sub-lieutenant at the time, but the job I was to do in Shetland was not a naval one, and I had orders to report there to an army officer, Major L. H. Mitchell. I had known for some time who Mitchell was and what he was doing, and had asked to be detached from naval service and sent north as his assistant. I thought his work promised excitement, and a degree of independence and a chance to use one's wits which are seldom granted to a junior officer in wartime. I had a slight knowledge of the Norwegian language and a more thorough knowledge of the Norwegian coast, because I had spent my holidays in Norway for many years; and I knew something about small boats. I was very fond of Norway and the Norwegians, and felt I wanted nothing more than to help them in some small way.

So I was delighted, after months of delay, when my request was granted and I was flying at last to Shetland. As the plane, after leaving the mainland of Scotland near John o' Groats, skirting the balloon barrage over Scapa Flow and passing the last of the Orkney Islands, flew low over a grey turbulent sea, I looked forward eagerly to see the gaunt rock called Sumburgh Head, and beyond it the narrow line of bare brown hills where our adventure was to begin.

Mitchell met me at the airport: a thin young man in an army officer's uniform, with the slight forward stoop and anxious expression of short-sightedness. In wartime some people are obscured by their uniform, so that on seeing them one thinks, there is a major, or there is an airman; but others continue to appear as individuals, and one says, that is a pleasant or intelligent-looking fellow, and only notices later his rank and service. Mitchell was the latter kind. He was always himself, and never primarily a major. He had a wise, kindly face, which did not accord well with brass buttons, and he had too much sense of the ridiculous and of his own fallibility to be a good parade-ground officer. But he had in plenty the much more valuable qualities of sympathy and humour, and freedom from prejudice and false pride.

In London I had been told that Mitchell would tell me every thing when I arrived; and he began at once, as we drove away from the airport, to share an encyclopedic knowledge of Norwegian politics and psychology, and of German and British strategy in the north, as well as to tell me what we ourselves were to do and to discuss how we should do it.

It was just over a year since the king and government of Norway had left their country and brought to an end the struggle in Norway itself against the Germans. The thoroughness and efficiency of the German preparations for the invasion of Norway, and the lack of Norwegian preparations for defence, had made the battle hopeless; but brave actions by both British and Norwegians had delayed its inevitable end; and when the end came the fighting had aroused in Norwegians an intense national emotion. I had known well before the war the complacency which decades of neutrality had induced in Norwegians. Mitchell, who had been in Oslo when the Germans arrived and had followed the whole of the campaign, had seen this complacency change to a strong positive loyalty to their king, a conscious love of their country and a hatred of Germans which far exceeded the feeling of most Englishmen.

Many thousands of Norwegians had found themselves in exile with the king, and thousands more had followed him, escaping from Norway in fishing boats, yachts, small steamers and even rowing boats across the North Sea, or crossing the border into Sweden and travelling through Finland and Russia eastwards round the world. But in Norway there still remained a large army, disorganised and disbanded and only partly trained, but still ready to risk a lot to drive the Germans out of the country. It had become the first duty of the exiled government to get into touch with potential leaders of this army, and under British direction to reorganise, train and equip it.

The first necessity in attempting this task was a means of regular transport between Great Britain and Norway for sending messengers, leaders, instructors, trained radio operators and saboteurs, and cargoes of weapons; and it was this transport which we were to provide.

It was the lack of any alternative which had first made the British and Norwegian authorities consider using fishing boats for this traffic. In 1941 British resources had still not recovered from the losses of Dunkirk, and neither aircraft nor naval vessels could be used for work which did not bring immediate results. Besides, it was questionable whether either would have been suitable. Unstable weather and the mountainous country made

Norway a difficult place for landing by parachute, and aircraft at the most could only have carried a small proportion of the traffic which was already planned. And no naval vessels at that time were both seaworthy enough to make such long voyages in winter and yet small enough to approach, with a reasonable chance of avoiding detection, a coast held by the enemy.

However, fishing boats had been constantly arriving from Norway manned by refugees. The best of them were certainly seaworthy: many had fished the Iceland and Greenland grounds in summer. Yet they were small; and above all, when they arrived in Norwegian waters it would be difficult for the Germans to distinguish them from similar boats which were still fishing there, so that they might, it was thought, be able to move about on the coast without causing suspicion.

In the winter of 1940, which was just past, several crews of fishing boats which had arrived from Norway were asked to sail back again, land a passenger and then return to this country. All these return trips had been successful, and at the end of the year Mitchell had been sent to Shetland to organise a base for continuous traffic. A couple of dozen Norwegian fishermen and merchant seamen had been recruited as civilian volunteers, and six fishing boats had been requisitioned. In the early part of 1941 they had made several successful voyages; but by the time I arrived the increasing daylight had put an end to their operations till the following autumn.

All this I learned from Mitchell as we went about our work, or sat in the evening by the peat fire in a large farmhouse which he had taken as his headquarters. The name of this place was Flemington. It was a comfortable dilapidated house, famous in Shetland for the tree which grew before it; for it stood in the sheltered valley of Weisdale, and besides its one fully grown tree it was surrounded by plantations of stunted birches, oaks, conifers and rowans, the only ones of any considerable size in the islands. In this house Mitchell had entertained some strange visitors in the past winter: agents waiting for passage to Norway, refugees exhausted by a crossing of the North Sea, and parties of saboteurs in training, with their instructors. The saboteurs had already given the place a doubtful reputation among the Shetlanders, and the house and garden were full of their devices. They had a childish delight in entertaining visitors with incendiary bombs and booby traps. Soon after I arrived I noticed a suitcase under my bed, but I did not bother to open it; and it lay there for nearly six months before I found it contained three hundred small bottles of chloroform and some detonators.

But my own main concern was not with such gadgets but with the boats. The Norwegians who had sailed on the winter journeys were mostly on leave in Scotland. One crew, to fill up the time, made a weekly trip to Aberdeen, taking fish on the southward journey and bringing back cabbages for the army – a profitable trade which continued throughout the summer. The other boats were being repaired by a local firm.

Norwegian fishing boats are a delight to a connoisseur of small seaworthy craft. To a casual observer they all look the same: two-masted wooden vessels, unusually high in the bow, and with a very large wheelhouse aft. The bulwarks and upper works are white, and the hull is not painted but treated with linseed oil. But to a fisherman there are many differences between boats from different parts of the coast. Those built in the south are what British yachtsmen know as the Colin Archer type, with a curved stem, a canoe stern and an external rudder. North of these are found the Hardanger cutters, fast straight-stemmed craft with a high sheer, a very low freeboard amidships and a long fine counter. Next is the Möre type, also a cutter, but more compact in its lines and with a wheelhouse of more elaborate construction. Within these three main types there are endless small variations, and in recent years the Norwegian government has helped to evolve a design which combines the Möre bow with a cruiser stern, and in profile resembles the modern craft on the east coast of Scotland.

Of all fishing craft the Möre cutter is the queen. The south Norway boats are slow in a head sea, the Hardanger type is not so well or so strongly built; but a good Möre cutter is fit to sail round the world and will stand any storm in nature.

The most noticeable feature of all these Norwegian craft is their engine, for with only a few exceptions it is a single-cylinder semi-diesel machine with a large reverberant exhaust pipe which comes out of the top of the wheelhouse and emits a slow, solemn, very loud tonk-tonk-tonk. This tonk can be heard miles away in calm weather, and it is a nostalgic sound to all who have happy memories of the Norwegian coast.

To a British shipwright these boats seem strange, for their construction breaks most of the traditional rules by which boats are built in Great Britain. There is usually no hardwood in them at all, except in some cases the stem. Keel, frames and planking are all of fir. The frames of the boats are double, each part six inches square, and they are spaced so closely that they form almost a solid block of timber. The outer planking is from two and a half to three inches thick, and the whole of the hull is lined or ceiled with an inner skin of from two to two and a half inches. Both these skins and the frames are through-fastened with trenails, that is to say, wooden pegs which are driven through and then tightened with a wooden wedge at each end — a form of construction which has been little used in this country since Nelson's day. Iron nails are only used in the garboard strake and the butts, and they do not hold well in the soft wood.

This method of building is enormously strong, but has one disadvantage: there is very little ventilation between the two skins of the boat, and the little there is becomes a matter of chance; and therefore dry rot often arises in the frames. This is a most insidious as well as a dangerous fault. More than once when we were overhauling our boats and took out a deck plank or stanchion which showed a suspicion of rot, we found we had to rebuild a large part of the ship before we were sure we had got rid of the trouble.

Most of the vessels we used were of fifty to seventy feet in overall length, with a beam of about eighteen feet and a draught of eight feet six inches. They had bunks for six or eight men in the forecastle, and for two in a small cabin aft. The hold amidships could carry eight or ten tons of small arms and explosives, and the wheelhouse, which was built on top of the engine casing, usually had a small chart-room opening off it, and a galley behind. There were few comforts aboard them, and with a speed of seven or eight knots they were absurdly slow by wartime standards. But for ability to keep the sea few boats of a similar size could rival them.

Mitchell's explanations, and my own memories of the Norwegian coast, soon made it clear to me what a powerful weapon these fishing boats could be. In Shetland we were a little over a hundred miles north-north-east of the mainland of Scotland. The islands lie strung out for sixty miles north and south, and a hundred and eighty miles to the eastward lies Bergen in Norway. From Bergen the Norwegian coast runs north for a hundred and twenty miles, and then north-north-east for nearly a thousand miles into the Arctic zone. Any part of this coast would be accessible to a fishing boat fitted with extra fuel and water tanks, and the nearest point on it was only twenty-four hours' steaming away.

It seemed, in theory, that having once reached the enemy coast a fishing boat should be in reasonable safety, although if it should have the bad luck to be detected it would stand no chance at all of getting back across the North Sea to Shetland. The western part of Norway is a high plateau, which was eroded during the Ice Age into a series of great valleys, some filled by the sea and thus forming fjords, and all separated by high mountains which, at the time of year when our boats would be operating, would be thickly covered with snow. On the coast itself the erosion of the sea has been added to that of the ice, and has cut up the land into tens of thousands of islands.

The channels between these islands form a lead of sheltered water which extends along the whole of the coast, with only a few points at which coastal shipping is exposed to the open sea. This 'inner lead', besides being very beautiful, is the principal thoroughfare of Norway for all kinds of traffic; and the minor channels which form a maze between the inner lead and the sea are constantly used by thousands of fishing boats of all sizes from rowing boats to seventy-foot whalers.

We could assume that it was out of the question for the Germans to prohibit either the coastal traffic or the fishing; but we were also sure that as soon as we and our passengers began to achieve our object of being a nuisance to them, they would do their best to control the movements of even the smallest of boats. In fact, as time went on, they used every possible means to achieve control. All boats had to carry quantities of passes and get them stamped at each port of call. Patrol boats were stationed in the leads to inspect these passes and search suspicious ships, and large numbers of observation and artillery posts were gradually established on shore. All lighthouses showing to seaward were extinguished or obscured. Fishing was restricted to a zone of fifty miles from the coast, and the limit of this zone was patrolled by aircraft. Arbitrary 'forbidden areas' were declared from time to time, and controls in general were varied with ever-increasing frequency in the hope, presumably, that our boats would give themselves away by showing ignorance of new regulations.

It would undoubtedly have been difficult to penetrate this hedge of controls had it not been for the stream of refugees which flowed from Norway to Shetland and Orkney. These refugees brought us the latest German orders almost as quickly as the Germans could disseminate them in Norway. We kept details of the defences plotted on large-scale charts and card-indexed, and one member of our unit used to boast that he knew every German N.C.O. in charge of a watchpost in Norway by his Christian name.

Since the job we had to do was to land men and materials in secret, it followed that our crews had to avoid the Germans, though they often wanted to try their hands in a scrap. We armed the ships as best we could against chance encounters, always bearing in mind that to appear as innocent fishing boats might often be their best chance of survival, so that the armament had to be invisible except at close quarters. In the open sea the chance of meeting a German ship was negligible, but aircraft were a considerable danger, particularly along the fifty-mile limit. Our aim was usually for the boats to approach this limit at night, so that dawn found them within the fishing zone. Here they could expect to be reasonably safe, provided they looked and behaved sufficiently like ordinary fishermen to deceive passing aircraft. They could approach the coast in the evening, so that the skipper could fix his position before darkness fell and thus be sure of making an accurate landfall however dark the night. Once inside the leads success and safety would depend on luck, bravado and a good look-out.

Such were our expectations; but in the summer of 1941 we had a lot of administrative work to do, with no precedents other than those of fiction to guide us, before we could put these theories into practice. Such boats as were not undergoing repair in the harbour of Lerwick, which is the only town in Shetland, were anchored in an inlet called Cat Firth, which lay about ten miles north of the town, and three miles from Mitchell's house of Flemington. The coasts of Shetland are so deeply indented that it is said no point on the islands is more than three miles from some arm of the sea. But most of the fjords, or voes, as they are called in the islands, are straight, and the gales, which blow from every direction in winter, drive steep and dangerous seas into each of them in turn. Cat Firth was the safest anchorage in the neighbourhood of Lerwick; but it was by no means ideal for our purpose. We thought we must keep our boats in a deserted spot so that their cargoes could be loaded without causing too much gossip. Lerwick itself was therefore ruled out as a base. But though Cat Firth was sufficiently deserted, the water alongside its pier was only deep enough for dinghies. Also we needed some kind of accommodation ashore, and there was none in Cat Firth. The crews of the boats had been living aboard, but this was too uncomfortable and too bad for their health. The very least we could do with ashore would be a canteen, a bath house and a drying-room for clothes. Besides, as I was to look after the boats we thought I ought to live close enough to them to keep an eye on them at all times, so that I too needed some kind of shelter near the shore.

So Mitchell and I spent many of our evenings during June of that year looking for a better anchorage. It was a delightful occupation. At supper we would choose a promising place from the map, and afterwards get out the car and set off to visit it. In the calm and serene 'white nights' of the northern summer, which Shetlanders call the Simmer Dim, the islands are very beautiful; and I have happy recollections of exploring deserted bays and coves, where the seals watched us with inquisitive stares, and the seabirds swooped at our heads in protest at our intrusion; and of watching the yellow sunlight gilding the sea and the skerries and the barren hills till it faded into a gentle dusk which soon became dawn; and of coming back to the queer and sinister house at Flemington to make tea and talk ourselves to sleep. It was many years before I enjoyed again such carefree days in Shetland, and it was then that I first felt a fondness for the islands, which, through all the troubles which lay before us, I never lost.

But we did not find what we were seeking, and I began to make plans for rebuilding the pier at Cat Firth and putting up Nissen huts on shore. However, one Sunday in July, when I was just shifting the first lorry-loads of shingle to the pier, Mitchell went with one of the staff officers of our London headquarters to a place we had often considered on the map, but always turned down because it was twenty-seven miles from Lerwick, which we thought was too far. It was called Lunna Voe, and when they came back they told me they thought it was hopeful. I persuaded them to drive out there again the same evening, and as soon as I saw Lunna Voe I felt sure it was the place for us.

To get there, we had to drive north on the main road of Shetland for ten miles, as far as the hamlet of Voe. Then we turned to the right by a moor road, which ran down to the head of a firth after two or three miles, and there, at first glance, seemed to stop. But there was a gate, and beyond it the road, a little diminished, wound on along the side of the firth, and crossed a plain dotted with crofts. Then came the head of another firth, with a cluster of cottages, and again an apparent end. But again a gate gave on to a farther road, by now no more than a track with a grass-grown centre, which led by a rocky shore grown with yellow flags, up a hill and across a desolate moor. At a turn in the road we suddenly saw on our left the magnificent sweep of Yell Sound, and beyond it the northern islands of Yell and Fetlar and Unst, and the rocks called the Ramna Stacks pricking the sunset like monstrous fangs. At the next turn there was Lunna: a small patch of green in the midst of brown heather, a small landlocked bay with a quay and a roofless stone building at its head, and above, on the hillside, a large, gaunt, grey house.

I have always had a liking for bleak and lonely places, and perhaps it was on romantic grounds that I first determined that Lunna should be our base. I think Mitchell and our friend from headquarters were influenced in the same way; for the wild, desolate and deserted appearance of the place, and its remoteness, suggested perfectly the smugglers' haunt of fiction. But we had to support our romance with reason. Luckily that was not difficult. The house was to let, and it could accommodate thirty-five men. There were plenty of outhouses for stores and explosives and ammunition. The quay was built of great blocks of stone and had enough water for our boats to lie alongside for six hours of the tide. The only other buildings in sight were a farm, a manse and an ancient church; and the bay was so placed that our boats could come and go on their errands without being seen by anyone, even the coastguards. The anchorage seemed to be safe, and when a few days later I brought one of the boats up to survey it I found that the depth was just right — from four to five fathoms.

All these advantages seemed well to outweigh the disadvantage of the distance from Lerwick, which was our only source of supply, and of the indifferent road. We reported to headquarters on the virtues of Lunna, answered the questions which convention compelled them to ask, and very soon leased the place furnished.

The acquisition of Lunna completed the material resources which we could foresee we should need during the coming winter. Lunna was to house the operational crews, with myself in charge, and the boats were to be anchored there. Our office remained in Lerwick, where communications were more reliable and the naval and army headquarters were close at hand, so that the ciphers and other secret documents we kept were under better protection than we could have given them outside the town. Flemington was retained as a place where agents could be kept in seclusion while they waited for passage, and Mitchell continued to live there. Stocks of arms and explosives which we were to export were cached in a number of dumps throughout the islands, one of which was in the dungeon of the ruined medieval castle of the Earls of Zetland in the village of Scalloway. We had a lorry, a big shooting brake, and a small Ford.

Our human resources were less adequate. We were a queer mixture of military and civilian. Mitchell and I were the only commissioned officers – he army and I navy. The forty-odd Norwegian seamen were civilians, paid a weekly wage of £4, with free food and lodging and a bonus of £10 for each trip they made to Norway. The shore staff consisted of three British sergeants, Almond, Sherwood and Olsen; a civilian British shorthand typist and cipherer, Mr Norman Edwards; a Norwegian cook at Lunna; and two local girls as cook and house maid at Flemington. It became obvious as soon as our operations started that this staff was much too small, but there was naturally a delay before it could be increased, and by the time help arrived, towards the end of the year, we were all exhausted.

But during the summer, although there was plenty to do, nothing was of immediate importance, and we were able to enjoy our work. I was particularly happy on the days I spent at Lunna, making preparations at the house and the anchorage for the arrival of the boats and their crews. There were inventories to be made, supplies of peat and coal and food and paraffin to collect, and much shifting of furniture. The pier had to be repaired and resurfaced. The installation of the telephone needed six miles of new poles and lines. Outhouses had to be adapted as stores for large stocks of arms, navigational equipment and ships' stores, and a small standing stock of saboteurs' implements — explosives, fuses and firing devices of different kinds, incendiary bombs, hand grenades and such things as knuckle-dusters, benzedrine tablets, compasses, torches, maps and Norwegian clothes.

I chose for myself a small room on the first floor as an office and sitting-room, and a smaller one next to it as bedroom; and most of my idle moments were spent in admiring the view from the windows. Although Lunna was on the east side of the island, the house was built on the western slope of a hill, and its front windows overlooked an isthmus, two hundred yards wide, which joined the long narrow peninsula of Lunna Ness to the mainland. On the left or south side of the isthmus was a wide, open inlet called Vidlin Voe, full of skerries and reefs, where the last echoes of the Atlantic swell always broke in a slow, powerful rhythm. On the right was our anchorage. At one time it had been an open bay with two small islands in its mouth; but each of the islands had joined to the mainland with a spit of shingle, and in this way the bay had been nearly enclosed. It was four hundred yards in diameter, and almost a perfect natural harbour. In the prosperous days of herring curing in Shetland it had been used as a landing-place for fish, and to this fact we owed our pier, as well as the roofless stone building near it, which I was told had once been a curing station, and which I intended to turn into a workshop.

On the isthmus itself there were signs of more ancient buildings, which the Ordnance Survey maps marked as a monastery. There was also the very old, very small church, which perhaps had been built by the monks, for even before the eviction of crofters in the nineteenth century, Lunna can hardly have been the centre of a parish. No legend or record remained of the people who had built it; but I thought I could understand why they had chosen to build there, for the place had a remote and simple beauty.

Our anchorage opened north-west to an arm of Yell Sound, and from my windows I could see, beyond the islands which guarded the entrance, a series of inlets – Swining Voe, Colla Firth, Dales Voe – in the mainland of Shetland; and out to the right the holms and rocks where the tides from the Atlantic to the North Sea swept through the sound in an eight-knot race. Beyond all were the Shetland hills, whose colours and contours were always changing under the slanting sunlight and the fast-driven mist and rain; and winding up and down among them the narrow rough road which led back, in the end, to Lerwick.

Such was the place where our saga was begun. To me it gave endless pleasure, even in darkness and storm and snow; but to tell the truth I met few other people who liked it; and as I made ready that summer I constantly wondered what the men of the crews would say when they saw it. I had met very few of them, and I had been told they were difficult people to please or control; so I waited with some foreboding for them to come back from their leave.

A day came at the end of July when the house was ready, and the crews with five of the boats were waiting in Lerwick. Mitchell was away in England, but he had left orders for us to move in as soon as we could. So I told the crews to start on the three hours' sea passage to Lunna, and drove there myself with the Norwegian cook and Sergeant Sherwood. I spent the afternoon giving some kind of warning to the farmer and the minister of the church concerning the disturbance of their peace which might be expected, and asking them and others to help to foster discretion among the few local people who might pass by Lunna and see something of what we were doing. Sherwood finished the fifty-nine blackout shutters, and Harald Albertsen the cook, an amiable rascally retired ship's steward with a passion for photographs of the nude and of the royal family, pottered about in the kitchen. It grew late; the boats were long overdue (boats usually are), and I began to wonder how they would manage the

11

entrance to the bay in the dark. Then at dusk, as if symbolic of our future at Lunna, everything happened at once; a pressure lamp started leaking and burst into flames, Albertsen complained that the supper was spoiling, and I pulled the plug of a water-closet which had not been used, and found a few minutes later a cascade of water down the stairs. As I ran for a mop and a bucket I heard the tonk-tonk of our engines and saw the five ships coming into the voe.

We put out the lamp, and I gave Sherwood the bucket and ran down to the pier to point out the best places to anchor. When the boats were secured I brought the crews up to the house, and they took off their caps and wiped their feet, and went in on tip-toe, saying, 'But this is a palace,' and 'Does the king of Shetland live here?' I was pleased; but, I thought, you will soon get used to all this and want something better; and so they did.

There was still a month before the nights would be long enough for operations to begin, and that month gave me time to study the characters of the men of the crews and to discover the delicate nature of my own position. Most of the men were fishermen, and no fisherman of any nation can be driven; he is brought up to depend on nobody and to call nobody his master. Our men had been recruited among the Norwegian refugees in London, where it had been emphasised that they were volunteering for a dangerous job, and where they had been offered rates of pay which were much higher than those in the services. This had increased their natural unwillingness to be ordered about by anyone. Fortunately both Mitchell and I disliked doing anything without knowing the reason for it, and therefore had no desire to make other people do so; and, in fact, neither of us had any means of punishing a man or of enforcing our orders; we could only dismiss an offender from the unit, and that, as everyone knew, we did not want to do because it was difficult to get new recruits. I soon learned that unless I was able and willing to explain step by step the connection between any job at Lunna and the success of our voyages, it was better to leave the job undone. This principle was a strain on our patience and wasted a good lot of time. But it was both inevitable and fundamentally just; and it had its small triumphs in the end.

But petty troubles were forgotten as soon as our first operation was arranged. In the middle of August we were told to make ready to take a messenger to a point a little north of Bergen in order to re-establish contact with a party of army officers who had begun to form an 'underground' force in Bergen itself. The messenger's orders were to find a certain lieutenant, hand him a good supply of Norwegian money, and tell him we had a cargo of eight tons of sabotage stores ready in Shetland to be shipped. They were to arrange a landing place for the stores, and we were to pick up the messenger again a week after landing him.

The boat which we chose for this first trip was the *Aksel*, a cutter of medium size, sixty-five feet in overall length, with a hundred horse-power engine. Her skipper was a young fisherman called August Naeröy, who had done several trips before and had a high reputation as a seaman. His engineer was Mindur Berge, a gentle young giant who lived near Ålesund, and had an instinctive and loving understanding of machinery, together with a patent honesty and a quiet common sense which made him one of the leaders of public opinion in our gang. There were three others in the crew: Ivar Brekke, a quiet boy who was inclined to go on doing his job with so little fuss that he got less credit for it than he deserved; Andrew Gjertsen, a second mate from the merchant service; and Bård Grotle. Bård was one of our greatest characters, though at that time he had not begun to emerge as a leader, and I saw him only as a tall and untidy west-coast fisherman, with a shock of tow hair and a merry twinkle in a pair of bright blue eyes.

Fitting out the messenger himself was my first experience of dealing with an agent's needs, and like most novices I began with a childish enjoyment of the whole business which in time gave way to an admiration for the courage of the agents themselves, coupled with a cynical belief that much of the gear we supplied them with might have been invented by grown-up schoolboys playing at spies. This messenger's wad of Norwegian notes had to be hidden, and I spent a whole day unsealing a tin of Norwegian tobacco, packing the money inside it, and soldering it together again. I was rather pleased with the result. It was only by a stain on the label that he could distinguish his money from a tin of real tobacco which he also took with him. But he was carrying so much more compromising stuff about his person that I cannot, looking back, remember the point of hiding his money. We fixed him up with Norwegian food from a refugee vessel, some plug tobacco which was supposed to be useful for bribing fishermen, and a supply of cigarettes which had been specially manufactured without any name on the paper, but which would have given themselves away as British by the first whiff of Virginia smoke.

The registration number of *Aksel* was also a thing which called for some forgery. All fishing boats carry a number which identifies both the port of registration and the boat itself, and our boats therefore had to undergo frequent changes, using a number belonging to a boat from a port near, but not too near, their objective, and of similar size and type which had neither escaped to England nor been requisitioned by the Germans. We chose the numbers from a copy of the *Norwegian Fishing Boat Register*, and I had a set of stencils cut to simplify the business of painting the letters and figures on the bows.

The crew and the boat on this first trip gave Mitchell and me a foretaste of difficulties to come; for on the day before they were due to sail they told me that a main bearing in the engine was running hot, and we had to send the boat in haste to Lerwick and mobilise an unwilling local firm to work overtime to repair it. (Hot bearings later became a nightmare to us, and so did lack of foresight among the crews, though both troubles were possibly partly our fault.) However, we managed to get her back to Lunna an hour before sailing time. As she came into the bay our lorry drove down to the pier with the food and the guns and equipment for the trip, and in a few minutes it was all stowed on board. The registration number was quickly painted, and the skipper, the messenger, Mitchell and I went up to my room for a cup of coffee and a last look at the charts, and to check over the messenger's pockets and kit to make sure that nothing was omitted, and that nothing which ought not to be there had been left there by mistake.

By nine in the evening everything was ready, and all of us went down to the harbour to give this first venture a send-off. Mitchell and I went on board and wished the crew bad luck, which we had agreed with them might deceive the fates and have the opposite effect. Mindur started up the engine, and I saw him gleaming with sweat under the bright lights of the engine-room, and caressing his one great cylinder with a piece of cotton waste. A change had come over the crew. I had never seen them so happy, or so efficient. August, the skipper, was laughing at Gjertsen, who had chosen to sail in a rather smart grey lounge suit, a collar and tie and a homburg hat, and carrying a small attache case containing nothing but a razor and a towel. Bård shouted some wisecrack to the rest of the party on shore. Ivar Brekke said little, as usual, but there was a new sparkle in his eyes.

When Mitchell and I had shaken hands with them all we rowed ashore and joined the rest of my household, whose cigarettes were glowing in the darkness on the pierhead. *Aksel* dropped her moorings with a splash. The tonk-tonk of the engine grew quicker, and we could just see the outline of her hull as she swung to the open sea. Then she gathered way and disappeared into the dark night. As she passed the entrance to the bay, and we turned to go back to the house, she sounded her siren. It was the letter V. 'Fine fellows,' said a voice in Norwegian at my side. For the first time we began to feel pride in our adventure.

CHAPTER TWO

ACROSS TO NORWAY

WE were anxious, of course, about *Aksel*. The success of her trip was important to give a good start to the winter season, and we could not be sure that our information about German defences and fishing controls was correct. She might give herself away by infringing some new regulation; the men she was going to meet might have been captured and the meeting-place learned by the enemy; or the ship herself, or her gear, might lack some necessity which we had not foreseen or which had been forgotten in the rush of her departure.

Days passed, and our anxiety grew. She had left on 30th August. She should have reached the Norwegian coast in twenty-four hours, and either have gone in to her rendezvous at once or perhaps waited in the fishing zone offshore till the following evening. In either event she should have been back by the morning of 3rd September. But that day brought no reports from the coastguards or the R.A.F., and at Lunna we paused at our work every few minutes in the hope of hearing her engine. By the evening we were seriously worried, and Mitchell asked the R.A.F. station at Sumburgh, in the south of Shetland, to divert one of their patrols to see if they could find her. They willingly sent two Blenheims to search her whole track, and one of the pilots reported that he had sighted her close to the Norwegian coast. He had circled the ship, and the crew had waved.

This report raised our spirits for a moment; but when we had time to reflect on it we realised that it was far from conclusive. The pilot had not seen her registration number, and apart from this number the description we gave him would have fitted thousands of ships on the coast; and certainly any Norwegian crew would have waved to a Blenheim which circled their ship out of sight of the Germans. Our hopes fell again, and we spent a wakeful night.

The next morning the R.A.F. sent a Beaufighter to have another look, and this time we had definite news. She was half-way home, and still under way. That made her due early in the morning of 5th September. We slept better for the news, and at 5 a.m. a coastguard report came through to me at Lunna. At half-past six I heard the tonk-tonk we had been expecting, and went down to the quay to welcome her back.

The first thing I noticed as the ship came alongside was that she was decorated with bunches of heather and boughs of birch. That did not look like a sign of trouble; and when I went on board I heard a story which taught me never to worry again without something definite to worry about.

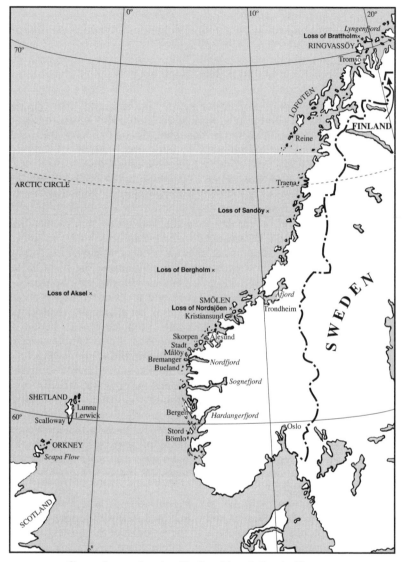

General map showing Shetland in relation to Norway.

They had had bad weather on the outward journey, and had made landfall a few hours late — about midnight — and about twenty miles too far south. This made them too late to reach their rendezvous that night and to get out again in darkness, so they lay off in the fishing zone all the following day. It was very clear, and they kept their guns ready, but nobody took any notice of them. In the evening they put in to the island of Bueland and landed. Everything was peaceful. They went to the house of a man called Dagfinn, whom we knew as the organiser of several escape parties. He took the messenger in a motor boat to his destination farther in the fjords, and the crew settled down to enjoy the hospitality of compatriots: in particular, of the local girls.

They stayed there for two days before their consciences told them they ought to return. No Germans came near them. They went to a dance, and invited their girl friends aboard for some real coffee and white bread. They distributed tobacco and flour, and when at last they decided to go they were given a regal send-off.

This story put us all in the highest of spirits at Lunna, and each crew was impatient to sail in the hope of enjoying an equally good reception.

Our next job was to pick up the messenger again. We had arranged to meet him, seven days after his landing, in the bay of Vetvik, on the mountainous island of Bremanger in the mouth of Nordfjord, about twenty miles north of Bueland. Several of our men and one of the boats — the *Igland* — came from Bremanger, and this boat had therefore been standing by for the job. Her skipper, Ole Grotle, was a young Bremanger fisherman. *Igland* was one of the smallest of our boats, only fifty feet long, and Ole sailed her with a crew of three: Henrik Igland the engineer, Anfinn Grotle* and Ove Aalen. Ole Grotle was the only one of our skippers who kept an informative log. This is his log of the trip to Bremanger:

Sept. 5	1800	Sailed from Lunna, bound for Norway.
	1945	Passed Out Skerries and set log. Course E by N $\frac{3}{4}$ N.
	2400	Log reading 34 miles. Light northerly breeze, cloudy.
Sept. 6	0400	Log reading 65 miles. Wind freshening. All well.
	0915	Aircraft sighted flying north about three miles off. We take it to be British. Wind still increasing and sea getting up. Cloudy with some rain.
	1130	Log 121 miles. Heave-to to secure oil barrels in the hold.
	1200	We are going full speed again.
	1600	Log 147 miles.
	1650	We sight land and get a bearing on Alden of E by S $\frac{1}{2}$ S.

* On the west coast of Norway one may take either one's father's name or the name of one's birthplace as surname. In addition, fishing boats are often called after the homes of their owners. This is sometimes confusing. Igland and Grotle, for example, are both hamlets in Bremanger. Thus the ship and its engineer were both called Igland, and Ole and Anfinn Grotle were neighbours, not brothers. On the other hand, one sometimes met brothers who used different surnames.

Alter course to ENE ½ N. Wind north-easterly and a head sea. We are now on a course for Olderveggen.

Sept. 7   0100   We are entering Bremangerfjord. Moonlight with occasional showers. We plan to sail up the middle of fjord. I shall try to get ashore quietly in the lifeboat. I must get hold of my father to find out whether the messenger has contacted him.

0130   We hear a boat coming out of the fjord and alter course toward Grotlevik to avoid being seen.

1530   I have been home and found that the messenger has made contact with my father. My father and brother have gone to Vetvik. We are on the way there now. Weather is awful – storm and rain. Hear that three people have spotted us. They rowed past the boat while I was at home, but promised not to talk about having seen us. Can't be certain of this as some people can never hold their tongues. God help them if anything happens to my family through having been mixed up with me. If they give us away it wil be the last thing they do.

1700   We have arrived at Vetvik. Dropped anchor but have left the engine running as it is blowing hard and there is a risk of being blown ashore. We have got the guns ready. Aalen and I turn in while Igland and Anfinn keep watch.

1900   The messenger and my brother are on board. We agree to wait till the evening before putting to sea. I am going ashore to meet my father who is in one of the farms here.

1930   Back on board and getting ready for sea. We have found we are to have more passengers, four men and two girls.

2000   Streamed the log off Olderveggen and set course for Shetland. We left ashore two barrels of lubricating oil in Vetvik. All passengers are on board. All well.

Sept. 8   0530   Log 70 miles. North-easter still blowing and rolling like hell. Passengers seasick, particularly the ladies. All sails set.

1200   Log 121 miles. A light north-easterly breeze now and sunshine.

1600   Land sighted.

2000   We are closing the shore off Unst, the northern island of Shetland. Follow the coast southwards.

Sept. 9   0300   Back at Lunna.

The success of these first two trips gave us confidence, and the report of the messenger was also encouraging. The men we had been sent over to find — ex-officers of the Norwegian Army — were waiting to take two cargoes of arms and explosives, and to hide them till they could be distributed to the sabotage organisation which was then growing in Bergen. A third boat was ready in Lunna to take the first of these cargoes — about eight tons of goods — and we began to assemble it from the dumps we had made in different parts of Shetland.

But in the meantime two other jobs had to be done. A party of Norwegian flying officers and other trained men were waiting to be picked up on an island north of Trondheim, and over four hundred miles from Shetland; and we had with us in Shetland two agents who were urgently required in Ålesund.

The fact that we had three trips so early in the season, all of which must be made as soon as possible, might have given us warning of trouble ahead. Mitchell and I had made all our plans in the expectation that we should not have to organise, on an average, more than three trips in two weeks. With crews at our disposal, we thought that the base should be self-supporting. We intended to send all the boats which needed major repairs into Lerwick; and I was to double the part of O.C. at Lunna with that of engineer and shipwright in Lerwick. Mitchell, apart from being my senior officer, was to look after the Lerwick office, the administrative problems of maintaining the base, the planning of operations in advance (which entailed a mass of correspondence in cipher), and the fitting out of agents and assembly of cargoes. As assistants we had only the three sergeants, Almond, Sherwood and Olsen.

After the first three weeks of September, during which we made eight trips instead of the four we had been led to expect, Mitchell and I and the sergeants were exhausted. However hard we worked, there were still things left undone which we ought to have done. It became obvious to us that our plans could not carry the burden of twice the number of trips we had aimed at.

In early September, however, things still seemed to be going well, and we set about preparing the next three trips. *Siglaos* was the boat for the cargo run to Bueland, and *Vita* for the Trondheim pick-up. *Aksel*, after her return from the first trip, was made ready to take the Ålesund agents.

The skipper of *Siglaos* was Petter Salen. Salen was a merchant service mate who had sailed all over the world, and had therefore a much wider experience than most of the crew. He usually acted in those days as their spokesman. He had learned his seamanship in a tough school, and his training had made him not only an expert at his trade but also a tough character. His relationship with Mitchell and me was always more difficult than that of the rest of the men. Although he had faults, this difficulty was by no means all his fault. I was the only one of the British staff, either in Shetland or in London, who made any claim to a knowledge of seamanship, and I was by no means a professional seaman. But Salen had been an officer in the merchant service, and it was hard for him to accept the status of a petty officer in our gang, although he had volunteered for the job. On the other hand, it was neither desirable nor within our powers to make one of the skippers an officer.

However, we could not fail to respect Salen's ability as a seaman, and presumably he found something to respect in us, for he stayed with the unit for nearly four years and carried out many successful trips.

He sailed for Bueland on the 14th of September with about eight tons of cargo in the fish-hold of *Siglaos*. This cargo consisted primarily of implements for sabotage – high explosives with primers and detonators and a variety of fuses and igniters for use in different circumstances, together with a large quantity of incendiary bombs and hand grenades. There were also defensive weapons for the saboteurs, including .32 and 9 mm. automatics, knuckle-dusters, rubber truncheons and fighting knives.

At dusk on the 15th *Siglaos* closed the Norwegian coast, but the crew mistook one mountain for another farther north, with the result that they entered, in the dark, the channel north of the island of Kinn instead of the one south of it. The northern channel is full of skerries, whereas the southern one is clear, and they soon got involved with unexpected rocks on all sides. While they were feeling their way around people started flashing lights from several points on shore, and soon four men rowed out from Kinn and asked if they needed a pilot. Salen told them he was going in to get bait and had taken the wrong entrance, but while he was talking to them one of his crew gave the game away by lighting a cigarette. Cigarettes were very scarce in Norway, and the men in the boat asked for one each. After the first puff of real Virginia tobacco these men put two and two together and asked Salen to take them 'back west.' Three of them were ready to leave everything and climb aboard there and then. The fourth wanted to go ashore to tell his fiancée he was leaving, but as Salen had not yet carried out his mission he thought it would be unwise to let any of them leave the ship. With little hesitation all four came on board.

With these four passengers as pilots *Siglaos* arrived at the meeting place at 1.30 in the morning. A party of men were waiting with a motor boat, and cargo was transferred to it till it would hold no more. By the time this work was finished the first light of dawn could be seen in the eastern sky above the mountains, and Salen took *Siglaos* to a sheltered creek, surrounded by high cliffs, where they could lie safely through the hours of daylight.

This creek was very near the main convoy channel, and during the day several German convoys passed within a few hundred yards of *Siglaos*, but if the Germans saw her they took no notice, and the day passed without trouble. Salen told me later that he wished he had had a torpedo – a remark that perhaps took root in my mind and influenced later events.

During the night our principal 'contact' in this area, who had been helping with the unloading of the cargo, told Salen that he had twelve men in hiding in his district who were waiting for a chance to cross to Shetland. Salen agreed to take them, and the 'contact' promised to collect them during the day and bring them on board the following evening.

At dusk therefore another small motor boat entered the creek bringing these twelve passengers, and Salen weighed anchor. On the return voyage a strong southerly wind and a beam sea made *Siglaos* roll so heavily that her port rail was stove in and the deckhouse on the port side of the wheelhouse was smashed. The overcrowded boat, with bunks for only eight of the twenty-two men on board, was appallingly uncomfortable, and none of the crew was able to lie down or sleep during the forty hours' passage. Salen sensibly took his passengers to Lerwick instead of to Lunna – we did not want too many strangers to pass through our base. But three of the four men he had kidnapped from Kinn volunteered straight away to join up in our unit. There were two brothers, Leif and Olaf Kinn, and their half-brother A. B. Albertsen. Olaf Kinn and Albertsen both lost their lives in the service. Leif stayed with us to the end, and married an English girl.

While *Siglaos* was at sea both *Aksel* and *Vita* made successful trips. *Aksel* had to land two agents who were to organise resistance in the Ålesund district. One of these agents was the elder of two brothers, known as Karl-Johan or K.J., and Knut. These brothers formed one of the most successful of our permanent stations on the coast; between them they kept a radio transmitter and a flourishing organisation in Ålesund throughout the whole of the occupation. About every six months we would pick up one of them and land the other, so that one was always on duty in Norway while the other was in training or on holiday in England, and they and their organisation rescued many of our men who were cast ashore or otherwise in trouble in their district.

On this first occasion *Aksel* made landfall many miles south of the point she was bound for. She had steered to pass north of Stadtland, where the north-and-south line of the coast turns to run to the north-north-east; but at dawn on the morning after she sailed the crew saw land ahead where no land should have been. They recognised Bueland, over thirty miles south of Stadtland. They altered course to the northward, but the weather was thick, and as the compass was evidently not to be trusted, they did not try to close the land again till the following dawn. Then they found themselves off the island of Skorpen, and saw two men rowing out towards them.

One of these men, whose name was Johan Skorpen, knew Mindur

Berge, the engineer of *Aksel*, and volunteered to take the two agents ashore and to see them on their way to Ålesund. He also became well known to us. His farm on the island became one of our most regular meeting places on the whole of the coast, and many agents and shipwrecked men passed in and out of Norway through it.

Meanwhile *Vita* had carried out the longest trip we had so far undertaken, a round trip of eight hundred and seventy miles to a small island north of Trondheim, where a party of men organised by our agent in Trondheim were waiting to be picked up.

The crew of *Vita* were only five in number, but they were all old hands who had sailed in the previous spring. Ingvald Johansen was the skipper, a cheerful roguish fellow who seemed middle-aged compared with most of the men in the unit, and was therefore known to the British staff as Old Joe. He had contrived in the spring to break one of our strictest rules and to be forgiven. He had posted a letter in Norway. This was forbidden because letters in Norway were liable to be censored, and if many had been posted the Germans could easily have traced our movements. But this was not all. His letter was addressed to a lady he knew. It told her (and anyone else who happened to see it) the exact point he was to visit on his next trip, and it asked her to meet him there and to marry him. She accepted this romantic proposal, turned up at the rendezvous, and came over with him to Shetland.

This private operation was so successful that nobody had the heart to take action against him, except to point out that he had put both his own life and hers, and those of his crew, in the greatest of danger – but this he had known all the time. Arrangements were made for the pair to be married in Aberdeen, and in due course, as Fru Johansen, or Mrs Joe, the lady joined us at Lunna to help in running the house.

Old Joe's engineer was a stout merry lad whom everyone liked. His name was Hermansen, but he also was one of those people for whom a nickname seems natural, and he was always called Tromsö, since he lived in the town of that name in north Norway. Two of the deck hands were Sandvik and H. W. Olsen. These two were such close friends that they seemed to have no separate existence, and one always thought of them as a pair. At first I found them difficult to deal with; we seemed instinctively to mistrust each other. But in September Sandvik injured his foot, and it fell to me as man-of-all-work to dress it each evening. Olsen would sit in my room and watch. It was painful for Sandvik, and I was by no means an expert, but in hurting him I somehow grew quite fond of him, and therefore of Olsen as well; and at the same time their attitude to me seemed to change to a trust which it was not always easy to live up to. Later on these two friends spent over three years in concentration camps together, and it was no surprise to me when they turned up, still together, in Shetland after

1. Lunna — its peace soon to be disturbed by Norwegian freedom fighters.

2. Crew of the *Vita* at Lunna, Ingvald ('Old Joe') Johansen, A. S. Sandvik and J. A. ('Tromsö') Hermansen.

3. Lunna with Norwegian boats at anchor in the winter of 1941-42.

4. A fishing boat heads for Shetland in heavy weather, photo still from the film *Suicide Mission*. *Courtesy of Columbia Pictures*

5. *Arthur* **leaving Lunna with three agents (on the right). Crewmen (from left) are Leif Larsen Kinn, Kåre Iversen, Leif Larsen (captain). In the wheelhouse is Palmer Björnöy. Pevik, the agent on the far right, was killed in Norway.**

6. Still from the film *Suicide Mission*, showing the Twin Lewis gun, disguised in an oil barrel. *Courtesy of Columbia Pictures*

7. The two-man chariots — the devices used in an attempt to sink the German battleship *Tirpitz*. *Photo: Imperial War Museum*

the war, and asked me for a gold watch which Sandvik had given me to get repaired four years before. I had entirely forgotten the watch, but fortunately found in our archives some papers which reminded me what I had done with it.

The last of the crew of *Vita* was Jens Haldorsen. He was a quiet, gentle and studious man. His quietness made him conspicuous in our gang, most of whose members were extrovert and noisy, and his appearance also was not what one would expect in a seaman of proven toughness. With a thin ascetic face, and large calm and innocent brown eyes, he looked more like a priest or a poet. He spoke fluent English with an idiom all his own, and I always enjoyed hearing him telling a story in a slow, rather mournful voice, in which the most powerful swear words passed almost unnoticed. One such story remains in my mind. We were sitting on the hillside below the house screwing together lengths of pipe to supply the boats with water at the pier, and he was telling me about a dance which the men had attended on the neighbouring island of Whalsay.

'Oh, there's very nice people in Whalsay,' he said. 'They was very nice to us there. And they was telling me there is a bloody big shark in the bay, and that's bad for the fishing, you see, he's chasing those fishes away. So they's wanting to shoot on that bloody big shark, and they ask me have I got a reefle ? And I say, no, we're only poor Norwegian fisher boys, they doesn't give us no reefles. (This was a security lie.) And I'm sorry, because I am wanting to shoot on the bloody old shark, because they was nice people and I am wanting to help them.'

No-one could help liking Haldorsen.

These five men took *Vita* on her long trip without incident, and after six days at sea brought ten refugees into Lerwick. On the way back the weather was bad and the passengers were seasick, so that the crew had to give up their bunks and, according to their own account, spend most of the time holding buckets.

Old Joe also brought us a letter from Trondheim, which (translated) read as follows:

' To the Captain in Shetland   8 September 1941

'A number of people, airmen, officers, radio operators, etc. must go over [to Shetland]. They are already assembled and hidden in Trondelag. The police are already searching for many of them. It is requested that the boat which brings you this letter should be put on a regular run to the same meeting-place on the following dates:

'September 23, October 4, 15 and 26, November 6, 17 and 28, December 9.

'If difficulties are encountered in making the rendezvous at the pre-arranged time, a second attempt should be made twenty-four hours later.

'On each trip the boat must bring three days' iron rations for ten men, for the use of the next boat's party during the period of waiting, plus a total of one hundred litres of diesel oil and ten litres of lubricating oil in small cans for local transport.

'If this plan cannot be approved in its entirety, the boat must at all events come on the 23rd and give your full decision in a sealed letter to our representative at the rendezvous.'

With our slender resources, and the other work we had in hand, this was an ambitious programme, but we determined to do the best we could for the Trondheim agent, who was a trustworthy and efficient man. It so happened that *Igland* was due to leave the day after *Vita* returned, to pick up some men farther south. This party had also been organised in Trondheim, and we expected that one of our agent's men would turn up at the rendezvous. We therefore gave Ole Grotle in *Igland* a letter, written on silk so that it could be concealed in clothing, addressed to the agent. We told him we could not undertake a definite schedule of trips, but that we would in any case try to send over the boat on the 23rd, and that her skipper would be able to give him the date for the next meeting.

The rendezvous arranged for *Igland* was at a place we would certainly not have agreed to after we became more experienced. It was at the head of Vinjefjord, forty miles from the open sea, and with no alternative route of escape if the boat had been detected after she had entered. To get there, she had first to enter Griphölen, a sound about two miles wide just north of Kristiansund, passing the German watchpost which we knew was established in the lighthouse on the southern shore of the sound. Thence she would steam up Edöyfjord, which was the main route for coastal traffic, and she must cross to the southern side to keep clear of a battery of guns on the north shore. From Edöyfjord she would turn south down one of three narrow sounds which led after five or six miles into Vinjefjord itself, and there she had yet another ten miles to go up the cul-de-sac towards the head of the fjord.

It must be confessed that this was a foolish plan. The place was proposed by the people in Trondheim, but we should have known better than to accept it. Throughout our four years of operations inexperienced agents always tried to persuade us to send boats far into the fjords to meet them; they probably felt safer as soon as they boarded the boats. But in fact, as we very soon learned, it was much safer for the agent himself to make his own way to the outermost islands, either by using a local boat, which if necessary could pass an unexpected control, or at worst by walking and rowing by night. This was also, of course, much the safer plan for our boats and their crews.

But we had not yet learned this lesson, and on 17th September *Igland* left Lunna. Ole Grotle again kept a log in his own style:

Sept. 17 2130 Left Lunna with order to go to Vinjefjord. Exact place is Hovde, where we are to collect four men.

 2255 Log set to zero off Fetlar. Weather fine.

Sept. 18 0930 Log reads 82 miles. N.W. wind. Fog.

 1935 Log reads 158 miles. Wind N.W. Nearly dark. All well.

Sept. 19 0630 Log reads 236 miles. Wind W.

 1200 Log reads 275 miles. Course altered $\frac{1}{2}$ point to N. Trying to recognise coast. Lighthouse 2 points to starboard. Resembles Grip Light.

 1530 Grip now abeam about three miles off. According to our information there should be a German watch on the lighthouse. If so they certainly have seen us. We decide to go in at once, following the old proverb which says, 'It is better to jump in than crawl in.'

 1645 We are now in Skeia. A German trawler is going along the other side of the fjord on a southerly course. I believe it is a watch boat. We are trying to keep as close in to Smölen as possible to avoid being seen by this boat.

 1845 We are now half way along Edöyfjord, making course for Aursund. Nothing suspicious observed. Can just make out a watchboat off the Kristiansund coast.

 1930 Proceeding down Aursund. Reckon to be off Hovde by 2100.

 2100 Off Hovde. Hove to waiting for someone to come on board.

 2130 This all seems very mysterious. Have been waiting half an hour but no-one has turned up. Can see there are people up at the farm as a light is showing and they must have heard us coming. I am going ashore to see what's up. Taking Anfinn with me.

 2215 Going full speed down the fjord. We got bad news ashore. At the first place we came to we learned nothing. We asked whether there were any strangers living there or at any of the other farms. At first they wouldn't say anything. They seemed to think we were Gestapo, they looked very upset. Then they advised us to go to the farm Hovde which was five minutes away, there they would tell us what we wanted to know. I felt so sorry for the wife in the house, she was trembling with fright, so I knew there was something devilish afoot. A girl offered to show us the way to the other farm. When we got half way we met two girls and a man. One of the girls was the daughter of the farmer at Hovde, and she told us what had happened. It was true they had had three strangers on the farm, but yesterday afternoon a lot of German soldiers came and arrested all three. They had taken two men on another farm, so they got five altogether. The Germans are also searching for ships which were to pick up the men. They have been patrolling in and out of the fjord since midday today. The girl said all ships passing on the main lead were being stopped and asked for passes. The fishermen had even been made to break open their herring barrels to show they really contained herrings. They had made a thorough search. Yes, this really was news. And we were lying in the middle of a fjord not much more than a stone's throw in width and six hours from the open sea. So we didn't have time for talk. We got on board in a hell of a hurry and got cleared away for action. We were very angry both with the Germans and the people who had sent us, but we are going to put up a fight however many there are in the pack. As we managed to get in, we must be able to get out, I believe.

2330 Have got through Aursund. Passed two boats in the middle of the sound. One of them seemed to be standing still, so I thought it was a watchboat, but fortunately it was a small steamer with very little speed. It had one boat in tow.

Sept. 20 0100 Now going south along Edöyfjord. Stiff breeze from the S.W. As dark as a coffin. Can't see the lighthouse, so I am navigating by time and compass. It will be very difficult to reach open sea without seeing anything. But it looks as though we have good luck with us, so we think everything will be O.K.

0430 We have passed Grip to the open sea and set the log again. We got too far south on the shoals on the east side of Grip Light, and saw nothing till the sea was breaking on the rocks on all sides. Fortunately we saw the lighthouse at once, close ahead, so we knew exactly where we were. I had to go hard astern, and went cautiously to the north to get into clear water. Then set course to the west. Strong wind from south and a choppy sea. Doing seven knots now. Everything is jumping about, but it's good to be clear to the west.

After this narrow escape we never attempted to send a boat so far into the fjords — except on one memorable occasion. It taught us also that 'pick-ups' had their special dangers, for it was only the fact that the men waiting in Vinjefjord had been compromised which put *Igland* into any special danger. Had she been landing men there, instead of trying to embark them, the operation would have been accomplished without any incident, except for the manner in which she so nearly ran on the rocks at the feet of the German sentries on Grip.

But this lesson was soon to be taught in an even more serious manner. On the day that *Igland* returned, *Vita* was due to sail on the first of the pick-ups requested in the letter from Trondheim. She had actually sailed an hour before *Igland* returned, but as soon as we heard of the arrests in Vinjefjord we inquired from headquarters whether there was any connection between the arrested men and the party who were waiting for *Vita*. If there were, it was more than likely that the second party would have been arrested as well, and it was not yet too late to send out an aircraft to intercept *Vita* and tell her to return. But we were informed that there was no known connection between them, and *Vita* was allowed to continue her voyage.

I shall always remember her sailing. *Aksel* was in Lerwick with engine trouble, and *Siglaos* was having her deckhouse rebuilt, so *Vita* had had a large share of the work for some time. After she had returned with the first party of refugees, she had had to take a couple of agents across to an island near Bergen, which she accomplished without any trouble. She had only twenty-four hours in harbour between her return from this trip and her sailing for the pick-up. Old Joe had decided that he and his crew deserved a night off in Lerwick, and I entirely agreed.

After his last trip to pick up refugees, when the crew had suffered from the congestion in the cabins with ten seasick passengers, I had promised to sling some hammocks in the fish hold, and to cut a door in the forward bulkhead to give access to the hold without the necessity of opening the fish hatch. With Joe and his men enjoying themselves in town, I was the only person at Lunna who could possibly do this small job, and after my day's work was over I spent most of the night in sawing a hole in the tough inaccessible bulkhead in order to have the ship ready in time.

Joe got back to Lunna a few minutes before his sailing time, in a happy and contented condition: like most of our gang he liked a good drink at the base, but was almost teetotal at sea. Tromsö and Haldorsen, and Sandvik and Olsen, were all ready and in the best of humours. Joe looked at my door and the hammock hooks in the hold, and said, 'Thanks, Hovart, you did a fine job to get that ready for us.'

It was rare to be thanked or commended by any Norwegian, and I was glad to know I had pleased him. But I specially remembered this remark because it was the last thing he said as his ship drew away from the pier; and he never returned.

On this occasion, the first time we had lost a ship, news of her came very soon. She had sailed on 22nd September, and she might have been back on the 28th. The 29th and the 30th passed without sign of her, but we were not very worried; so many things might have delayed her on a passage of such a length. Then on the 30th we deciphered a signal from London:

'Ship number SS 18 F arrested with all hands.
Is this *Vita*'s number?
Telegraph Most Immediate.'

This news was only too certain. The number painted on *Vita* just then was SF 18 F; the coincidence was too close to leave any room for doubt.

But as soon as we had told London that the boat was undoubtedly *Vita*, we received a second 'Most Immediate' signal. We were told that the news of the arrest had come from a man in so perilous a position that we must not pass on the news to anyone else under any circumstances whatever.

This was a cruel thing to be ordered to do. Mrs Joe was still at Lunna, and as the days passed she grew more and more anxious about her husband. It was true that the knowledge which Mitchell and I had would not have been much comfort to her, because it was generally believed that to be captured and delivered to the Gestapo was worse than to be killed; but any news would have been better for her than none. Both Mitchell and I were hard tempted to tell her what we knew; but apart from knowing the seriousness of such an offence we also knew the importance of the source of the news. If we had told the crews that we already knew what had happened, and if another boat was captured and its crew revealed by mistake or under torture that they knew about the *Vita*, many other lives would have been lost. No humanitarian consideration would justify taking this risk.

So poor Mrs Joe had to suffer uncertainty for several weeks, till more detailed news began to come through from our agents in Trondheim. Then we learned that the Germans had traced the party of refugees to their rendezvous. The refugees had escaped, but a German warship was posted to wait for *Vita*. *Vita* met it at point-blank range in a bend in a narrow channel, and was swept with fire before she could turn to escape.

But the crew all survived for four years in captivity and were not badly treated. Old Joe and Mrs Joe, I presume, are now reunited, and if she should ever see these pages I hope she will forgive me.

CHAPTER THREE

AIR ATTACK

AMONG our diverse jobs at Lunna that autumn was the fitting out of a fishing boat called *Nordsjöen* as a 'Q-ship' minelayer. We worked on this boat for six weeks, and finally sailed her to Norway on 9th October. She should have come back in five days; but weeks passed without news of her, and on our trips that month the crews left under the shadow of the fear that she had been lost. Her story is told in the next chapter.

Meanwhile a further anxiety, on the heels of the news about *Vita*, had been for the safety of *Aksel*. She had left before *Vita* was due to return, and before we had heard of the capture, to pick up another party of Trondheim refugees at a point even farther north – the island of Traena, right on the Arctic Circle. We knew that both parties were connected with the same organisation in Trondheim, and as soon as we heard about *Vita* we started desperate attempts to recall *Aksel* before she could reach her rendezvous where, we felt sure, she would fall into another German ambush.

At that time each ship had been fitted with an ordinary domestic wireless receiver so that the crews could hear the weather forecasts and have a little entertainment on their watches below. But no arrangements had been made for sending messages to them, and the crews of course had no training in ciphers or telegraphy.

So our first step was to appeal to the R.A.F. for a search. We gave them a description of *Aksel*, with the registration number which she was using at the moment, and an area in the neighbourhood of 63°N where we hoped they would find her. We asked the pilot to signal 'return' very slowly with his Aldis lamp if he should sight her. A Sunderland took off from Shetland, but it returned in the evening with the report that nothing had been seen and that visibility in the area of the search was only five hundred yards.

By the following day *Aksel* should have been close in to the coast, and we wondered whether it was right to ask another air crew to run the risk of searching in enemy waters, six hundred miles from home, on the slender chance of finding her. The only aircraft at that time which could have reached and searched the sea round Traena were Sunderlands and Catalinas, neither of which had much chance of escape if they were detected within fighter range of the German bases. Mitchell and I drove during the night to the R.A.F. station at Sullom Voe, in the north of Shetland, and put the problem to the station commander. He telephoned to his group headquarters. The Group Captain said that our boys were doing a tough job, and he didn't like to think of them putting their heads in a noose. The next morning a Catalina from a base in Scotland flew eight hundred miles to Traena; but visibility in the district was very low and a forty-five knot wind was blowing. They could find nothing.

On the same morning we heard from our head office that they could arrange with the B.B.C. to broadcast a fake S. O. S. message in the six o'clock news, to which the crews usually listened. We made up some bogus names to include the name of the boat and several of those of the crew: 'Will *Aksel* August Berge, at present believed to be fishing, return at once to port, as his brother Ivar Mindur Berge is dangerously ill.' This duly went out at the beginning of the news. If the crew heard it they would know very well what we meant.

After this there was no more we could do, as *Aksel* must either have reached Traena or given up the attempt.

For twelve days we had no news, and we began to despair of seeing her again. But on the night of 10th October, as I was undressing to go to bed, I heard it: that distant tonk-tonk of the engine, so faint at first that for several minutes I could not be sure whether I heard it or whether my wish to hear it had made me imagine it among the sounds of the wind and sea. But it grew louder till I was certain; and everyone in the base went down to the quay to hear what had happened.

After these long periods of waiting it was often a surprise to find the returning crew in a different frame of mind from our own. Sometimes when we had been most worried they turned up cheerful, nonchalant or even hilarious. But on this occasion the crew of *Aksel* was tired and disgruntled. They had had an uncomfortable three days' journey north in storm and fog. Their compass on a previous trip had led them astray, and we had had a new one fitted and corrected, but they had again made landfall far south of the proper place, and had to follow the coast for thirty-six hours. They had also collided with some wreckage in darkness and damaged their rudder, so that when they ran into heavy weather later they were afraid it was going to drop off. It was the fact that all hands were busy trying to make the rudder fast in a storm which prevented any of them hearing the B.B.C. message.

In spite of all this they had arrived in Traena and gone ashore. They learned from local people that a week before a number of Gestapo men had arrived in the islands and searched them high and low. There were no strangers in the place, but three men with rucksacks had come in the mail boat on the day after the search had been made, and on hearing of it had left again in a hurry.

The mail boat was due in again on the day after *Aksel* arrived, so August Naeröy the skipper decided to wait for her. When she came in one of the crew went aboard her and bought some beer, but there was nobody on the boat who could have been a refugee; so the crew spent the afternoon in buying salt fish, newspapers, matches and a large baulk of timber to steer with in case the rudder gave way; and in the evening they put to sea again.

On their second day out, when they were off Ålesund, they spotted what they thought was a periscope, and to their dismay it began to follow them. They worked *Aksel* up to nine knots – a knot faster than her usual top speed. But the periscope followed behind for three hours, when darkness began to fall and they lost sight of it. All night they held on at full speed in a thick fog. At dawn a main bearing of the engine failed.

They had to heave-to for two days before they could get the bearing repaired. It was a hard job with the boat tossing unevenly in a confused sea, and to add to their discomfort their food was beginning to run short. The trip had already taken three times as long as it should have.

In view of their difficulties and the failure of their mission it was hardly surprising that they came back to Lunna fed up. But all of us were learning all the time, and their experience led us first to make sure that all boats which sailed later carried a month's iron rations in watertight cases; and secondly to ask London to send us radio receivers which could pick up naval stations, some small transmitters and an instructor to teach the crews to use them.

By the time *Aksel* returned the deckhouse of *Siglaos*, which had been stove in in a storm, had been rebuilt and she was ready for sea. With Salen as skipper she carried out a good routine trip, taking an agent to Bremnes in the island of Bömlo near Haugesund. The sea was heavy and confused throughout the trip, and the deckhouse was demolished a second time in exactly the same manner as before.

With *Nordsjöen* already overdue, *Vita* lost and *Aksel* in Lerwick getting her bearing properly repaired, we were short of ships. A new boat called the *Jakk* was being made ready for sea by a crew under a skipper called Gundersen – a cheerful merchant service man who had travelled the world and spoke English with a delightful Hollywood accent. But a second trip to the Haugesund district was urgently needed, to take an agent who was to travel farther inland; and as the *Jakk* was not ready and the crew of the *Siglaos* were tired, Gundersen took over *Siglaos*, the deckhouse was quickly repaired and she set off again for Bömlo.

The exact point for this landing was the village of Øklandsvaag. Among Gundersen's crew was a young man called Økland who lived in this village, and another, called Nils Nesse, who came from the larger neighbouring village of Bremnes. *Siglaos* made landfall as dusk was falling, and by ten in the evening the two local boys had piloted her into the little bay on which Øklandsvaag stands. Nesse went ashore to find the doctor from Bremnes, who was to look after the agent, and about midnight he brought him on board.

A dance was in progress in Øklandsvaag, and there were too many people on the Bremnes road for the agent's luggage, which included a radio transmitter as well as some crates of arms, to be carried along it. So they dumped it on the quay, where it looked less out of place. Some men and women from the dance came aboard, but when they found out what was happening they went back on shore, and kept other sightseers away by telling them that *Siglaos* was a German boat, and that anyone who went near her would be asked to show his papers. When the dance broke up in the early morning the luggage was taken to Bremnes; and during the day the agent crossed safely to the town of Lervik, on the next island, which was the first stage of his journey.

By the time these arrangements had been made it was too late for *Siglaos* to get clear of the coast before dawn, so she lay alongside the quay till the following evening. Both Økland and Nesse visited their families and found them in good health, and the doctor turned up again and asked if he could put some passengers on board for the return trip. Gundersen said he could only take people who were in serious trouble, but the doctor returned in the evening with two men, two women and three children. One of the women, the mother of two of the children, was the Norwegian wife of an American citizen who had escaped a year earlier. She had been lying low in Lervik waiting for a chance to follow him. The other woman was a Norwegian nurse who had been in the Channel Islands when they were invaded. The Germans had kept her for four months in a prison in France, and had then sent her back to her own country; and ever since her arrival there she had been trying to get back to Britain. On the strength of these two stories Gundersen agreed to take them all, though he never found out who the two men were, or the third of the children.

They left Øklandsvaag just before midnight on 27th October. On their way over the weather had been bad, but now it was worse. A whole gale was blowing from the north-west, on their starboard bow, and by dawn they were only fifty miles from the coast. As the first grey light came into the sky they sighted a twin-engined aircraft to the southward. Gundersen was in the charthouse, Nesse at the wheel, Bård Grotle, the engineer, in the engine-room. The rest of the crew and all the passengers were in the cabin.

At that time our boats were armed with anti-tank rifles, Bren guns and tommy guns, the Brens being mounted on detachable mountings on deck. But the weather was so bad, with seas sweeping the deck, that all the arms had been taken inside and lashed down. Before anything could be done to mount them the aircraft turned, approached *Siglaos* at mast height from astern, and opened fire with cannon. Gundersen ran to the forecastle hatch, with Bård Grotle behind him, and as they reached the door the first burst of fire smashed it to pieces. The cabin was full of luggage belonging to the refugees, which had cast loose on the floor, and before they could get the guns up on deck the aircraft had made a second run over the ship from the bow, firing with cannon from nose and tail. On its third run, from astern, Bård Grotle emptied a tommy gun magazine at it. It immediately turned in a wide circle and disappeared towards the east.

Nils Nesse had stuck to the wheel throughout the attack, but they saw him fall. He was hit in the head and the leg. With the help of the nurse they bandaged his wounds and carried him to a bunk, but there was no hope that he would recover. He died an hour later without regaining consciousness.

Siglaos had continued under way during the attack, and when the nurse had attended to Nesse, Gundersen put the boat on its course again and inspected the damage. It was widespread but superficial. The upper works and lifeboat were riddled with shell holes, the sails in rags, and the mizzen mast cut nearly through, but the hull itself was undamaged. They continued throughout the day to plug into a heavy head sea. After night fall they came up under Sumburgh Head, in the south of Shetland, and hove-to until dawn. At first light they made their way into Lerwick.

Nesse was the first man to lose his life in our unit. He was little more than a boy, like many of the members of our crews, and all of us, both British and Norwegian, were saddened by the sudden premature ending of a young happy life.

In a morning of calm and winter sunshine we buried him at Lunna, in the graveyard of the ancient church below the house. There was nobody to conduct his funeral in Norwegian; but many of the other young ones wept as the Scottish service, which they could hardly understand, was read in the sombre grey stone church. After the committal the Last Post was sounded, and one of the men started to sing the Norwegian National Anthem. All joined in. I saluted the grave and the other officers present followed suit.

We were a solemn and silent party as we climbed the hill to the house. Not only had the loss of Nesse depressed us. The capture of the *Vita* was still fresh in our minds, and now the *Nordsjöen*, which had left three weeks before on her mine-laying expedition, was so long overdue that we knew that something serious must have happened, and had little hope of seeing the seven men of her crew again. I myself, as I walked up the hill, was reflecting on all these disasters, and I thought that at that moment we could not have sailed another operation. It was too much to expect that with thirteen of our number missing — a third of our seagoing strength — the remaining men would be willing to sail into a danger which was unknown, and which it seemed must be greater than any of us had supposed.

But in this I had underrated the courage of one man who had newly arrived, and whom at that time I hardly knew. His name was Per Blystad.

At lunchtime he approached Mitchell, and told him that he had taken a fancy to a very small boat called the *Olaf* which was lying in Cat Firth. He asked if he could take over this boat and fit her himself, and then, if he could muster a crew, sail her as skipper. We knew he had the technical skill to do this, and the fact that he made his proposal at such a moment proved in itself that he had the courage to do it. We accepted his suggestion gladly; but we could not know then how well we should come to know Per or how implicitly we should rely on his judgment.

After dinner I wandered down to the pier with one of the London staff who was with us on a visit, and we discussed the situation. It seemed pretty serious. He was asking me whether I thought Blystad would be able to find a crew. I was doubtful; unless, I said, we got some good news of the *Nordsjöen*. As I said these words we both stopped. We listened. Was it. . . ? Seconds passed and we heard nothing. Then a shift of the breeze and it came unmistakably: tonk-tonk-tonk. A Norwegian engine. But whose ? 'It can't be one of ours,' I said; 'every single man's here. Can't be a refugee, nobody in Norway knows the way into this harbour.' 'And yet,' someone said, 'the *Nordsjöen*? If it's her, where on earth has she been all this time?'

The sound grew louder. We watched with aching suspense the point of land to the northward where the boat would first be seen. It was impossible to imagine that *Nordsjöen* could be coming in under her own power after three weeks at sea; she would have run out of fuel long ago. Unless she'd broken down and been drifting.

A mast appeared first. It grew downwards as the boat cleared the slope of the hill, until the stem was visible. A tall topmast. 'It's not one of ours,' I said. And then — the V sign on the siren. 'But it's our boys', I added, and jumped into a dinghy and rowed out to meet them.

As the strange vessel slowed and I closed her I saw Larsen, then Björnöy. Norwegian quite failed me. 'By God, I'm glad to see you,' I shouted. 'Larsen, Björnöy, Pletten, Sangolt, Nipen. Where are the others? Where's Gjertsen and Merkesdal? And what the devil's this boat you've got?' But by then everyone from the house had packed into dinghies and come alongside, and so many questions were being hurled at the crew that no-one could make out what really had happened. So we anchored the boat and took them ashore, and as they wolfed bacon and eggs I began to hear a remarkable story.

CHAPTER FOUR

SHIPWRECK

I DO not know who first thought of laying mines from fishing boats. The idea had been discussed for months. Some people argued against it, on the ground that a mine laid in the shipping leads in Norway was more likely to sink a Norwegian ship than a German, since Norwegians were still in the majority. But during the summer a small party of men had been trained for the job, and the hold of one of our spare boats contained dozens of R-type mines – a small contact mine about eighteen inches high. These had been made in the days before France fell, to be launched in the Rhine and Moselle in the hope that they would float downstream towards the Ruhr, and many were actually used for this purpose. In the spring of 1941 one of our boats had carried eighteen of them on deck and had laid them in one of the main leads on the Norwegian coast. It was rumoured that a ship had been sunk; but it had been difficult to lay the things quickly in the dark, and before the crew had finished the job a coastal battery grew suspicious and fired some shots at them. There was obviously more room for ingenuity in the matter of stowage and laying, and in September we started to fit out one of our boats for the purpose.

The general idea was to stow all the mines in troughs in the hold, and to cut a camouflaged watertight door in the hull through which the mines could be laid without the necessity of bringing them up on deck. The *Nordsjöen* had been chosen, and Gjertsen was made her skipper. Soon after we had started work on her the party of men who had been trained with the mines arrived and were formed into a crew: Leif Larsen, Karsten Sangolt, Merkesdal, Björnöy, Pletten and Nils Nipen. With them was Chief Petty Officer Percy, R.N., an expert who had been on the expedition to the Rhine, and whom we managed to keep in our party for over a year before the Admiralty dug in their heels and demanded him back.

We put a lot of hard work into *Nordsjöen*, with the help of some carpenters at the R.A.F. station on the other side of the island, and the results were quite promising. We first cut the hole in the hull, on the starboard side at the forward end of the hold. It was about two feet square, and was closed on the outside by a hinged wooden door, carefully stained to match the rest of the ship. Inside was a steel door-frame, which replaced the strength we had cut out and also carried a steel watertight door which opened inwards. From ten yards away nothing suspicious could be seen.

Opposite the door, in the hold, were a pair of steel rollers, and running aft from the rollers for the whole length of the hold we built two strong wooden rails. Seven troughs for the mines lay athwartships on top of the rails. For laying the mines, the first trough was pulled on to the rollers and rolled lengthways till its end projected a foot beyond the door. The first mine, which had a sinker attached to it by a long length of line, was pushed off the end of the trough. The sinker sank to the bottom, unwinding its line, and as the mine floated astern it pulled out a coil of grassline made fast to the second mine. When the grassline tightened it pulled out the second mine. Each trough contained six mines with a hundred feet of line between each, so that at eight knots we could lay a five-hundred-foot string of mines in under a minute. As soon as the first trough was emptied, the next was pulled into its place, and in another minute it also was ready for launching.

We practised this technique round and round Lunna Voe, and by the middle of October the *Nordsjöen* was ready to sail.

There were not many places in the main shipping lead where it was possible to lay these mines, because most of the lead is very deep, and our home-made sinkers became difficult to manage with more than seventy fathoms of line. After searching the charts of the whole coast of western Norway we decided to try the laying in Edöyfjord, just north of Kristiansund, which was the main channel from the south to the important anchorage of Trondheim. This could be reached in the dark by passing the German watchpost in the lighthouse in the mouth of the wide fjord called Griphölen, and there were plenty of small islands to the north of the fjord among which a boat could hide during daylight.

Nordsjöen left Lunna on the morning of 19th October with a cargo of forty-two mines. The weather forecast predicted a wind of ten to fifteen miles an hour. But on the morning of the 20th we woke at Lunna to hear the familiar roaring of wind and rattling of tiles and windows; and when I looked out I saw the spray whipping over the pier in a full north-westerly gale. We felt anxious about the boat and her cargo. In particular C.P.O. Percy and I, who had made the hole in her hull and stowed the mines in her hold, wished we were with her to share the consequences, for better or worse, of our calculations and workmanship. We hoped she would turn back and wait for a better chance. But the next day brought no sign of her; and in fact (as we heard three weeks later) she weathered this storm without damage, and made landfall at Stadtland after a passage of twenty-four hours.

From Stadtland she sailed all day and all night up the coast. But the storm had delayed her, and by the time she arrived off Kristiansund it was too late to get in past the watchpost in Griphölen and to hide among the islands before dawn. So the skipper decided to make for the island of Smölen, which forms the north side of both Griphölen and Edöyfjord, and to try a very difficult inshore passage through the maze of small islands and rocks which fringes this part of the coast. This passage is not very dangerous, because the rocks lie so thickly for several miles offshore that once the right entrance has been found and negotiated the waters are well sheltered. But there are so many small shallow sounds and so many hundreds of low-lying islands that without local knowledge the channel is almost impossible to find. By midday, after four or five hours of taking wrong turnings, they had only made six of the twelve miles to Edöyfjord. But then they met two local men in a rowing boat, and asked them on board. These men could see at a glance that some dirty work was afoot, and did not seem inclined to take part in it. But a bribe of two hundred and fifty kroner, and an offer of coffee and food, won them over, and by four in the afternoon they had piloted *Nordsjöen* to the lee of an island on the north shore of the fjord. Here the crew anchored, got rid of the pilots, and set to work to unlash the mines, fit the detonators and clock mechanisms inside them and make everything ready for laying.

All day the wind had been rising, and when after dark they came out into the open fjord they found such a sea on their beam that waves came in through the mine door, and on the heaviest roll some of the mines in the last trough started sliding and crashed into the bottom of the hold. (A mine is not 'live' until a certain time after its clock has been put in and started, but it is always rather alarming to drop one.) They therefore turned more to the east to bring the sea farther astern; and on this course the first eighteen mines were successfully laid. Then, according to plan, they made a wide turn to starboard and laid a second row diagonally across the fjord.

As soon as the last trough was empty they headed west for the open sea. But as they passed through Griphölen they met the full force of another north-wester and a high sea against them. Under normal conditions they would have hove-to in such weather, or gone back to shelter; but the skipper had made up his mind to be far from the minefield by dawn, when the mines would be live and things might begin to happen; so he kept going full speed into the head sea. The ship was coming clear of the wave crests for half of her length and was pounding heavily into the troughs: yet they were barely making three knots. It was more than she could stand. A little after midnight, when they were seven or eight miles out, the engineer on watch saw a spray of water thrown up by the flywheel of the engine. He called all hands, and Sangolt went down into the hold. There were two feet of water in it. More was coming in through the inner planking on the starboard side of the forecastle, and the cement ballast in the hold was breaking up, which showed that her bottom was stove in or her keel broken. The mine door was intact, but later on it began to leak too.

They turned and ran with the storm towards the coast. As the engine was awash they set sail, and no sooner had they done so than water started pouring from the exhaust pipe and the engine stopped. A moment later the foresail and mizzen burst into shreds and vanished. Nothing could be seen in the lashing of rain and spray; and with only the small triangular mainsail set, and with the ship very low in the water, they drove at six knots towards the rock-bound coast.

Either by luck or by instinct or skill they sailed straight into Griphölen again. For a time, with the ship sinking under them, even a known German watchpost had seemed like safety, and they felt that if they could beach *Nordsjöen* below the lighthouse it would be the best they could hope for. But as they came into quieter seas the water in the hold did not rise so quickly, and they decided to push on into the fjord. Inside Griphölen the channel divides into two. The northern arm was the one they had mined, so they turned south; but before they could reach the southern arm they felt that *Nordsjöen* was going. With the ship sailing more and more sluggishly they steered for the first of the series of islands which divides the two arms, and hove-to in its lee. They let go the anchor, but a shackle jammed in the hawse and before they could free it the deck was awash. As she sank they got the lifeboat clear and rowed ashore on the island. It was half-past three in the morning.

They pulled up the boat, turned it upside down on the beach and lay down underneath it. They were wet and cold and exhausted, and three hundred miles from the nearest friendly land. But each of them still had a pistol, and when they came to take stock they found they had salvaged between them four hundred and fifty kroner and six English pounds, a tin of ship's biscuits and half a bottle of rum. Someone said things might have been worse.

When dawn broke they saw that the masts and part of the bow of *Nordsjöen* were showing above the water. This was unfortunate, because when the first German patrol saw the wreck they would certainly connect it with the mines a few miles away and would begin to search the neighbourhood. They agreed that they must get away from Edöyfjord without losing time.

Larsen had noticed before they lost their charts that four houses were marked on a neighbouring island. The first thing they needed was to get dry and warm, so they rowed across to the island, hid the boat in the bed of a stream and walked over the hills towards the houses. It was still early, but some men were already working in the fields. They approached them and told them they had lost their ship, and asked to be allowed to go into a house and sit in front of the fire. All of the crew were wearing some part of their uniform, so it was useless to pretend they had not come from 'the other side'; but they told the men they had been sent from England to pick up some refugees who had not arrived at their meeting-place.

The men took them into a house, but they were plainly frightened. One of them produced a small poster which the Germans had decreed must

8. Dinapore on Scalloway's Main Street, the headquarters for the Scalloway base.

9. Local people watch with interest as the slipway at Scalloway prepares to take its first vessel for repairs.

10. & 11. Hardanger cutters at anchor off Scalloway, *Feie* (above) and *Jakk* (below).

12. *Andholmen* at anchor in Scalloway Harbour. She was an example of a modern type of Möre cutter.

13. Camping equipment, uniforms and arms being packed into German cases and Norwegian paint drums at Scalloway.

14. Harald Angeltveit and Erling Roswall with other Norwegian engineers in the Scalloway workshop.

be displayed in the wheelhouse of every fishing boat. It said, 'Contact with the enemy is punished with death.'

'Yes,' said Larsen, 'we've seen that before. But the question is, who is 'the enemy'? If you think we are your enemies, just say so and we'll go.'

'No, no,' the man protested, 'we are all good Norwegians here. But we shall be glad,' he added, 'if you will go away as soon as possible.'

While they were getting dry they thought over their situation. The obvious plan was for them to make their way to one of the districts farther south in which they had friends. The nearest of these was Ålesund, where Björnöy lived, and where he was certain his father would help them to find a boat to take them back to Lunna. But even that was seventy miles away, and to get there by land three wide fjords had to be crossed, with snow-covered mountains between them rising to six thousand feet.

Their best chance, it was clear, was to get there by sea; and while they were wondering how they could arrange this a large fishing boat dropped anchor off the island. The men of the house recognised it and told them it was bound for the south; so with high hopes five of them hurried down to it to try to get a passage from the skipper.

By then they had cut the brass buttons off their tunics and fastened them with nails, and they put on their oilskins in order to hide what remained of their uniforms. But the skipper of the boat was suspicious and asked if their passes were in order; and when they admitted that they were not he refused to help them.

They decided at once that they would take the boat by force, and one of them ran back to the houses to fetch the two men they had left behind — Gjertsen the skipper and Merkesdal.

They had disappeared.

The men of the house did not know where they had gone. But one of them cautiously added that he had heard that the Germans were searching all ships in the fjord.

This made it useless to attack the fishing boat; and after a moment's reflection it led them to suspect the men of the island. How had they heard the news? Somebody must have used the telephone. Had they rung up the police? If so, time was short. The remaining five of the crew packed all that they could of the stores they had salved into their pockets and set off into the forest which covered the central part of the island.

They walked through the woods for some hours. The thick trees would give them a few hours of security and rest; among them, at least, it felt safer than in the open fields. As evening approached they found a small hut in a clearing. It was empty except for two of the things they needed most – a bed and a stove. They collected some wood for the stove and some berries to eat with the ship's biscuits, and then settled down, with one man on watch, for a long night's sleep.

Rest and warmth brought back their strength, and they woke in high spirits. Early in the morning they approached the shore at a point farther up the fjord and began to search for a boat to take them off the island. After many cautious conversations with local people they found a farmer who was willing to take them across to the southern shore of the fjord in a motor boat. But he warned them not to come to his house before six in the evening because, he said, two Nazis were coming that afternoon to assess his stock of corn. So they waited in the woods till half-past six. But the Nazis were late. As the five men in ill-disguised uniform walked up to the door of the house, it opened and the two Nazis came out. Five hands gripped pistol butts in oilskin pockets and waited. The Nazis walked past without a word.

Inside the house the farmer was wiping sweat from his face. For half an hour he had been trying to get rid of his unwelcome visitors, and expecting every moment that the crew of the *Nordsjöen* would walk cheerfully in and give him and themselves away. There was another man with him. He brought the news that Gjertsen and Merkesdal had been taken safely across the fjord the previous night. He suggested that it would be unwise for more men to take the same route, and offered to give them an old rowing boat in which they could make their way as far as possible down the fjord before landing. They agreed to this plan and gave him £2 10s in English notes for the boat. He was delighted, and threw in some bread and some maps of the district.

After four or five miles in the boat they had to pass close to a small island on which there was a battery of German coast defence guns. It was a very dark night, and they expected to pass it without any trouble, but as they came abreast of it some very bright lights were suddenly switched on. They were rather alarmed, and turning back into the comfort of the darkness, they landed on the south side of the fjord to wait for the lights to go off. Here they struck lucky, for they met a most friendly farmer who gave them a very large meal. At 11 p.m. they embarked again in their boat and successfully passed the battery. They rowed on till dawn, and then landed on the island of Averö. They had covered twenty miles in the boat, and they slept soundly in a haystack till late in the afternoon.

When they woke up the wind had shifted to the south-west, and it was impossible to row farther down the fjord. But success had given them even more confidence than they had when they started; so they rowed across the fjord to the mainland, went into a farm which had a telephone, and rang up the village of Eide for a taxi. The taxi owner replied, 'All right. Of course you've got your petrol coupons.' This question took them by surprise, so they hurriedly replaced the receiver and rowed back to Averö.

In Averö they made discreet attempts to hire a motor boat, but without success. However, they heard that the local passenger boat was due in a few hours, and they made up their minds to travel in comfort to Eide. When the boat arrived they marched on board with all the assurance they could show, and bought tickets. There were not many passengers on board, and those who noticed the strangeness of five men all wearing identical oilskins and seaboots probably thought they had escaped from the German labour service. One man asked casually whether they had come from the airfield which the Germans were building on Averö.

In Eide they struck lucky again. Forewarned about petrol coupons, they hired a car whose driver was another 'good Norwegian,' and started on the next stage of the journey, across the mountains to the northern shore of Romsdalsfjord. The driver pointed out the risks of going too near the town of Molde, and took them to the house of a friend who, he said, would be able to find them a boat for the five-mile crossing of the fjord. The friend, when he heard that they were 'in a mess,' and came from 'the other side,' promised to do all that he could, and took them into his house. But all the rest of that day and the whole of the next went by in a tiring search, before they at last found an old man who was willing to take them across the fjord and to ask no questions in return for a fee of two hundred kroner. They slept for a night in his boat to be ready for an early start, and to keep him up to his promise.

In the morning the old man arrived and brought his two sons with him. He himself did not much like the job he had undertaken, and he liked it still less when his passengers thoughtlessly drew their pistols and began to clean them. But his sons were very keen to join up with the *Nordsjöen* crew. The father sternly refused his permission, but a family quarrel was avoided because the crew said a party of seven would be too large.

They safely crossed the fjord by midday. Before they left him, the old man asked if they had enough money, and offered to give back some of their two hundred kroner if they would remember him after the war; but they were rather tired of him by then, and told him they had plenty, though in fact they had only sixty kroner left – about £3.

On the southern side of the fjord they again tried to telephone to the nearest village for a taxi, but could not get through. So Björnöy, who was now in his own district and spoke the local dialect, volunteered to walk the ten miles to the village to find one. He succeeded in getting a car; but it had been snowing all day, and when in the evening the driver arrived to pick up the party he told them he had no chains for his wheels, and could not go over the high mountain passes which still separated them from Björnöy's home. He took them part of the way, and asked another driver if he would tackle the mountain road. But the second man also refused, and as they did not like the look of him they set off to walk the five miles across the first of the passes.

In the darkness and snow these five miles were the most trying of all their journey. But they noticed with pleasure that the pattern on the rubber soles of their British seaboots left a V-sign imprinted on the snow at every step; and in the early morning they arrived at the next settlement, crawled into a hay stack and tried to sleep.

The next day was the last lap of their journey by land. They walked a few miles and then found a driver who was willing, for the last few of their kroner, to take them to the village where Björnöy lived. On the way they came round a corner and found a convoy of about forty German lorries standing by the roadside. They drove past with a nonchalant air, and the Germans stared at them without the slightest sign of interest. Thus they arrived, in their taxi, at Björnöy's home, after coming over a hundred miles by land and sea in five and a half days.

I have often wondered what the parents of our men said when their sons arrived secretly at home after years of absence. But it was too personal a question to ask. It must have been a great shock to them; but whenever it happened the parents behaved in the most practical manner. Björnöy wisely took the party to a neighbour's house and sent a message to his father and mother to tell them what had happened; and in the evening his father arrived to say that he had already started to try to find a boat for the passage to Shetland, and to send a message to London through an organisation he knew of in Ålesund which had a radio transmitter. For the present the men were to stay in hiding in the neighbour's house.

There they remained for two days, sleeping in comfort and eating special dishes which Fru Björnöy and the neighbours cooked for them. In the afternoon of the second day Björnöy's father came to tell them that he had still not been able to get a boat but that he knew of one which was theirs for the taking. It was the *Arthur*. She was in first-class condition — the owners had only just finished paying the hire purchase instalments for her — and she was lying not two miles away ready to be laid up for the next fishing season.

They decided to steal her that night. Fru Björnöy promised them a special dinner before they left, and in the meantime they took a few hours' more sleep.

But early that evening Fru Björnöy ran in an alarm. They must hurry! The Gestapo were here. They had been asking the children if they had seen five men in oilskins and seaboots. Just now they were searching a house down the road. It was a matter of minutes.

At that moment the air raid warnings sounded. Immediately after came the crash of R.A.F. bombs from the harbour, and the German defences went into action. The five men picked up their clothes and ran for a rowing boat which they had seen on the beach. They took it and hid with it in the lee of the land till they were sure there was no-one on board the *Arthur*. Then they rowed quietly out and climbed aboard.

The *Arthur* was lying close inshore, so they crawled about the deck on all fours to inspect her. Björnöy looked over the engine, Larsen searched for charts, and the others measured the oil in the tanks and found food and bedclothes. She was completely equipped for the journey. There was even a new suit of sails in the cabin. Björnöy's father came out to them with more food and charts and a log, and told them where a barrel of oil was cached.

Under cover of the noise of the air raid they started the engine and slipped quietly out into the darkness. They stopped to pick up the barrel, then headed for the sound which led to the open sea. This sound had a seaplane base on one side and a German watchpost on the other; but the R.A.F. were keeping the Germans busy, and safely through the sound the *Arthur* set course for Shetland.

Meanwhile the two men who had vanished on the first day after the wreck were also making their way across country. They decided to make for the island of Bueland, where Gjertsen had spent several days on the first trip of the season in *Aksel*. This was a journey of two hundred miles, and they achieved it less by audacity than by endurance. Almost all of the journey was made by rowing boat and on foot, and took over three weeks.

For the first five days they marched over the mountains to the head of Romsdalsfjord, avoiding the roads and asking no help except in crossing the fjords. But on the sixth night, when they were trying to cross the high mountains towards Andalsnes, they slept in a mountain hut, and it snowed so heavily during the night that they could not get out again. They were snow-bound for four and a half days, and by then they were so cold and hungry that they realised it was useless to try to go on without help from the local people.

So they retraced their steps to the fjord, and were lucky enough to find a friend at once. He was the local schoolmaster. He gave them food, money, a bed for the night, and the first of a series of introductions which carried them from one friendly house to another for more than half of their journey.

After another day's walk they were warned by a friend of the schoolmaster that the Germans were building fortifications on the road ahead, and that the road itself was closed by two gates where passes had to be shown. The snow was too deep at that point for a detour to be made on foot; but the friend told them that the sentries would not ask for their passes if they went through in a car, and he gave them a note to a local car driver. This unfortunate driver was not told who they were, so that he should not be too deeply involved if the plan miscarried; but he seemed to assume that they were British spies, and volunteered a lot of information about German defences in the neighbourhood.

As they drove up to the gates of the fortification they saw a dozen

German soldiers and a group of officers standing in the road. A sentry with a rifle stepped out and signalled for them to stop. It was a bad moment. But as the car drew to a stand-still the sentry opened the gate and waved them on. The driver hooted, and the officers stepped aside. They drove through. Gjertsen told me it was the finest experience of his life.

Their next problem was two ferries which had been taken over by the Germans. Norwegian passengers were supposed to show passes. They by-passed the first by hiring an old man to row them across the fjord. This poor old man pointed out that the ferry was soon due to leave, and that it would get there sooner than he could; and when they insisted that they wanted to go in his boat he was convinced they were crazy. However, he took them; and this was fortunate, because the ferry, which passed them on the way, was full of German officers, of whom one appeared to be a colonel.

At the second ferry there was no boat to be had, and the only possible means of crossing was the German-manned ferry itself. They watched it coming and going for some time and could see no inspection of passes, so they decided to risk it. There were plenty of German officers and men on board, but none showed any interest in two curiously dressed passengers.

Some further days' walking, and a rather unsuccessful expedition on some borrowed skis, brought them in the end to the shores of Nordfjord. Their feet were in bad condition, so they bought an old rowing boat for forty kroner (£2). It leaked, and needed one man to bail while the other rowed; but in the next twenty-four hours they managed to row it for forty miles down the main shipping lead to the island of Bueland.

In Bueland they were among friends. In particular Merkesdal's fiancée was there. So was Dagfinn Hugöy, the organiser of many successful escapes, whose name was already well known to us in Shetland.

They learned that Dagfinn himself had decided to leave, and was getting a boat ready for the journey. There were some days to wait, so Gjertsen sent a message to his fiancée, who was in Bergen, asking her to join him. She arrived in Bueland in time and the passage to Shetland was made in safety. Thus the last two of the *Nordsjöen* crew turned up in Lerwick bringing their future wives with them. Dagfinn joined our unit and remained with us to the end.

CHAPTER FIVE

DOMESTIC AFFAIRS

THERE was a fundamental difficulty in our organisation which we could
never completely overcome. The base had to be under British command,
yet it was necessary to use Norwegian boats and Norwegian crews. No
British boat, of course, could have passed as a fisherman on the Norwegian
coast, and no British crew would have had the advantage of local
knowledge, or have been able to land unnoticed in a Norwegian village.
Nor would they have had so much chance of escape if they had been cast
away on the Norwegian shore.

The British officers in charge of the base were therefore in a very odd
position. Each of us inevitably had a fairly wide knowledge of future plans
and of organisations in Norway, and it was believed that if one of us had
been captured by the Germans he would not have had the protection of the
conventions regulating treatment of prisoners of war. If anyone who had
useful information fell into the hands of the Gestapo, it was to be assumed
that he would be unable to refuse to tell them all he knew. We were
therefore forbidden most strictly to sail on operations with the men under
our command.

We all chafed at this restriction, not only because it injured our self-
respect but because it was so much more difficult to be an efficient officer
when one could not observe the honourable tradition that an officer should
share every risk with his men. But we were not so foolish as to fail to see
that it was necessary, and that we must pocket our personal pride. Besides,
there was another argument against our sailing: if a crew had to go ashore
and escape across country, they would have been very much hampered by
the presence of a British officer who spoke Norwegian with an obviously
foreign accent. As the success of the mine-laying trip in the *Nordsjöen*
particularly depended on an idea of my own I made a special plea to be
allowed to sail with her, feeling that if my idea had been wrong I had better
share the consequences; but I was refused, and when the crew had returned
from their shipwreck I realised that they would probably not have escaped
if I had been with them. So I did not press the point any more.

This was a difficulty which it lay in our hands to overcome, and on
the whole we succeeded. But another source of trouble was outside our
control. In the early days we and our seniors in London recruited civilians
from among the merchant seamen and fishermen who were continually
arriving from Norway, and they remained civilians at the base. But
meanwhile the Norwegian Navy was beginning to reorganise in Britain.

They had no ships of first-line quality, and for a time our little base was waging a much more direct and conspicuous kind of warfare than they were. They naturally coveted command of the base, and in London discussions went on about this continually over our heads. We were always too busy and too isolated to take any part in them ourselves, and perhaps for this reason we remained in charge of the base throughout the whole of its evolution from a civilian force of thirty men to a 'private navy' with one hundred and fifty men and its own well-armed warships. But for a long time we never knew from day to day when we should find ourselves suddenly subordinated to a Norwegian whose ideas could not have been expected to coincide with ours, or else have to try to put into practice some political compromise which would divide command of the base between the two nationalities.

In the autumn of 1941 we took the first step in our evolution towards becoming a private navy by buying Norwegian naval uniforms for the men. We all thought that if they were captured in uniform they would stand a better chance of being treated as prisoners of war, although they might still wear fishermen's clothes when it suited their purpose better. We now know that it did not make much difference what they wore, for the crew of the *Vita*, who were captured in civilian clothes, were not badly treated, whereas a crew captured in uniform a year later, when the temper of the Germans was roused by our activities, were executed without trial. But this decision brought with it the question of the rank which could be given to the men. It was impossible to dress any of them in officers' uniform because none of them had had any training in an officer's responsibilities. They themselves wanted all to be dressed alike; but in the end we issued petty officer's rig to all the skippers and some of the engineers, and dressed the rest as seamen. They still remained volunteers and were given their civilian pay and bonuses; they could still give us as their employers a week's notice; and each individual member of a crew was free to decide whether he should sail on each operation or not.

Peculiar questions of discipline therefore arose. Our thirty-odd crew-men were temperamental individualists who had not the slightest notion of military behaviour, but had been recruited specifically to sail the ships. Many of them were very good at that, but they were naturally not very willing to do anything else, and it was clear to Mitchell and myself that if we tried to run our unit on military lines we would inevitably fail to carry out successful operations. We could already see that if our men could be allowed to work in their own way, with all the help we could give them, but with the least possible interference, they would develop a pride in their job, a mutual loyalty and ultimately great skill in our kind of warfare. This could not be achieved by imposing on them a new uniform character as naval ratings; such an imposition would have stifled their independent judgment, on which the outcome of an operation depended from the moment they left the base. It was unjust as well as unwise to expect them to exercise this judgment at sea, and then when they were ashore to submit as ratings to the restrictions of naval or military discipline.

As their officers could not go to sea with them the role of the officers ashore must be limited. They might lead by persuasion, but they could never give orders; nor could they rest on the prestige of an officer's uniform, which, if it meant anything to the fishermen, was a symbol of ridicule and distrust. Their most simple duty was to serve the men who sailed by providing everything they could for their safety. Beyond this they should offer sympathy, which was always accepted if it was sincere, and should act as spokesmen for the crews in expressing their inarticulate wishes and suggestions to higher authorities, just as they were the medium through which the authorities' wishes were presented to the men.

Above all they should never try to deceive the men by even a half-truth. The men would have been hard to deceive in any case, and an officer who had tried it and been found out would have been of no value to the unit; and besides, we believed that with clear-headed direction of the policy of such a little unit as ours it should never be necessary to deceive the lowest of ranks.

It appeared to me that as the men could not be made into naval ratings it was necessary, in order to create as much homogeneity as was possible in a unit of two nationalities, for me to abandon for the moment my status as a naval officer and to approach the outward character of a fisherman as nearly as I could. At Lunna there was little distinction between myself, as the only officer, and the rest. (This was made easier by the fact that even a sixteen-year-old houseboy was paid more than I was, since he was nominally in special service and I was nominally still in the Royal Navy.) I kept a room for myself and had my meals there; but this concession to my liking for solitude was excusable on the grounds that both Mitchell and the men often had to speak to me in private. I usually looked like a fisherman; as, for example, when I was wading in the sea in a pair of ragged flannel trousers and a shirt without a collar, with my hair full of cement, and looked up to see, with astonishment, an admiral standing on the beach, who asked me where he could find a naval officer called Howarth. None of the crew-men showed Mitchell or me the slightest formal sign of respect.

In trying to identify myself with the crew-men I was inevitably guilty of a degree of disloyalty to those of my seniors who did not understand the life we led at Lunna; and I paid penalties for this. But I never needed to be disloyal to Mitchell. He called me the devil's advocate; but he did much more than I, in ways which the men did not see, to preserve their character as independent buccaneers outside the shadow of discipline. It was he who explained our mission and its implications to the senior naval and army officers in Shetland and Orkney, and who pleaded skilfully with the civil police when celebration of a successful operation led, as it frequently did, to the cells; till the phrase 'one of Mitchell's men' became reason enough for any eccentricity or misdemeanour.

In October 1941 we were joined by a third British officer, Captain A. W. Rogers.* He was able to help us build up an *esprit de corps* in a different way. He was a Royal Marine, who had been trained to a strict discipline and liked it. He had been used first to receive and later to give orders without questioning whether they would be obeyed, and the rigidity of life in the Marines had perfectly suited his character. He came from a family of landowners, and was a man accustomed to command whatever men he found about him: handsome, charming, extrovert and simple in his judgment of right and wrong; firmly illogical when logic did not suit him, but with a clear head and sufficient sense of humour to admit and yet to refuse to defend his prejudices. He was so different from me that we soon agreed that if we had met in peacetime we would have cut each other on a second meeting. But war, by imposing companionship, often creates friendship where one would not have thought of seeking it, and Rogers and I became friends, each of us enjoying astonished amusement at the idiosyncracies of the other, and each curbing the other's faults; and I, at least, learning from his virtues.

When Rogers arrived in Shetland he was horrified to find what a curious gang he had joined, and his first impression was that Mitchell and I must be lazy and inefficient disciplinarians. But he was very quick to understand the relationship between ourselves and the crews; and within a few weeks he was able to state it more clearly than we had seen it ourselves, and to aid it by deliberately taking upon himself, in the Lerwick office, the occasional necessity to use stern words, and thus sacrificing his own immediate popularity among the men in order to preserve the harmonious atmosphere which existed at Lunna.

By October a feeling of confidence had begun to grow up between the crews and the officers, in spite of the difference of nationality and the non-combatant role of the officers, and in spite of the efforts of some Norwegians of higher rank to discredit us. But our method of running the base, and the fact that we were organising twice as many operations as we had been led to expect, had exhausted our shore staff. Apart from the work of running the operations and maintaining the ships, the thirty-four crewmen had to be fed, clothed, paid, housed, doctored, armed, transported and entertained largely by a shore staff of seven: Mitchell,

* Rogers' real name was Arthur Sclater, but as he had many relations in Norway it was thought best for him to use an assumed name in our work. As few of us knew his real name, and all of us thought of him as Rogers, I have used this name here.

myself, C.P.O. Percy, (who had joined us as an expert on mines but could turn his hand to anything), Sergeants Almond, Sherwood and Olsen, and Albertsen the cook; and to provide these services at Lunna was no easy matter. We had to ask for more staff, road transport and workshops.

In the middle of that month several of our seniors came from London to discuss our needs with Mitchell. On the whole I think they sympathised with us in our difficulties, but some things distressed them. One, of course, was the lack of any outward sign of discipline at Lunna. We had given the house a whirlwind spring clean before they arrived, but it was still far from tidy. I think Mitchell explained that running our operations and trying to make fishermen into soldiers were two jobs which could not be mixed; but I could not miss the look on the face of one of the visitors when he lifted the lid of our clothes boiler and found it was full of old mouldy boots and other more horrible debris, and I knew a black mark had been put against my name.

Another thing which concerned them was the defence of Lunna against sea or air attack. We had no defence whatever, and to tell the truth it had never occurred to us that we might be worth attacking. But our chiefs had a higher opinion of our importance, and told me to think the matter over. For months we had slept peacefully at night without a sentry or any help within twenty miles. Now I lay awake realising that any German could have walked in and cut my throat if it was really worth while. The next morning I had to report that the place was indefensible. There were about thirty miles of uninhabited coast on which a commando force could have been landed to attack us without any risk of being detected; and against air attack our only hope was to remain an inconspicuous country mansion.

However, three results of this visit were of immediate benefit to us. First, more British troops for shore duties were promised and soon began to arrive; secondly, the Royal Navy agreed to undertake the maintenance of our boats; and, thirdly, the small but efficient engineering firm of William Moore and Son in the village of Scalloway was freed from naval work to help us.

It seemed a blessing to be able to hand over the maintenance of the boats to the Navy, for with the number of operations we had made from Lunna it had become quite impossible for me to supervise repairs in Lerwick. But as things turned out the arrangement did not work as well as we expected, because hard on its heels came an order that we were to take over all possible boats which arrived from Norway, and to keep them in Shetland for a purpose which was never disclosed to us. This was a difficult order to carry out. As I have already remarked there are few really safe anchorages in Shetland, and it was impossible in those days to get materials for laying down moorings. We had only two men we could spare to look after these boats, and the Navy had none. Finally, the worst of the winter weather was approaching.

So the maintenance officer whom the Navy appointed from the local naval staff found himself in charge of a rapidly growing fleet of Norwegian boats with almost no facilities for keeping them in repair or even making them safe. Nobody could have done more than he did, but it was far more than one man could manage. He could not give attention to the endless demands of our seagoing crews, for no sooner had he finished taking over a boat newly arrived with refugees from the other side, moving it to the best of our bad anchorages and pumping it dry, than another, or two or three more, would turn up in different parts of Shetland, and our London office, on hearing that they were above a certain size, would order us to keep them. We had thirty-six boats lying to their own anchors in different voes by the time in November when the first hurricane broke. In one night seven of them blew ashore and were wrecked, so that attempts to salvage them put a strain on our slender resources for the whole of the following year. The damage to these ships, each of which was the pride and the principal possession of some Norwegian family, naturally annoyed a lot of the Norwegians very much. They laid the blame on Mitchell, who of course was not responsible for it at all. The strong feelings which they showed, together with our increasing experience, made us realise that maintenance of the ships would always remain our responsibility in their eyes. It was in fact a thing we could not hand over to anyone else, and efficient maintenance was the most important factor in retaining their confidence in us and in making them feel they were being well provided with the tools for their job. During the next few months we therefore took this responsibility back into our own hands.

But in the meantime I had been freed to concentrate my attention on affairs at Lunna. I was always glad to get back to that bleak isolation. I had begun to look upon the fishermen as friends, and I enjoyed a hard day's work among them. In Lerwick one might get involved in political arguments, but at Lunna there was a straightforward and exacting job to be done; and whatever happened in our human affairs, there remained the surge of surf at the foot of the cliffs, the coarse winter grass bending to the blasts of wind from the sea, and in the air the undefinable smell of the first snow.

CHAPTER SIX

STORM

ON 10th November an exceptionally violent storm broke over Shetland. During that day the wind rose continually from the south. By the morning of the 11th it had reached hurricane force. It blew for five days and nights, often with a velocity of well over a hundred miles an hour. At Lunna the salt water snatched from the wave crests in Vidlin Voe streamed over the isthmus and over the house to a height of a hundred and fifty feet. From the upper windows the spray looked as solid as streamers of grey silk, whirled over the hills with the speed of an aeroplane, and the shrieking of the wind was unlike any natural sound – insane, hysterical, demoniac. To go out of the house for a few minutes on top of that hill was as exhausting as running a race. One returned breathless, with face and hands stinging with salt and the scouring of sand and small stones flung up by the wind, and legs sore with the lashing of oilskins which cracked like a whip.

Shipping was driven ashore in all harbours of Orkney and Shetland. Many seaplanes were sunk at their moorings. Nissen huts vanished, and stationary lorries were blown off the roads. At Lunna three boats dragged their moorings over to the far side of the Voe. We struggled for two days to get them clear, and in a moment of comparative calm which coincided with high water we managed to get them across the harbour and into a lee, with no serious damage.

But our main anxiety during that week of storm was for our ships at sea. *Arthur* had sailed on 8th November for Norway, taking Jonsen, the same messenger who had sailed with the first trip of the season, to re-establish contact with the agents in the district of Florö. And on the following day a ship called *Blia*, making her first trip since the spring, had sailed with a new crew, including her peacetime skipper and mate, to pick up our Haugesund agent.

Arthur should have been back on the evening of Monday the 10th, but in view of the weather we did not expect her. We hoped she was sheltering in one of the many good hide-outs near Bueland or Kinn. But it was not till Saturday that she limped into the Voe, her mizzen mast down and her bulwarks smashed, and I heard her terrible story.

The crew of the *Arthur* included four of the first party of men who escaped from the *Nordsjöen* – Larsen, whom they had elected skipper, Sangolt, Björnöy and Pletten. There were also two of the men kidnapped from Kinn, Leif Kinn and Albertsen; a new engineer, Kåre Iversen; and Jonsen the messenger.

The trip had gone well to begin with. They had made landfall near Kinn after a passage of thirty hours, and Larsen allowed the two kidnapped men to land there to reassure their parents, who thought they had been taken by the Germans. They went on and found the local agent; landed their cargo of explosives and helped him to hide it under some rocks; and gave him some coffee, flour and tobacco and a bottle of rum we had sent him for Christmas.

They sailed for Shetland at 1 a.m. on Monday. The weather was then quite good, but the wind rose steadily all day on their port quarter, and by 4 p.m., when they were ninety miles out, it was blowing so hard that Larsen decided to make for the north end of Shetland and come up under lee of the land.

At 6 a.m. on Tuesday their dead reckoning put them within a mile or two of the north end of Unst, and with the approach of dawn they were looking out for land. The wind had reached hurricane force, and a very heavy sea was running. Larsen decided to lie stern to wind till daylight came and land could be seen. But the mizzen sail was still set. Sangolt, who was in the wheelhouse with Larsen, volunteered to get it in, and after calling the other hands he went aft.

A minute later two very large seas broke over the ship. The engine-room door of *Arthur* was on the starboard side of the wheelhouse, and was in two halves. The lower half was bolted, but as the door was on the lee side the upper half, about four feet above the deck, had been left open for ventilation. One would have said it was impossible for the boat to take water through it; but the breakers which now crashed down upon her must have flooded her decks to a depth of over six feet. Before she could shake off these hundreds of tons of green water the engine-room was flooded. The engine stopped, and the boat drifted broadside to the storm.

The motor bilge pump was driven from the main engine, so it was useless till the engine could be started. With the boat lying low in the water and out of control, seas were constantly breaking inboard. All hands set to pumping by hand and bailing with buckets. To lower the level of water in the engine-room was an immediate matter of life or death.

In this extremity it was not for an hour that they noticed Sangolt was gone. Outside on deck it was impossible to hear anything above the howling of wind and the crash of seas against the hull; it was impossible to see unless the eyes were shielded against the lashing salt spray, and impossible to stand without a firm grip on the wheelhouse or the shrouds. They searched the ship, hoping he might have been injured and be lying below decks. But a few moments were enough to show that the sea had taken him. Perhaps the first breaker had swept him of the stern as he was working with the mizzen: they could not tell. The sail which he had gone to take in was still set; but he had vanished, without a sound or a trace, from the solid tangible microcosm of the ship which encompassed their lives, into the wilderness of the storm.

This discovery, I believe, made the younger members of the crew feel that death was very near them, but they did not relax their fight against it. After an hour they succeeded in getting the water level down to the crankcase of the engine, so that the engine could be started. Then, with the motor bilge pump working, the remaining water was soon cleared. But the clutch, which had been submerged, could not be engaged, and it was ten hours from the first disaster before they could get way on the ship. By then she had probably drifted twenty miles away to the north of Shetland. During those ten hours two of the crew had made three attempts to get out a sea-anchor which would stand the strain, in order to make the ship lie more easily, but each time it carried away. They also worked with oil buckets, which helped to prevent more seas breaking over her.

When the engine was started the crew entered upon a period of nightmarish inaction which lasted for four days. So long as the engine kept going the ship was not in immediate danger. By steaming very slowly ahead they could keep steerage way on her and so keep her head to sea. This called for constant attention and muscular effort from the helmsman. But to attempt to make headway would have been to risk breaking her up when she pitched into the troughs of the seas, and even at dead slow she buried her stemhead into most of the seas which swept down on her, so that a wave of green water rushed over her deck and smashed against the front of the wheelhouse.

The crew were already exhausted, and as soon as the ship was under control Larsen assembled all hands in the wheelhouse. With the disappearance of Sangolt fresh in his mind, he knew that every man who tried to go forward to the forecastle, across thirty feet of open deck, might too easily lose his life on the way, and that if any did reach the forward hatch it would be impossible to recall them in an emergency.

The six surviving members of the crew, and the passenger Jonsen, crowded into the wheelhouse, which was six feet by four. Most of them sat down on the floor and, leaning against one another, fell asleep.

They could never remember afterwards the time at which later incidents happened. Some time during the second day after the accident one of them fixed some battens in the engine room, which was accessible by an inner door from the wheel house, in such a way that three men could lie down there and sleep without the risk of sliding into the flywheel or propeller shaft. Later they cut a hole in the bulkhead between the engine room and the after cabin, so that they could crawl through and use the two bunks, as well as a small stock of food which had been stored there. Even then they had little rest. Everything was soaked with salt water, and the quick and violent motion of the ship made relaxation impossible.

For four days the storm beat upon them. The dim winter light of day could hardly penetrate the heavy clouds and spray, and they could see no more than a few yards of grey-green sea and white foam, which bore down upon them in waves mast-high and vanished instantly in the spindrift astern. Each day the men grew weaker and less able to make the effort of holding the ship on the course and maintaining the engine.

Some time during those four days the rigging screws on the mizzen forestays broke and the mast came down, but none of them heard or saw it.

One evening a large aircraft suddenly passed low overhead and fired a burst of cannon fire at them. It made a second run from astern. By then the crew had made ready a Bren gun which they carried in the wheelhouse, but neither of the wheelhouse doors would open against the wind, so they were unable to return the fire. The plane vanished again as suddenly as it had come. Looking back on the incident later, some of the crew began to think it was hallucination, and I myself disbelieved it; but after we had argued the matter for several days we found the star-shaped scar of a cannon shell on the *Arthur*'s hull. None of them had heard it explode.

On the evening of the fourth day they began to feel a slight moderation of the wind. The seas became gradually less steep, and Larsen slowly increased the revolutions of the engine. As darkness fell they were making a little headway. During the night the improvement continued, and he was able to work her up to four knots on a southerly course. Some of the men were able to reach the forecastle to fetch more food, and to boil some coffee. The sea was still high, but the dreadful tumult of the last four days diminished, and with the comparative calm, and the knowledge that they had saved themselves, most of the men fell into an exhausted sleep.

At dawn they saw land. Probably if visibility had been good they would have been within sight of Shetland all the time; but even if they had been able to see it they would not have been able to reach it. As the light improved they recognised the island of Fetlar and set course for the base.

In the early afternoon we at Lunna heard an engine with a feeling of great thankfulness. *Arthur* and *Blia* were both five days overdue, and as we ran down to the pier we watched the headland to see which ship was coming. The mizzen mast was lying on the stern in a tangle of rigging. The bulwarks were smashed and the gun mountings swept off her decks. Down below was a chaos of broken crockery and spilt food and of broken lockers. But she was a fine ship; she had not leaked at all or suffered any structural damage.

It was our custom at Lunna to have a drink ready for the men when they returned from operations. It happened that on that day we had none in the house, and C.P.O. Percy went to the village of Voe to get some. All he could find was some cheap champagne. One of my many curious recollections of Lunna is of the scene that evening as we sat sipping this incongruously festive drink, while the seven men told me their story and discussed the loss of their comrade, and first Otto Pletten and then Albertsen and Björnöy fell asleep in their chairs.

Meanwhile our anxiety about *Blia* was not allayed, and as days of calmer weather passed it became certain she was lost. It was tragic to have to admit to ourselves that seven men who had set off in particularly high spirits had met with disaster and were never to return, but it was many months before we learned the full extent of the tragedy.

Blia was different from our other ships. She was a southern type, with a curved stem and a cruiser stern with an external rudder, and she was built with valves in the hold so that sea water could be let in for carrying live fish. She had rather less displacement than the other ships of the same length, and correspondingly more speed – about eight and a half knots.

Her peacetime skipper and mate, two brothers called Leröy, had joined us in the early autumn, and had been busy on the slipway in Lerwick getting her ready for operations. They were among the keenest of the men, and when we got orders to pick up our Haugesund agent at Bremnes on the island of Stord they were delighted at the chance of going. Bremnes was near their home and they knew it well. They had collected the nucleus of a crew – Fagerlid, Svinöy and Björnsen – and as this was to be their first trip we asked a pilot from Bremnes, called Økland, to go with them.

Afterwards we often looked back on the pride and enthusiasm with which they put the finishing touches to their ship in the bay at Lunna. After many months of struggling with inadequate resources and insufficient staff, we had just got a fully trained carpenter to work ashore at the base, a young man called Kvalheim; and he also entered into the spirit of the Leröys, fitting gun mountings and doing other odd jobs on board with a care and a pleasure in workmanship which it was a joy to see.

The rendezvous with the Haugesund agent was fixed for the night of Monday, 10th November. The morning of Sunday the 9th was sunny and calm, and when we all went down to the pier where *Blia* was moored to see her off there was an even happier atmosphere than was usual when a boat was sailing. This crew going on their first trip were like children waiting to go for a picnic. They shouted jokes to myself and Kvalheim and the others who stood on the pier. I cast off the stern ropes, and Kvalheim stood by the forward spring. He was admiring the gun mountings he had installed.

'You damn well ought to be able to bring back a plane with those,' he shouted.

Leröy shouted back, 'You'd better come with us and show us how.'

'Will you take me?' Kvalheim asked eagerly; and when Leröy and the rest of the crew shouted yes, Kvalheim turned to me.

'Can I go?' he asked. 'I'd like to do just one trip.'

The ship was already cast off, and I had to answer at once. I knew very well how he felt. I was another shore-based sailor, and I also wanted to do just one trip. It would have been a great help to my self-esteem. There were plausible reasons, and definite orders, against my going, but they did not apply to him.

'All right,' I said. 'But don't forget we want you ashore when you come back. Can you jump it?'

He shook my hand vigorously, then jumped about six feet from the quay to the ship's rail.

As *Blia* turned to head for the harbour mouth the crew were waving, and Kvalheim was doing a fantastic dance on the forecastle. In this cheerful manner six men left for their fatal trip, and I, by a quick decision, sent a seventh with them.

We pieced together some of the story of what happened to *Blia* from scraps of information which we received during the next few months, but her end will never be known except to our imagination.

She arrived safely at her rendezvous in Bremnes, and met the agent. He was in touch with an efficient military 'cell' in the island of Stord, which also acted, like most of the local organisations on the coast, as an escaping club. This cell had at that time a large number of people waiting for a chance to get away to Shetland. Some of the men were in danger of arrest by the Gestapo, and others wanted to come across to join the Norwegian forces; with their families they totalled nearly forty people. Plans were in hand to obtain a ship for them, but when the head of the organisation heard from our agent that *Blia* was in Bremnes he decided quickly to assemble the party and embark them with her the following night.

To collect so many people on one of the outer islands was always a difficult task. Trustworthy messengers had to be sent round to tell them when they should leave their homes or hiding-places and exactly how they should travel to the rendezvous. There was a considerable risk that the movement of so many people converging on a normally isolated spot would be noticed by the Germans or by quislings; and if one of them had been arrested for any suspicious action German patrols would at once be called out, and not only the whole party but the ship and the military cell itself might be detected. Above all the operation had to be carried out quickly. Many of this party were professional men and local workers. They could not leave their homes until after dark, and by the next morning when they failed to report at their works and offices the ship must be safely away from the coast.

However, thanks to the efficient organisation in Stord, the whole party were safely embarked, and *Blia* sailed with between forty and forty-five people aboard.

The congestion on board her must have been appalling. She was fifty-five feet in overall length. Forward was a cabin with six bunks enclosing a small triangular space containing two benches and a table. Amidships was the fish hold. This was damp and dark and without ventilation. Some of the passengers might have found room to sit down there, but it could only be reached by opening the fish hatch, which would be impossible in very bad weather. Aft of the hold was the engine-room, with a minute wheelhouse and galley above it; and in the stern the skipper's cabin, with two bunks and four feet of floor space between them.

On a calm summer's day the discomfort would have been intense; but on her passage back to Shetland *Blia* ran into the storm with which *Arthur* was struggling a few miles to the northward. It would have been suicidal for her to put back to Norway. By the time she arrived there the disappearance of her passengers would be known and the coast on the alert. She had to try to fight her way through it to Shetland. Somewhere on the way she failed. We shall never know why. Did she break up? The two Leröys, at least, would have denied that such a thing could ever happen. Was the hold being used as a cabin? Perhaps the hatch was left open too long, to give light and air to passengers down below, till a sea suddenly broke aboard and partly filled her. One could imagine that before the passengers could be got out of the hold, with the boat flooded and dangerously low in the water, following seas might quickly have completed her destruction. Perhaps the congestion of people aboard her prevented the crew from working the ship in some crisis; Larsen doubted whether he could have kept *Arthur* afloat with so many aboard. After the Germans found out that so many people had escaped they claimed to have sunk her, and this may have been true; but on the other hand they may have said this to discourage others from leaving Norway by the same means, and may not have known that she was really lost.

When our friends in the base disappeared in this way we could not forbear to speculate on the possible causes of their deaths, though we knew such speculation was useless. From the loss of *Blia* the image of a dreadful scene of suffering and fear, of revolt against an inescapable fate, or of resignation as the end could be seen to be approaching, will always remain with us and haunt us, and remind us that though wars can still bring adventures which can stir the heart, their true nature is of innumerable personal tragedies, of grief, waste and sacrifice, wholly evil and not redeemed by glory.

CHAPTER SEVEN

TWO SKIPPERS

WHEN we invited the crews to elect their own skippers they seldom made a mistake. Leif Larsen was the first to be elected by the vote of the men who had sailed with him, and he turned out to be the finest leader of them all. He did not look the part. He was a stockily built man in his thirties, with china-blue eyes, a broken nose, and a wide humorous mouth; and he had so quiet and modest a manner that it might have taken us a long time to find out his latent powers. But after he became skipper of *Arthur* he soon showed astonishing qualities of a rough and ready leadership and perfectly unshakable courage, and a combination of confidence, bravado and luck which brought him through one adventure after another that would have broken the nerve of most men. By the end of the war he had become the subject of legendary stories in Norway, and the object of devotion among the crews, affection and admiration among his British colleagues, and a certain natural jealousy and mistrust among officers of the Norwegian Navy; all of which left him unmoved, unchanged and unspoilt. He was not only an outstanding figure of our little unit, but one of the most remarkable characters of the war. For his work in our unit he was awarded the Conspicuous Gallantry Medal, the Distinguished Service Medal and Bar, the Distinguished Service Cross and the Distinguished Service Order, besides, of course, Norwegian decorations. No other man, either British or foreign, has ever received all these British military honours; and this succession of awards was in fact the highest expression of regard which the British Crown could offer, for as a foreigner Larsen was not eligible for the award of the Victoria Cross.

I think the most notable quality of Larsen's character was its stability. He was always the same. I was often in his company with people of every rank, from the Commander-in-Chief Home Fleet and the Crown Prince of Norway to the cook of his own crew, the British army privates of our shore staff, or the humblest of Shetlanders. He remained himself with them all, never raising his soft gentle voice with his juniors, and never being obsequious or overawed with his seniors; so of course both seniors and juniors liked him. His men said he remained the same in a battle, equally unruffled and quiet as he stood at his wheel unscratched while his wheelhouse was slowly shot to matchwood around him, or as he sat in the cabin of the *Arthur* discussing with a German examination officer the cargo of peat in his hold which concealed tons of war machines and six British sailors; equally unruffled hove-to in a hurricane, or in his dinghy, with wounded and dying comrades, abandoning his sinking ship a hundred miles from shore and four hundred from home. Yet this was not the calm which can be shown in danger by people of little imagination, and which sometimes passes for courage. He once told me in a confidence which I now break that he had been scared stiff on his last adventure, and I believe he had the sense to be often afraid, but could always overcome his fear by that mixture of a sense of duty and self-respect and of strength of will which is true courage.

He was reticent by nature, and though I came to know him well I never heard much of his earlier life. It was said he had fought in the Spanish Civil War and in Finland, but this may have been part of the legend; and before he took to fighting he had been skipper of a ferry boat in Bergen. But he never spoke about these things. Nor was I or anyone among us in his confidence in more intimate matters than our work and daily life. Yet I am sure I am not mistaken in thinking that for all his formidable deeds he was a humble, gentle and peaceful person by nature. His gentleness showed in his expression, and in his relations with people under his control and in his indignation at oppression and infringement of human rights, whether on a national or an individual scale; and in his modest readiness to defer to our judgment, and in his expressed mistrust of his own brains. He never pretended to be anything but an ordinary fellow of peasant stock, and when he made light of his exploits it was not in affected modesty, but in the genuine belief that he had done the only possible thing under the circumstances. He hated writing. I usually wrote a report on each trip after hearing the skipper's story of it, but a time came when we tried to get Larsen to write his own log. It became a joke, because his log usually contained three entries: '0830 Jan. 16. Left Lunna. 2300 Jan. 17. Arrived at objective. Carried out operation. N.W. gale. 1100 Jan. 20. Arrived Lunna.' It was only over the drink which celebrated his return that we were able to extract the whole story, which would either be of an operation completed with unerring skill, or of some fantastic adventure caused by unforeseeable circumstances.

I have said that Norwegian officers in general were jealous of him and mistrusted him. They can hardly be blamed for at that time he despised the Norwegian Navy, and frequently said so, though he greatly respected the Royal Navy. There was, of course, a difference between them. The Royal Navy is so secure in its tradition of discipline that it can afford to tolerate and encourage a man of his kind who knows nothing of formal discipline, but leads by pure force of character and skill; whereas the Norwegians must have been aware that the authority of their officers over their men was precarious and needed the support which formality can give. Ultimately we had to make Larsen a sub-lieutenant – not because he cared, but so that we could give him ciphers which were only issued to officers.

The Norwegian Navy were not very willing that he should be promoted and he, for his part, absolutely refused to go to one of their officers' training schools. After exhausting all other arguments they discovered that he was disqualified by being colour blind; but in the end common sense won, and Larsen, without training, and still remaining his unalterable self, became both the most unofficer-like and the most successful sublieutenant one could imagine.

It was typical of him and his crew that in the depression which overcame us after the loss of *Blia* and of Sangolt they were the first to report themselves ready for another trip. When *Arthur*'s mast had been restepped and rerigged and her bulwarks repaired, and the crew had had a few days' rest to recover from their ordeal in the storm, they set off again to drop a radio operator at a point near Florö, between Nordfjord and Sognfjord, for watching coastal traffic. On their return I wrote to London that it was a pleasure to be able to report an uneventful trip again; but re-reading my report reminds me of the severity of the conditions we had become accustomed to, for *Arthur* was hove-to in a storm for five hours on the outward journey, and approached the unlit coast at night in a gale and fog, so that the first thing the crew saw was the sea breaking on skerries, which they could not identify, on both sides of them – a situation which in normal times, a seaman would hardly describe as uneventful.

As it was impossible to find out where they were they stood off the coast till dawn, when they identified the lighthouse on the island of Utvaer. They made their way in to Bueland to tell the local people that Dagfinn's boat, in which Gjertsen and Merkesdal had escaped after the loss of the *Nordsjöen*, had arrived safely in Shetland. While they were lying in the harbour at Bueland the fog thickened so much that they could not move, and they had to wait there two days before they could grope their way on to the point farther in the fjords where the radio operator was to be landed. When they got there, at night, they helped him to carry his apparatus and stores ashore and to stow them in the upper storey of an empty house; and by the time this was finished it was getting light, so that they had to spend a fourth day on the coast, lying securely in a creek surrounded by high hills.

By now we had satisfied ourselves that a fishing boat could lie up on the coast, or in the fishing zone offshore, for a long time in safety, provided of course that she kept away from the German control points, and that the crew were discreet in their contacts with the local people. The men felt quite at home there. There was always a feeling of suspense during the actual performance of an operation. While they were ferrying ashore the radio transmitter, for example, they listened and watched for any vessel approaching through the darkness and fog, feeling, I think, like any small boy doing something naughty but pleasant and hoping not to be found out.

But while they were waiting before or after the job there was often no need to keep watch, and after making sure that their arms were concealed but ready they all turned in and slept in peace.

On other trips at this time the practice of lying innocently waiting on the coast was carried a stage further. Per Blystad, who had volunteered to fit out the *Olaf*, took over the *Siglaos* for one trip, as her regular skipper was away. It was his first trip as skipper. He had to land two agents at a point from which they could get to the town of Ålesund. He left Lunna in a moderate gale, which increased to a full westerly gale during the passage. When he made land the wind was blowing onshore, and the sound which he had intended to enter was a mass of breakers. This meant that the agents could not reach the man whom they had expected to help them in the next stage of their journey, so the only thing to do was to make inquiries to find an alternative route to Ålesund. Blystad therefore sailed into a wider fjord a few miles away, and dropped anchor among a large number of other fishing boats in the little harbour of Svinö. Then he rowed ashore with one of his crew who lived in the village there. This man greeted many acquaintances as they walked up the village street and called on his family. They told him there were no Germans on the island, and gave him the name of a local boat which had a permit to go to Ålesund that same afternoon to fetch some new nets. The crew of this boat, which was lying at the quay, were quite willing to help. The two agents took the places of two of the lawful crew, borrowing their passes to show at a control point through which the boat had to pass; and thus they arrived very easily at their destination.

During the day, in this friendly spot, it occurred to Blystad to order some spare parts for some of our engines. It was difficult and expensive to get parts for Norwegian engines specially made in Britain, but I confess it had never occurred to me to get them from Norway, though as it turned out nothing could have been simpler. Blystad ordered as much as he could afford with the Norwegian money we always issued to each man in case of emergency, and a few weeks later one of the other boats was able to return and collect them. Some of our staff suggested that it was illegal to trade with the enemy, but we were delighted when we received our first consignment from the German-run factories, and we placed many more orders at different places on the coast, buying among other things spare cylinder-head castings which weighed several hundredweights each and cost a king's ransom in England.

While *Siglaos* was lying in Svinö, Blystad was surprised to find that nobody from the other boats went aboard her, though the people he met ashore were all so helpful. Before he left he discovered the reason. For the registration number which was painted on her bows at that time we had chosen that of her sister ship, which was still in Norway and was one of the few with her rather unusual type of stern. But unknown to us this ship had been requisitioned by the Gestapo, and, on seeing the number, of course everyone gave her a wide berth. Blystad found this so useful in keeping inquisitive visitors away that we kept the same number on her throughout the winter, and she was able to move on the coast like a pariah, quite free from the callers who embarrassed the rest of our crews.

The successful audacity of this visit to Svinö made us take notice of Blystad, who for the past month had been quietly working at the fitting out of his little boat *Olaf*. He had received a better education than most of our men, for his father was a well-known civil engineer; and he shared with me a fondness for mechanical gadgets. By then I was giving a lot of thought to new kinds of gun-mountings for our boats, on which the guns would be hidden when they were not being used, so that the boats could still use disguise as a first line of defence, but could be brought into action within a few seconds if disguise should fail. Blystad (or Pete, as everyone called him) was the only one of the skippers who could understand a mechanical drawing at a glance, and he used to spend hours with me inventing all kinds of Q-ship equipment, some practical and some of the kind which pleases nobody but the inventor. Thus I got to know him quite well and to respect him greatly.

Like Larsen he was the kind of Norwegian who rouses friendly feelings in every Englishman, and he also made many friends among the people of Scalloway, where he spent most of his time ashore. But unlike Larsen he was a man of mercurial temperament. He worked very hard for day after day and far into the night, and then one morning would unexpectedly stay in bed until noon, and spend the rest of the day trout-fishing in the hill lochs. He expected everyone else to work hard too, and would occasionally get almost speechless with anger over somebody's slackness or inefficiency. This kept everyone who worked on his boat on the move, and he completed his fitting-out in record time.

With his brains and energy and fearlessness Pete would have become a great skipper if he had lived. But he lost his life in the following year in carrying out one of his own daring and ingenious plans. No loss was more sincerely mourned, both in our unit and in many Shetland homes.

Pete was a great believer in disguise, and he went so far as to carry fishing nets and buoys, or 'sculls' of lines, according to the season, on the deck of the *Olaf*. But at the same time she was well protected. He took out the sliding windows of her wheelhouse and filled the space between its inner and outer lining with concrete, afterwards replacing the windows on hinges, and he fitted half-inch steel plates inside the bulwarks at her bow and stern. This simple and invisible armour plating would certainly have given his crew some protection against cannon-shell splinters, which caused most casualties in air attacks, and perhaps even against machine-gun bullets, and we adopted it for all our boats. He also carried a Bren gun in the wheelhouse, and fitted a kind of medieval loophole in each of the four sides; but I think the main object of this was that he himself, while standing at the wheel, might be able to take part in any fight that was going on.

My own most successful gun-mounting was one made for twin stripped-Lewis machine guns. I mounted these guns on a telescopic stand inside an ordinary forty-gallon diesel oil drum. The drum was bolted to the deck, and lashed, for appearance's sake, to the bulwark, and its top was sawn off and refitted as a removable lid. Oil drums are a common sight on fishing boats, and with the lid on nothing suspicious could be seen unless a very close inspection revealed the saw-cut near the top. But as soon as the lid was given a sharp pull the guns, ready loaded, sprang up into the firing position, being attached to a counter-weight in the hold underneath. The inside of the barrel was lined with two inches of concrete all round to protect the gunner, and a folded shield of steel plates unrolled automatically as the mounting rose. This mounting passed the test of being ready for use in three seconds, even when the ship was rolling and the mounting was frozen or covered with salt spray; and the efficiency of its camouflage was proved when one of our boats was searched in the North Sea by a suspicious British destroyer, which removed all her weapons but did not discover the two twin Lewises mounted on deck. I believe it was adopted in other theatres of war, and when some examples of it were captured by the Germans it elicited a rather patronising description in the Berlin papers.

We also made special low mountings for twin .5 Colt machine guns which were installed in the net ponds at the sterns of the boats. These were not thoroughly concealed, but by fitting folding handles, triggers, shields and sights, all of which could be raised for action, we managed to keep the height of the whole mounting down to two feet, so that it could hardly be seen above the bulwarks and could easily have a net or sail thrown over it. In the same way a mounting for a Colt in the bows, with a tarpaulin over it, looked very much like the harpoon gun with which many of the larger Norwegian boats are fitted.

P.A.C. rockets were a defensive gadget which was very easily concealed in the roof of the wheelhouse of each boat. They fired a rocket which, at the top of its flight, released a parachute with a long trailing wire attached to it. I never heard of any enemy plane which suffered any hardship from these, but at least the pilots could see the rockets going up, which helped to discourage the low-level attacks which are the greatest danger to a small boat.

All these things came gradually, as our resources for making them and our experience increased, so that in time our humble fishing boats, once startled out of their humility, could bring to bear seven or eight mounted machine guns, as well as a sub-machine gun in the hands of any passenger or spare member of the crew. With this armament they put up a respectable volume of fire against attackers.

CHAPTER EIGHT

RAID ON LOFOTEN

At Christmas we became involved, rather unwillingly, in the commando raid on the village of Målöy and the occupation by a naval force of the harbour of Reine in the Lofoten Islands. The raid on Målöy was judged a success, in that it took the German garrison by surprise and put an end to it without greatly injuring the Norwegian people. In Norway it will always be remembered as the last battle of Captain Martin Linge, who was killed in leading a troop of Norwegian commandos. Captain Linge was another Norwegian who won a legendary reputation among the Norwegian forces; he was one of the few officers who was able to inspire unqualified devotion in all men of junior rank. I myself only met him the day before his death, so I can only render a passing tribute to a man whose record was a model for Norwegian soldiers long after his death, and whose name was given to the company of volunteers from which the agents we landed in Norway were drawn.

The occupation of Reine seemed to us to be a less successful operation. We did not know enough to justify us in holding an opinion of its strategical value, but we could not help being aware that it had a bad effect on morale in Norway.

Reine is a little fishing village tucked away among high precipitous mountains at the extreme end of the Lofoten group of islands, well north of the Arctic Circle, and about six hundred miles from Shetland as the crow flies. In midwinter the sun did not rise, and the only light was an uneasy dusk for a few hours at midday. Ships in the little harbour beneath the fantastic icy crags which tower over it would be very diffcult to attack from the air or sea, and impossible to reach by land; and a British force established there could have been a serious menace to German communications with the whole of the north of Norway. When a British cruiser and several destroyers arrived all Norwegians were under the impression that they had come to stay, and the more optimistic of them saw Reine as a bridge-head for a gradual reoccupation of Norway. There was great rejoicing all over the country, which was not concealed from the Germans and quislings; and there was bitter disappointment when the force left a few days later. From the point of view of the Norwegians the worst of it was that although the British took with them a good many quislings and 'good Norwegian' volunteers, some of each kind were left behind in the hurried departure, so that reprisals were quickly taken by the

Germans against all who were reported, rightly or wrongly, to have welcomed the British.

The withdrawal may well have been inevitable; but it had been decided to use fishing boats for a subsidiary part of the operation, and this was certainly a misconceived idea from the outset. Their job was to extinguish the navigational lights in the 'inner lead' for some distance south of Lofoten, so that any German naval force which steamed northwards in the darkness to counter-attack would at least have to move at low speed, and at best be forced out of the protected lead into the open sea.

Looking back I cannot help thinking that a single small warship could have accomplished this job with certainty by steaming at full speed up the well-lit lead and shooting out the lights as it passed them. But somebody must have persuaded the Admiralty that it was a suitable mission for fishing boats carrying demolition parties of commandos.

At all events, a week before Christmas we received orders from our headquarters to go to Invergordon and prepare for sea seven fishing boats which had been assembled there. We were to sail them to Lerwick and have them ready for an operation, too secret to mention, which was to start in seven days' time. I was sent south, and found a dreadful collection of crocks. Some of the boats were only forty feet in length, some were rotten, some had parts of their engines missing; and none had any equipment left which could possibly be unscrewed and stolen — no compasses or lights or cooking stoves, anchors or chains, sails or cordage, or any of the hundreds of things which the smallest of boats needs on a long sea passage. The crews and their commando passengers, who had been specially assembled, were waiting in the naval transit camp.

There followed the most desperate week of improvisation and placation we ever experienced. None of us in Shetland knew what the job was to be. We had been given a vague impression that it was a prelude to invasion and of enormous importance; and even we, rebellious though we sometimes were, had not then formed the habit of saying that things we were told to do were impossible. So we threw overboard all our standards of seaworthiness and preparation, and did our best to get seven boats away on time at all costs. There were three of the seven at Invergordon which could be got under way, and Mitchell collected three more from other ports and from our reserves. One was even a motor yacht which had been used by a travelling tobacco salesman on his rounds of the coast of Norway, and only one was really fit to undertake a round journey of fifteen hundred miles into the far north in midwinter. Eventually we got them all anchored in the roadstead at Lerwick, with a bored, nervous and seasick security corporal on each, and a somewhat disgruntled crew who were not allowed ashore. Three or four times a day Mitchell or I, or Sergeant Sherwood, or some of the officers who had come up from London for the occasion, would go the rounds of this fleet, returning each time with a formidable list of things which the crews had found they must have. The operation was delayed, and the longer they waited, of course, the more things they thought of, but luckily our quartermaster, Sergeant Almond, known as 'Q,' by that time was a past master at finding the most improbable articles at a moment's notice, and he was able to give them nearly everything they wanted except seaworthy ships.

One demand which had been foreseen was for acid for the ships' batteries, and this had been sent up from London in gallon glass jars. A weary sergeant distributed these to the ships one night, two to each ship. But the next morning someone discovered a further supply of acid, and in due course we found that fourteen gallons of rum had been sent in identical jars. The sergeant had issued the rum. So another tour of the fleet was made to hand out the acid and bring back the rum. Some crews had delightedly found out the mistake and were gay or insensible. Some had filled their batteries with rum, and some who had not opened their jars were extremely annoyed to hear of the opportunity they had missed. The more ingenious of these tried to take the jars of acid on board and then hand them back, retaining the rum, but they were foiled by Sergeant Sherwood, who was not easy to deceive.

When at last the order came to sail, the weather, which had been calm, was breaking, and by the time the boats were due to raise anchor a southerly gale was blowing and it was inky dark. I went out in the naval examination vessel to get them under way and give them a lead out of the harbour mouth. But by the time three were moving around in the darkness, waiting for the others who were showing no sign of life, it was evident that getting out of the harbour in itself, with seven invisible ships, was going to be so dangerous that we would have to wait until dawn. At dawn they all sailed; but as I watched them rounding the island of Bressay into the open, the smaller ones seeming to show more than half of their keels as they plunged into the oncoming seas, I felt sure it was impossible for them to make such a voyage in such weather; and by evening three of them had returned to their starting-point, and three had sought refuge in Lunna. None of them knew what had happened to the seventh, and we were afraid for her safety; but much later we learned that she managed to reach Reine, though without fulfilling her mission, and that her crew abandoned her there and came back in a British destroyer.

After another twenty-four hours of waiting for the storm to subside, it was very doubtful whether any of the remaining boats could get to Lofoten in time to carry out the demolitions, but the three at Lunna decided to try. One gave it up after going about a hundred miles. The other two lost sight of each other, but both carried on. Their original orders had been to join the British force at Reine after they had finished their job. As it turned out both were delayed so much by bad weather that they not only arrived too late to put out the lights, but steamed into Reine to find the British had gone.

The largest of the seven boats, *Havörn*, had no trouble throughout her trip; but she lost her way. After four days' steaming through continuous snow and heavy seas they had not had a glimpse of the sun or stars to fix their position, but their dead reckoning put them in the latitude of Lofoten. Then in a brief clear patch they saw two islands, which they wrongly identified as being on the main coastline south-east of Reine. So they steamed north-west. After thirty-six hours on that course they realised they had missed Lofoten altogether, so they set a course of east for twelve hours, and south-east for another twelve, knowing that in that direction they must reach some part of Norway sooner or later. Eventually they saw rocks ahead, and dropped anchor. Some of them rowed ashore, and after several attempts they managed to beach the dinghy safely. They found an old man, who said he had never heard of Lofoten. However, he showed them a safer anchorage, and after moving there the skipper went ashore and found a better informed farmer, who told him they were on the island of Andoya, eighty miles north of Reine. They set out again, and entered the fjord at Reine at 4 a.m. on New Year's Eve, nine days out from Shetland.

Where they had expected a welcome from a British fleet they found a deserted harbour, and when they went ashore the first dozen houses were empty. There was an eerie hush. The snow on the mountains glittered in the light of the moon, and a dog was howling. They had no idea what had happened, and felt that anything might happen at any moment. At last, as they prowled up the empty street they saw a light in the post office. There was a man in there, and when they went in he told them the British had gone, and that the Germans had been there two days ago. They had not done anything except make an inspection, but they were coming back that morning; and then, he said, all the people who had been so glad to see the British had better look out.

Just then the crew of the *Havörn* heard a ship coming into the fjord, so they hurried back on board, cast off and made for home.

Their journey south was uneventful. The engine ran smoothly day after day, and the ship was sound. But the weather had thickened again, and after they had run eight hundred miles on the log there was still no sign of land. They had to ration their fresh water and open their emergency tins of biscuits; but they held on the same course, knowing that even if they missed Shetland altogether they must fetch up somewhere in the British Isles. Eventually they did see land ahead, and skirted it to the eastward, more or less expecting to see Lerwick at any moment to starboard. Soon a port was sighted; but it turned out to be Stornoway in the Outer Hebrides.

They put in and tried to explain themselves to the naval authorities, which was no easy matter. Their engine had not been stopped for seventeen days.

The other boat which sailed from Lunna did not fare so well. She was in bad condition, and was making water all the time in the heavy weather on the northward journey. The head seas delayed her, and her engine was giving trouble, so that she took six days to get to Reine. The crew had to abandon their operation, and like the *Havörn* they arrived in Reine after the British had left. They also found the village deserted, but came across the local doctor, who told them what had happened.

The bilge pump of their boat had broken, and the gale had backed to the south-west, which promised head seas again for the voyage home. So they abandoned the boat, and moved to a big old wooden freighter which was lying at anchor, and whose owner and crew, the doctor told them, had left with the British fleet. She had a full cargo and deck cargo of timber. They did not know who might be watching from the shore, or how soon the Germans might be coming, so to save time they dynamited the anchor chain and put to sea.

Against the heavy weather the old boat did not make much headway, and they soon found she was leaking so much that they had to stop the engine for fear of drawing water into the crank-case through the air inlets. They pumped her dry and started again. After a few hours the steering gear broke. They stopped again and lashed a batten from the cargo to the rudder head as a tiller. Finally, after two days during which they had not made much distance, the fuel tanks ran dry, and they found that some drums, which they had thought contained oil, were really full of water. They were left drifting back in the direction they had come.

There were no sails on board, so they rigged the hatch cover and another tarpaulin as a kind of squaresail, but of course it was hopeless to expect to be able to sail the heavy old ship to windward, and they could only wait in the hope that the gale would veer before they were blown ashore again on Lofoten.

Luckily, after they had drifted for a day and a half and were expecting at any moment to see rocks to leeward, the wind did shift, and blew strongly from the north. They set the improvised sail and got steerage way on her; and rolling sluggishly before a mercifully steady gale for over a week they made Shetland – perhaps the most ill-equipped vessel ever to succeed in such a voyage under sail.

No-one could miss learning the lessons of this failure. First, it was a mistake to try to use fishing boats for a job which could be done by a warship, and which did not make use of the only advantage of fishing boats, which was their innocent appearance. This quality enabled fishing boats to go undetected to places which a warship could not reach without a fight, and so fitted them well for secret landings. But for an aggressive mission in which their presence must be known to the enemy they were hopelessly slow and inefficient, and to use them just because they were easily available was to take unnecessary risks with a very small chance of success. It was very lucky that no lives were lost in the Reine adventure. Secondly, the equipping of a fishing boat needed as much time and care as that of any small warship, and its crew needed time to 'shake down'. And thirdly, it was no use relying on a fishing boat, as one might on a battleship, to reach a spot hundreds of miles away in midwinter at an exact time; wind and sea must be allowed for.

These were the very points which we had all learned in Shetland and had already explained to the people who planned operations in London. On this occasion some of the planners had come to Shetland to see the boats sail, and they realised that they had set both us and the crews an impossible task, which we had all tried to carry out without comment only because we all thought the invasion of Norway was beginning. So our stock rose somewhat. Afterwards we were always asked our opinion of operational plans before they were completed, and as we always consulted the skippers who were to carry them out, so far as security permitted, there were no more fiascos.

CHAPTER NINE

LIFE AT LUNNA

AFTER the Reine episode it took us a few weeks to get ourselves organised again for ordinary operations; but when we did get started things went more smoothly than they had before. Most of the new base staff we had asked for had arrived, and those of us who had been there from the beginning had learned a lot. By the new year we had about fifteen British Army N.C.O.s and private soldiers to help 'Q' and Sergeant Sherwood. Most of them were billeted in Lerwick, and we only saw them at Lunna when they brought out rations and stores for shipment. 'Q' and Sherwood were also more and more needed in Lerwick, and Sergeant Olsen had had a misunderstanding with a revolver and shot himself through the palm of his hand, so that he was out of action for some time. I also found myself having to travel more to Lerwick and Flemington, and C.P.O. Percy and his assistant A.B. Hoad were often left at Lunna for long periods as the only British staff. They had been loaned to us by the Admiralty to look after our stock of mines and to train the men who had done the mine-laying in the *Nordsjöen*; but they enjoyed being with us, and they were so useful that we kidnapped them by simply not reporting that the mine-laying job was finished. Percy stayed till the summer, and I do not know how we would have got on without him. The Norwegians always respected an expert, and they could all see that he was not only an expert in mines, but a man with a life-long experience of the sea. So whenever I had to be away, we knew we could leave Lunna in his charge for as long as was necessary.

Life at Lunna had begun to settle down into a peculiar pattern of its own. It was rather a lonely life for me. Although every minute of it was filled with human contact, and there was plenty of excitement and plenty of humour, and although I liked the Norwegians and very much liked the four British N.C.O.s, I was separated from the former by nationality and a vast difference of background, and from the latter by the remnants of the gulf which stands between officers and men, and which no amount of mutual esteem can ever quite bridge with friendship. The N.C.O.s and I had a strong bond in being the only Englishmen among a crowd of foreigners, and I do not think I had ever properly appreciated Englishness before. After a tussle with a Norwegian who wanted something quite unreasonable, it was a tremendous blessing to see a sympathetic twinkle in the eye of 'Q,' and to hear his beautifully unruffled lugubrious Lancashire voice expressing exactly what I was feeling but could not say. Sometimes this bond made me feel such a fraternal affection for them that I would have liked to go beyond that delicate and rather absurd balance of relationship between junior officers and senior N.C.O.s; but having been a petty officer myself, I knew there was no more infuriating creature than the sub-lieutenant who wants to be 'called Alf' one day and to exercise his slender authority the next.

Luckily I had so much to do that I did not worry about loneliness, and did not feel the need of entertainment. But in that desolate lonely spot it was a job to keep the Norwegians amused in their spare time and yet to keep them out of mischief. The only sport they could enjoy at Lunna was shooting. They would shoot endlessly and pointlessly at anything living, or at any natural target that caught their eye. I think I am rather stingy by nature, and when I heard something like a battle going on in the hills or on the shore it annoyed me to think of the ammunition that was being wasted. But they had no idea that there was any limit to British supplies, or that the Home Guard thought themselves lucky to have ten rounds a man; and as they had access to stocks of machine-gun ammunition on their boats, which was practically inexhaustible when used in rifles, and as they had been encouraged to practice, I could not stop it but only struggle to keep it within something like reasonable bounds. The neighbourhood of Lunna is probably still covered with cartridge cases like a battlefield. It is a wonder that no-one (except Sergeant Olsen, who didn't deserve it) was shot. Once the minister, whose manse was one of the two other houses in sight of Lunna, came to ask me to curb their fire a little, as his wife had had to lie down in the ditch when she was walking back from the shop two miles down the road. But to soften her mild complaint she had baked me a splendid sponge cake and he had brought it with him. After that the Norwegians were forbidden to shoot across the road; and as this was an order they could see some sense in they complied with it quite willingly. But the rifle practice still spoilt the atmosphere of Lunna for me. I do not like shooting birds and animals myself, but I got a lot of pleasure from watching them, and found I could not enjoy walking along the sea cliffs when I knew that any seal or rabbit or seabird I saw might attract a fusillade at any moment.

The British sporting instinct produced a refinement of this shooting, invented I think by C.P.O. Percy, which was quite exciting and usually quite harmless: shooting rabbits, with pistols, on moonlight nights when snow was on the ground. This involved long cold stalks, with plenty of that discomfort for the hunter which somehow seems to make hunting more moral, and gave the rabbit more than a sporting chance. I recommend it to any sportsman who finds using a shotgun on driven pheasants too easy.

'Q' also used to do his best to prevent the Norwegians shooting uselessly. One day, when I was not there, it seems he was telling some of them who were shooting at seals that it was no good blazing away at long range: the only way to shoot a seal was in the eye, because to shoot it anywhere else spoilt the value of the skin. 'Like this,' he said; and taking a rifle from one of them fired one shot at a seal in the water two hundred yards away. The seal was killed, and when they retrieved it they found it was hit exactly in the eye. After that I don't think 'Q' ever risked his reputation as a dead shot by handling a rifle again.

Occasionally Mitchell used to go duck shooting. Considering that he was short-sighted he was a good shot, and used to floor his prey with surprising regularity, repeating more to himself than to anyone else a quotation he was inexplicably fond of: 'Fire the gun!' 'Can't see the target, sir.' 'Well, just fire the gun, you bloody fool!' But one was never quite sure what it was he had shot till he picked it up. I forget if it was he or somebody staying at Flemington who painstakingly stalked some duck on the burn and ultimately slew two with a right and left, to find that they were pet ducks of some rare breed belonging to a croft in the valley; but it was certainly Mitchell who shot the Great Northern Diver. He was sorry when he found what he had done, because this is a very rare and splendid bird; but as there was nobody who could stuff it we thought we might as well eat it. The cook at Flemington roasted it and made bread sauce and apple sauce and roast potatoes and cauliflower, and we invited our friends to dinner. It smelt and looked fine when it came to the table, and I was instructed to carve it. I set to work, then stopped to sharpen the knife and set to work again. It had a hide like linoleum, and I made no impression on it till I stood up and used brute force. Then, as soon as I made a small hole in the skin, a new smell arose: a smell so incredibly revolting that we fled from the room, and so penetrating that it seemed to cling to our clothes and our hair and to haunt our dreams for long afterwards.

Our social activities at Lunna were naturally very meagre. It was about twenty miles to the nearest place where any other troops were stationed, and we could not invite anyone to visit us. No doubt the few crofters and fishermen and their families who dwelt round about were as hospitable and friendly by nature as all Shetlanders are; but they kept aloof from the strange band of foreigners who had appeared there, and I cannot blame them, for we were not very desirable neighbours. Besides, spy-fever was at its height, and even the general store of the remotest hamlet had its posters about careless talk; and our base was so obviously something that it would be thought careless to talk about at all that the local people seemed to prefer to pretend that we did not exist, and the few who passed Lunna on the road, which led to five or six crofts on the peninsula beyond the house, walked by with a furtive air, looking neither to right nor left. After a time we discovered there was a weekly social, or a whist drive, at the village hall at Vidlin, a few miles down the road, and some of us used to go to them. I can hardly think that the people were very glad to see us, but when they met us like that away from our base they were very kind and made us welcome. After we had attended a few of their social evenings we gave one ourselves, which a great many people came to. That kind of entertainment is much the same in any country, and it seemed homely to all of us. Several Shetlanders sang songs, and we danced to an accordion and raffled a Norwegian cake for the hall funds; and then the minister called for a song in Norwegian. There was a long whispered consultation among our men, and several strongly resisting performers were pushed forward but were struck dumb by stage fright before they had started. I suggested they should make it a chorus, and in the end they managed to think of one song, and only one, which they all knew; so they sang it, in Norwegian, amid applause. The minister thanked them in a gracious speech, saying what a jolly tune it was, and how sorry they were that they could not understand the words; and I blushed, for although the tune had been pleasant the words had been vulgar in the extreme. The evening was quite a success.

Some of the men, of course, needed more sophisticated amusements, and we used to send them in a lorry once a week to Lerwick and turn them loose there. With their wage of £4 a week and the bonus of £10 for each trip to Norway they had far too much money to spend, and the ways which some of them found to get rid of it were annoying to the townspeople and to the hard-up British servicemen. But on the whole they were naughty rather than vicious. All Norwegians in regular service were also grossly overpaid by comparison with the British, and later on when Norwegian naval units were based in Lerwick we found that our men, with no kind of artificial discipline but with Mitchell and Sergeant Sherwood to take a fatherly interest in them, had been angels by comparison with the others.

But as the winter solstice approached and it got darker and wetter and colder and windier we thought less and less of outdoor amusements, and the journey of thirty miles to Lerwick seemed less and less worth while. In winter in Shetland, if one has outdoor work to do, one feels it is a whole-time job merely to keep alive. The dim yellowish daylight, which in December only lasts from nine o'clock till half-past three, and the incessant wind and rain make any work much harder and more tiring, and after the great storm in November all that most of us wanted at the end of each day was to doze in front of a big peat fire. We did not often get the chance. The boats used to sail at whatever time would bring them at a suitable time of day to their destination, or to the fishing zone, and on the shortest trips, to the Bergen or Haugesund districts, it was best for them to leave Lunna at nine or ten in the evening. I was always glad when one of them sailed at night, not only because it meant another job accomplished for the base staff but also because Mitchell would usually come out to Lunna to see them off, and I could count on an hour or two of conversation and gossip with him afterwards. Being both entirely absorbed in our jobs we usually talked shop, but it was a relief to be able to talk without any reserve, and he was always amusing and stimulating. He was a shrewd judge of the characters of the people we worked with, and his criticisms were forthright and witty and apt. When I was worried or depressed, as I often was, he always succeeded in making me laugh at my troubles and see how paltry they were, and when I was angry he made me laugh at myself. After these visits I used to see him off on his journey back to Flemington with a feeling that whatever went wrong there was someone who knew I was doing my best and who was more or less satisfied with it. As the lights of his car vanished among the folds of the moors I would turn back to my dark gloomy mansion and its curious household with a much lighter heart. He was the best of colleagues for the sort of life we led.

So at Lunna in midwinter we worked hard and did not have much energy or inclination for anything else. Running repairs on the boats had to be packed into the few hours of daylight, but other work went on long before dawn and after dusk. Some of it was gradually reduced to routine – getting the boat's stores and the cargoes ready for the next few trips. But succouring agents on their way into Norway and refugees on their way out, and fulfilling as best we could the multifarious needs of the crews, who were as much in their element at sea as seals but as helpless ashore – these were jobs which never came to an end and were always full of surprises. The only times we all deliberately relaxed were when the boats came back from Norway, when we always found enough drink somewhere to give us a glow inside. Some of our number were always at sea, and we did not know where they were or how they were faring, and each return was a reprieve. After a while I had stopped worrying about them all the time they were away: one cannot go on being anxious about a thing for ever. But whatever we were doing in the base the crews who were at sea were in the background of our thoughts, and when they were overdue, or when the wind rose, it was hard to concentrate on other things. When bad storms were mounting, our work multiplied and by evening we were tired out. But it was hard to sleep in a comfortable bed when one knew what the men at sea were facing. I used to lie awake listening to the swelling of the storm: first the familiar moaning in the chimney and the spattering of hail on the windows, stray gusts which died to a sigh and then to silence so that one could hear the sea stirring; then, as the speed of the wind increased, an ever shriller note which rose to a scream and a hollow roar so deep that it was felt as well as heard; and, at the height of the storm, the 'flans' which Shetlanders fear more than a steady blast — gusts or whirlwinds which one could hear far off as they roared in the hills like an approaching train, louder and louder till they struck the house with an impact which made its solid stone walls shudder and the slates rattle like a million metallic footsteps rushing from end to end of the roof. I would get up and look out of the window, hoping that in a gleam of moonlight or aurora between the clouds I could see whether the boats in the voe were dragging their moorings; but if I did catch a glimpse of them it usually only made me more uncertain, and I would dress and struggle down to the pier with a torch to watch each boat in turn and see if its wild veering was carrying it down to leeward. There was nothing whatever that I, or anyone else, could do to help the men at sea: their salvation lay in their own hands; but standing out there alone in the wind and darkness seemed to clear my head of morbid thoughts of my own unheroic status.

In January the weather began to improve. It grew colder and we had some weeks of calm clear days with snow showers. It was wonderful how we all cheered up, and how our work was done in half the time. The weather, and our growing experience, and the extra staff combined to enable us to undertake more operations, and with greater success, than we had achieved before. But the first trip of the new year was run in the opposite direction. The naval authorities in Lerwick rang up one day to say that a Norwegian boat had arrived in Unst, right in the north of Shetland, and that the skipper claimed to have an urgent message for us. They were rather sceptical about it, and had put an armed guard on board; but after some argument we got them to bring one of the crew to the telephone, and we found it was our old friend Knut, one of the two brothers who manned the radio station in Ålesund. We got him down to Flemington, where he arrived – I forget why – with at least six months' growth of hair and a wispy blond beard. He told us that a local fisherman from Ålesund, Sevrin Roald, had brought him over, and that the boat must get back quickly before its absence was noticed: the first time I heard of a man who was to become the best of my personal Norwegian friends. The Navy and security police were very dubious about letting the boat and its crew go back to Norway. They said it was unheard of for anyone to come over from an enemy country and go back again without at least passing through interrogations in London, which may very well have been true. Knut was impatient with this attitude, and thought it should be more than sufficient that he should vouch for the crew. He told us Sevrin Roald was willing to go on making crossings from Ålesund till it looked as though he was going to be found out, when he would come over and join us. He did not need to tell us how valuable it would be to the Ålesund organisation to have a boat immediately available for escape or urgent verbal messages; and we also liked the idea of having a boat operating from the other side which could fetch cargoes for so long as it could be made to last. Finally Mitchell managed to persuade the authorities to let the boat go, and we sent a private message to the skipper telling him to come to Lunna next time, where he could come and go, like our own boats, without anyone being any the wiser.

So one day a few weeks later, when I arrived at Lunna from Lerwick, I found a stranger in the voe – Roald's sixty-five-foot whaler *Heland*. When I went on board I found everyone asleep, but soon a tousled fair head emerged from the after hatch and a voice said, 'Good day. Sevrin Roald.' 'Howarth,' I said, in the Norwegian way, and shook hands with a broad twinkling man. 'Ah, yes,' he said in reply to my introduction, 'I have to bring you greetings from Karl Johan.' I asked him what had brought him over this time, and he told me of a plan that had been made in Ålesund for storing and distributing arms. If we approved, he was to take the cargo with him.

While we got permission from headquarters to give him a cargo and assembled it at Lunna from our dumps, he stayed with us there, and he and I had several discussions about boats and the war and life in general. I had already heard that although he was a fishing-boat owner and skipper he was also a very good shipwright. He was much concerned about the damage that had been done by the storm in Cat Firth, and sympathetic over our difficulties in repairing the boats there. He told me he did not think he would be able to go on for long crossing from Ålesund, as his long absences would be sure to be noticed; and he said, 'When it gets too difficult I'll come and look after your boats for you.' This might have been an embarrassing offer, and it was certainly one which we could not accept without making sure that it would be acceptable to the crews. But he saw my hesitation, and added, 'You give the orders and I'll do the work. You must ask the men what they think. I think it will be all right.' I began to see that he was a shrewd fellow.

Before he left I found that the crews were pleased at the idea of having him as a kind of foreman shipwright, and told him he could join us as soon as he found things too hot at home. When we were loading his cargo I asked him if there was anything else he wanted for the journey; and, looking round the store, he said with an air of childlike longing, 'You know, I always wanted a sextant.' This was another piece of shrewdness, for the sextants were the most valuable, and to a seaman the most desirable, of all the equipment in our stores. It was not in the least necessary to have a sextant for a journey from Shetland to Ålesund, and I could not give one away without permission; but I asked Mitchell, and he asked our headquarters, and they told us to give him one with their compliments; so he left with eight tons of arms and explosives in his fish hold, and the sextant lovingly stowed in his bunk, as happy as a king.

He turned up again at Lunna about three weeks later, bringing his wife and luggage for a long stay. He told us his last journey had aroused suspicions among Norwegians who could not be trusted, and, though he and the organisation had got the cargo safely hidden, he could see he was heading for arrest and had left home while the going was good. Now he and his boat were at our disposal. We sent him and his wife and crew to London to go through the usual security controls which were applied to refugees, and then he and his wife and his brother, who was a member of his crew, all joined us in Shetland.

Roald was immensely useful to us. He knew all there was to know about the hulls of Norwegian boats, and as he was a well-known owner and skipper himself the crews placed great faith in his judgment on any question of the shipwright's trade. So he stepped naturally into the position of chief shipwright. By the time he arrived I had had orders to take over again the responsibility for the maintenance of the boats, which for a few months had been in the hands of the naval base in Lerwick, and in this Roald became my right hand. One by one we collected half a dozen good carpenters to assist him, and the seagoing crews came to know that they could depend on prompt and efficient repair work being done as soon as they came in from sea.

He was another of those Norwegians, like Larsen and Blystad, whom English people liked at once. He never learned to speak much English, but he had curiously perfect and courtly manners, and an unpretentious confidence in his own expert knowledge. He managed to converse with our British troops in the pidgin language which had already evolved in our mixed base, and however difficult they found it to understand him they had an instinctive trust that whatever he was trying to say would be sensible. Unfortunately, like many of the Norwegian seamen and petty officers who hit it off best with the British, Roald could not abide Norwegian officers, and later on in the war, when Norwegian naval officers were attached to our base, he sometimes flew into such rages with them that it was a job to keep him out of gaol. It was a general defect of the Norwegian forces, so far as I had any experience of them, that the ratings had no innate respect for the officers; but in Roald's case it suggested those otherwise normal people who have a passionate and unreasoning dislike of cats. When he got involved in tempestuous arguments with his seniors he was usually right in his opinions, which made it all the more difficult for us to smooth over the regrettable way he expressed them. But we always managed to do so in the end. He was well worth the trouble of exercising diplomacy, because we could trust him completely and he never let us down.

While Roald was making his crossings from Ålesund, our boats were beginning the run of success which lasted till the spring. Most of the trips in this second half of the winter were concentrated on four areas of the coast: the island of Stord, south of Bergen; the island of Bremanger, in the mouth of Nordfjord; the neighbourhood of Ålesund; and the islands of Traena, on the Arctic Circle. Each of these areas had three, four or five visits between January and April, and most of the trips achieved their objectives. But on the first of them after the New Year there was such a series of small mishaps that the boat nearly met with disaster. Larsen was the skipper on this trip, and he was using a boat which was new to us, a Hardanger cutter called *Feie*. The job was a simple one: to land an agent with a radio transmitter at a point just north of Nordfjord.

The boat's sailing was delayed for three or four days by a southerly gale, but at the first sign that it was moderating they set off. Their troubles started when they were about half-way to Norway. The engine stopped without any warning, and the engineers found there was a lot of water in the fuel tanks. They got going again after about an hour's delay, but soon afterwards a bearing began to run hot through a fault in a lubricating oil pump, and they had to stop again. Next one of the limbers, or drainage holes beneath the frames of the boat, got choked up, and the bilge water accumulated on the forward side of it till it rose to the level of the flywheel, which sprayed it all over the engine-room. With the engine stopped for the third time, they were finding difficulty in making repairs because the gale was rising again and the motion of the boat was becoming very violent; so Larsen set all sail in order to reach sheltered water on the Norwegian coast where the engine could be attended to in comfort. But after some time under sail the engine got going again and the sails were lowered. Near the coast the engine faltered once more. By then it was very cold, and salt spray had frozen in the rigging so that the sails could not be hoisted. But luckily it was only a little more water in the fuel which had caused the trouble this time, and it cleared itself. So they reached the coast after thirty-six hours at sea; and, as the night was nearly over, they anchored in the lee of an island to wait through the daylight before beginning to penetrate the fjords to the point where the agent was to land.

The next difficulty became known to them when two fishermen turned up in a rowing boat and came on board. These two men had recognised *Feie* as a boat 'from the other side,' but they wanted to be helpful; and among other news they told Larsen that there was a new German control in a sound they would have to pass through on the way to the landing place. It was one of a number of new precautions the Germans had taken after the Målöy raid. One of the crew who lived on the island of Kinn, farther south, suggested that they should go down there and get his motor boat, which he had left in the care of his father. He thought his father would be able to take the agent through the control in it, and, failing that, the agent could borrow the boat and return it whenever there was an opportunity.

So the next evening they set off southwards through the islands towards Kinn. On the way they passed close to the place where Larsen had landed a radio operator on his last visit to that district, and it occurred to him to call on this man to see how he was getting on and to ask if he had a boat. They found he was still there, and he was more than pleased to see them, as he had never been able to make contact with England with his radio and had been trying to get a boat to take him back to Shetland. So he came on board, and the two agents rigged up a transmitter on the boat to ask for instructions from headquarters.

This involved starting a petrol generator, and as it made too much noise on deck they put it in the hold. After a time one of the crew felt sick and went to lie down in the cabin. A few minutes later they found he was unconscious. They looked up his symptoms in the first-aid book, but before they had made up their minds what to treat him for two more of them collapsed, and the others realised they had carbon monoxide poisoning from the generator. The ones who were still on their feet dragged the unconscious men up on deck and worked with artificial respiration for half an hour before they all came round.

Meanwhile the man from Kinn had been home in the dinghy, and returned to say that he had arranged for a motor boat to meet them at dawn. But when it arrived its owner said he had broken the water pump by starting it when it was full of ice, and it could not be used for anything more than a very short journey.

After this last straw the passenger decided to come back to Shetland, and the radio operator they had picked up came too.

Such a series of small mechanical faults, earlier in the year, would have annoyed the crew and made them eager to find someone to blame, but by then, besides Roald and his shipwrights, we had three Norwegian mechanics at the base. They were all from the biggest of the factories which made Norwegian fishing boat engines, and everyone knew they were the best experts at Norwegian marine engines who could be found. So the crews took engine troubles more philosophically, and were even inclined to blame themselves for some of them. Thus when Larsen and his crew got back to Lunna the only person in a bad temper was the passenger; and as the crew, who had so obviously done their best, did not think he had shown enough determination in the face of the first difficulties he had encountered, we did not take his complaints very much to heart.

At about this time we found we needed a new skipper, and the crews elected our old friend Bård Grotle for promotion. He had been with us from the beginning. Like Ole Grotle he was a fisherman from Bremanger, though the two were not related. He was one of our most eccentric characters, and in his own odd way he became one of our most successful skippers.

I often thought that Bård in another age would have been one of the famous buccaneers. Even in modern clothes, or in uniform, he looked a pirate. He never dressed without some flash of colour, usually a red spotted handkerchief round his neck, like a gipsy's; and after uniforms were issued to the men he showed his scorn of naval formality by never wearing all his uniform together. Sometimes he would have naval trousers and an army battledress blouse, and sometimes civilian trousers and a naval jacket; and always, however correct or incorrect his suit, he wore a decrepit and filthy trilby hat, from which long golden locks of hair escaped and blew about his face like the hair of a friendly sheepdog.

Bård was physically a splendid figure, tall and strong, with a classical nose and the blue eyes and fair complexion which tradition gives to all Norse pirates. But so arresting a character shone from his eyes and moulded his expression and his slouching seaman's walk that one was inclined not to notice his good looks. It was the character of a man who could not take a serious view of himself or anyone else. There was always the recollection or the anticipation of a joke in the twinkle of his eyes, and his mouth was always ready to break into a broad grin, or let out a hearty bellow of laughter, which might equally be at his own expense or at that of an admiral or a prince, or at some comic aspect of life in general, or at death. When I look back on my eighteen months of acquaintanceship with Bård, it is mostly these gusts of laughter which I remember; these, and the misgiving with which the base staff looked forward to sailing Bård's boat on operations. For much as we cherished him, and successful though he was, as a skipper he was rather a trial to us. We could never rely on him to start on a trip within a couple of days of the time he said he would be ready, and he set a bad example to his crew, and indeed to everyone else, by his dirty old clothes and unshaven face, his habit of staying in bed till dinner time, and his lack of interest in anything but the essentials of sailing his ship. He was the skipper, and nothing more. He would sail, at his own convenience, to anywhere between Bergen and Lofoten, and to hell with the Germans. But if a few nails had to be knocked in his boat, that was the job of the shore staff; and he seldom remembered to tell us about them, however kindly we prompted him, till he was due to sail.

But no-one could have helped being fond of him and forgiving him his faults, which were quite unimportant compared with his virtues. His imperturbable gaiety, and his careless acceptance of danger, and his luck and skill in escaping it, far outweighed all the trouble he gave us. It is a very valuable thing in a small isolated community to have someone who likes being laughed at, and Bård loved it. I suppose he wore his unseamanlike hat to amuse us, and it certainly did. One day, when I asked him whether he slept in it, he said, 'Of course,' and then added reflectively, 'Then, you see, when I get up I'm all ready for breakfast.' And it is valuable among men who have to face danger to have one or two who really do not seem to care about it, and who go on believing against all reason that whatever happens they themselves will come to no harm. Bård was attacked from the air many times; German patrol boats were sent out to search for him in a narrow fjord, and he sailed right through them; his boat sprang a leak and they pumped her by hand for two days in a gale; and still he would sail on trip after trip with an air of slight boredom, as if it were a crossing from Portsmouth to the Isle of Wight. Poor Bård, he died before the end.

In February Bård and his crew did a typically casual and successful trip to his home in Bremanger. One of their difficulties ever since they had been formed into a crew had been with the compass of their boat *Aksel* – the same boat which August Naeröy, who was now away, had skippered earlier in the winter. Several times they had been miles out in their landfall in Norway, and we got so used to hearing the blame laid on the compass or the compass adjuster that the words 'dårlig kompass' (bad compass) had become a stock joke. We changed their compass several times and had it readjusted, but still they fetched up in the wrong place. Hitherto I had never taken the risk of adjusting the compasses of the boats, because I knew I would be blamed for any eccentricity in the skippers' navigation. But I felt sure that the compass adjuster was not to blame for *Aksel*'s vagaries, and I made a bargain with Bård that I would adjust it once and for all if he promised not to be cross with me if he found his courses were still wrong. When I adjusted it I also fitted an extra compass in the forecastle, where there was no ironwork to cause a deviation, and I gave Bård a sympathetic lecture on magnetic variation. After that their courses were as accurate as anyone else's, and I found myself with a reputation as a compass adjuster. But I think Bård's reform was a result of the lecture, not of my adjusting, and I rather despised myself for being able to offer him a little bit of mere book learning, knowing that no amount of it would make me as good a seaman as he was.

But the trip in February was the last before the lecture, and they missed Bremanger by so much that they steamed on parallel to the coast in a northerly direction without sighting anything. It was not till they had gone nearly a hundred miles too far that they decided something had gone wrong again, and altered course to the eastward. When they did reach the coast and found they were somewhere near Ålesund, they had to go back on their track for twenty-four hours, and reached Bremanger after three days at sea instead of one.

Their job was to land a cargo in the bay of Vetvik, on the seaward side of the island. Vetvik is a very deep bay with no anchorage, surrounded by steep mountains and quite open to the westward. It is subject to violent gusts of wind from the mountains, and there is no landing place except a small jetty on the southern side. A westerly wind was blowing when they arrived, and it was impossible to land or even to lie there; but if they could not do the job at once they saw no reason for coming back to the base, and decided to stay there till they could complete it. So Bård sailed *Aksel* into the harbour of his own village on the other side of the island and settled down to wait for a change of weather.

They stayed there for a week, without seeing any signs of Germans and apparently without exciting much interest among the local people. Neither Bård nor another of the crew who lived there went ashore to see their relations. They took the sensible view that it was no good involving them in our activities unless it was necessary. But Ole Grotle's brother, who had helped us before, came on board and made arrangements to hide the cargo as soon as it could be landed.

In the end the wind shifted and Vetvik became calmer. They sailed round there and ferried the cargo ashore in dinghies. The one man who lived on the shore of the bay, and whom we knew from previous visits, helped them to stow it in caves where it would be safe till the local organisation came to take it away and distribute it among its members.

Meanwhile at Lunna we had been worrying more and more about Bård and his crew who were away for ten days instead of only three; and we were correspondingly pleased, and celebrated in a suitable manner, when they turned up in the best of spirits.

Bård's next three trips were all to the Arctic islands of Traena, which were the landing place for a fair-sized army organised in the Mosjön district by a Swede whom we had taken over earlier. Traena was a long way away, but it was an excellent place for landing. It is a group of small bare islands, with good anchorages in the sounds between them, lying far offshore and separated from the mainland by masses of skerries and reefs which would have made it difficult for a German ship, without a local pilot, to reach the islands from the eastward. The population was small and trustworthy, and everybody there was willing to store cargoes and hide agents and to take them to the mainland in small local boats as opportunities occurred. As usual this was a much safer plan than trying to penetrate far into the fjords with our ships, which would always be recognised as strangers.

Traena was therefore simply a long tedious voyage with no special risk attached to it except that of weather. The round journey was about twelve hundred miles: four and a half days north-north-east from Shetland, gradually closing the enemy coast all the way till the tops of the mountains could be seen to starboard and the boat's position could be fixed for a final approach to land; then four and a half days slogging back again. It could never be a small undertaking in winter with a sixty-foot boat, because it was unlikely that in nine days of winter, so far north, no days of gales would be encountered, and the boats just had to carry on through them. If they had suffered any engine trouble or damage to the hull which the crew could not repair there would not have been the slightest chance of rescuing them. The long trips somehow gave more emphasis to the emptiness of the sea; thousands and thousands of miles were added to the distance covered by our boats, and never a ship was sighted.

On Bård's first trip there were no incidents at all. His boat *Aksel* was laid up at the time with engine trouble, and he was using a big old iron boat called *Erkna*, which we kept as a spare. Most of our boats were fitted with extra fuel tanks in their holds, so that they could go as far as Traena without worrying about fuel, but we had not fitted out *Erkna* in this way, and Bård had to carry spare oil in forty-gallon drums. About half-way home the weather was bad, as usual, and the fuel in the tanks was running low; but the seas washing over the decks made it difficult to empty the drums into the tanks without getting seawater in too. So Bård turned east and sailed about a hundred miles in to the coast again to do the job in sheltered water. He never seemed to take any notice of what the Germans might do, or to treat the Norwegian coast with any more respect than he would have in peace-time.

A fortnight after his return he set off again, in *Aksel* this time, with a fresh load of weapons. By then he and his crew had made friends in Traena. He should have been back in nine days, but over a fortnight passed before he turned up again at Lunna, bringing with him several barrels of salt fish, some hams and Norwegian bread, a gross of boxes of matches and other such trophies. It seemed that he and his crew had just spent five days in Traena enjoying themselves. I did not inquire too closely what they had been up to, but one of the crew confided that they had had 'plenty of fun on the trip,' and they all wanted to go back there again.

Perhaps the prospect of more fun encouraged them on their next trip, when they were attacked twice by aircraft on their way north, but carried on and completed the job. This time they were carrying six passengers for the Mosjön army, as well as stores. The first attack was in the early morning, when *Aksel* was about three hundred and fifty miles out from base and a hundred miles off the Norwegian coast. A seaplane approached from astern and flew low over them, firing with cannon and machine guns. The crew of *Aksel* manned their guns, and the six passengers all armed themselves with sub-machine guns. A long fight developed. The seaplane circled round the boat at a good distance, and from time to time made further runs over her, six or eight in all. Each time it approached it fired at the boat, and the passengers and crew replied with their ten or twelve assorted machine guns. Probably their fire was not very accurate, because it is so difficult to shoot straight from a small boat in a seaway, but they thought they hit it; and at least they were throwing up a fine display of tracer bullets which must have made the pilot think twice. After nearly an hour of this intermittent, ineffective shooting the plane flew off towards the coast.

When the crew took stock of the damage they found it was

widespread but not very serious. Nobody had been hurt, and the hull was sound; but the sails were in rags and the rigging was cut to pieces, and the wheelhouse had several holes in it. It might have been worse, and they carried on on the same course up the coast.

This was an odd thing to do. It was still early morning, the seaplane's pilot would certainly report their course and speed, and it was very likely that a much more powerful attack would be made at any moment. But Bård stuck to his policy of not taking any notice of Germans except while they were actually engaged in annoying him, and I dare say it never occurred to him to turn back or to alter course in the hope of evading planes sent out to find him. As usual, his policy worked. The day passed and nothing more happened.

It was not till the afternoon of the following day, when they were 180 miles farther north, that they were attacked again, and this attack did not seem to be a sequel to the other. Two four-engined bombers came over, probably on some long-range reconnaissance. One stayed up high, but the other came down to mast height and made two runs over *Aksel*. This time the Germans' fire seemed to be just as erratic as that of the *Aksel*'s crew, and more half-hearted. A few more chips were knocked off the mast and rigging, and the galley funnel was shot away, but the aircraft soon broke off the attack. Bård still steamed on his course, and the following evening they arrived safely at Traena.

This time they did not stay there so long. On the previous trip they had only been landing a cargo, but now that they had six men to put ashore it was more obviously their duty to get clear of the district quickly, and so give the men the best chance of getting from Traena to the mainland without any suspicion. During the night after they arrived they put the passengers in the care of the shopkeeper on one of the islands and loaded as much as they could of the cargo into the shopkeeper's boat. The rest, mostly diesel oil for the local boats which ran the cargoes from the islands to the mainland, was stored in sheds round the shop for future use. One of these boats had been badly damaged while it was running a cargo, and as the owner could not claim on his insurance or afford to get it repaired himself, we had given Bård some money to pay for the repair work, and he handed it over to the owner.

The next evening they left Traena for the last time that season. The voyage back was just four days and five nights of steaming hour after hour on the same course, and they sighted nothing. But by then it was early April, the equinox was past, and although all was peaceful the long days of the Arctic summer were on the way, and Traena would be inaccessible until the autumn.

When *Aksel* got back to the base Bård and I looked over the damage together. When I went on board he was looking rather whimsically at his rigging. Both forestays and three of the foremast shrouds had been partly shot through, and the foremast was held up by a few straining strands of wire. The foresail and mainsail were hanging in ribbons, like those scarred battle standards which are carefully sewn on to nets and hung up in cathedrals. Yet the rest of the boat only had a few holes in it, mostly near the top of the wheelhouse. It dawned on me that practically all of the damage had been caused not by the aircraft but by the enthusiastic barrage put up by Bård's passengers and crew. I looked at Bård, and saw that he knew, and was waiting to see whether I would put two and two together. He saw that I had and burst out laughing. 'Damned bad shooting,' he said. 'Here is Jerry trying to shoot us, and he only hits the sea, and we are trying to shoot him and we only shoot down our own rigging. Hovart, we must have new wire. And sails.' And he went below to sleep, still laughing. Damned bad shooting it was, but from his point of view it had been successful; and perhaps it was not a bad idea in a small boat, when good shooting was impossible, just to throw up a vast volume of fire in all directions like a porcupine rattling its quills, and so make one's enemy think one was not worth the trouble of eating.

While Bård was making his trips to Traena the other skippers were all busy crossing to places farther south. Larsen, Salen and Blystad were making regular trips, and a new crew of men from the island of Godöy, near Ålesund, whose skipper's name was also Godöy, made two towards the end of the season. As the spring approached and the weather gradually improved, we were able to sail more and more often, till in April our five crews completed ten successful operations, and for two or three days in the middle of the month were all at sea, or in Norway, at once. We were able to build up stocks for each of the main organisations in west Norway against the summer, when daylight would cut them off from us, and to take out of the country the agents whose position was getting too precarious.

Landing stores had become tolerably easy, but picking up agents was still difficult and dangerous – difficult because we had to make a rendezvous at a more or less definite time, and dangerous because once the agents had left their normal cover and were making their way to the coast they were much more liable to be captured, so that there was always the risk of an ambush awaiting the boat. But as radio communications improved, our headquarters were better able to keep in touch with the agents till the last moment, and the agents themselves had learned that it was better for them to get to the outer islands by ordinary routes than to expect our boats to go too far in to fetch them. And the skippers were getting to know the politics of such people as shopkeepers and ferry skippers so well that they could often suggest a good meeting place and a way for the agents to get there. We had one such case in March. Larsen had tried to pick up a party from Trondheim on an island off the mouth of

15. British soldiers load equipment onto the *Andholmen* at Scalloway.

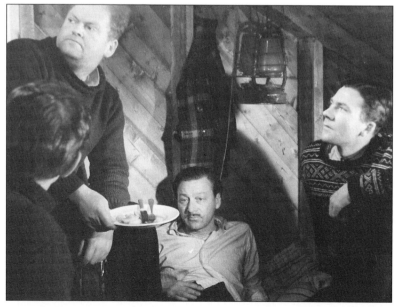

16. Rudolph Hansen, Finn Klausen and Johann Kalve in hiding after the *Bergholm* was sunk. Photo still from the film *Suicide Mission*. *Courtesy of Columbia Pictures*

17. Norwegian fishing boats and submarine chasers riding out a south-westerly gale at Scalloway.

18. Egil Karlsen inspects a 0.5 Colt machine gun on the *Aksel*.

19. A submarine chaser is manoeuvred onto the cradle at the Scalloway slipway.

20. Sevrin Roald, chief shipwright at the Scalloway base, watches anxiously as the first submarine chaser is hauled up on the slipway at Scalloway.

21. The submarine chaser *Vigra* at Scalloway.

22. From left Pål Krokenes, Louis Rasmussen and Torleif Fagertun take a break around a Bofors gun.

Trondheimfjord. But when he reached the neighbourhood he heard of an area newly closed to shipping which made it impossible for him to reach the island in daylight, and an onshore gale prevented him from getting in through the skerries which surrounded it in the dark, so that after several attempts he had to give it up. When he got back to the base he suggested that the agents should take the mail steamer from Trondheim to Kristiansund, and then the mailboat which ran twice a week from there to the village of Bratvaer on an outlying island farther south. He had been to Bratvaer before, and knew that the mail skipper was reliable, and if he had a few days' notice of the time they were due to arrive there he was sure he could be there at the same moment.

This plan was sent by radio to the men in Trondheim, and it worked excellently. When they were ready to start they sent a signal to headquarters. It was forwarded to us, and Larsen sailed. He was off the island forty-eight hours later, and as the mailboat left the village harbour he sailed in. He anchored his boat and rowed ashore, and saw five likely-looking men on the quay. He asked if they were waiting for transport, and they said they were. So he brought his boat alongside, took the men and their luggage on board, and was off again within a quarter of an hour.

Forty-eight hours later he was back at Lunna. The passengers came ashore, had hot baths and some dinner, and were sent to Lerwick, where they were passed, as refugees, by the doctor, security police and customs. Then, to the surprise of some of these officials, they were taken straight to the airport at Sumburgh, where an R.A.F. plane was waiting to take them to London. The journey from Trondheim to London could not have been made much quicker in peace-time.

A long series of operations like this made us feel, by the end of the winter, that we were getting the measure of the German defences, and that now we must concentrate our efforts on winning the battle with the weather. But as it turned out both enemies had some ugly surprises in store for us.

CHAPTER TEN

SUMMER REFIT

WHEN the nights became too short for the boats to make the crossing safely, we were able to take stock of our first winter's work with a certain amount of satisfaction. We had made forty trips to Norway; landed forty-three agents and picked up nine; landed a hundred and thirty tons of arms and equipment; and brought forty-six refugees across to Shetland. We could see that we might have done much more if we had known as much at the beginning of the winter as we knew at the end of it. But experience in such an odd kind of warfare had to be bought, and we felt that perhaps the most valuable result of that winter's operations was that all of us, both crews and shore staff, had gained in knowledge and experience and were confident we could keep open communications with every part of the coast in the following winter. By that spring our crews and our boats were good, and our base organisation was working smoothly. We were all agreed about the things we still needed, and had made plans to provide them for ourselves during the surnmer. Above all, we had been through a hard winter together and had confidence in each other.

We intended to make several changes in our base for the next season. The main one was to move the operational crews and boats from Lunna to the village of Scalloway. There were many reasons for this change of plan. A year earlier we had chosen Lunna because it was so far from anywhere that very few people would know of our goings-on. Since then, of course, some Shetlanders had learned more or less what we were doing; but they had been so discreet that we thought there was no longer any harm in working in a village. Besides, every man, woman and child in Norway knew about us, and referred to our route as the Shetland Bus; and we had succeeded in inflicting enough flea-bites on the Germans for them to know very well what kind of insect we were, and where we came from. So the only things which still had to be kept secret were the actual destinations of the boats.

Thus the main reason for using Lunna had disappeared; and much as I personally liked it, it had many disadvantages as a base. It was so remote that it was difficult to supply in winter. A bad snowstorm would soon cut it off, and the road had given us some anxiety, for it was built on peat, and when a heavy lorry passed over it one could easily see it subsiding under the weight and springing up again like a feather bed afterwards. It still remained difficult to amuse the crews at Lunna when they were ashore. And worst of all, there were endless problems in repairing the boats there.

It caused too much delay to send them to Lerwick for all the repairs they needed, and sometimes, of course, when they needed them most, they could not get to Lerwick under their own steam and had to be towed. Besides, we had come to the conclusion that we would have to run our own engineers' and shipwrights' workshops. We already had the Norwegian craftsmen, but to build adequate workshops at Lunna would have cost a lot of money and made the place conspicuous from the air. And furthermore, before an engineering workshop can be really resourceful at emergency repairs it needs to be in existence for years, and to accumulate stacks of useful scrap in every corner.

So everything pointed to a move either to Lerwick or Scalloway, which are the only places in Shetland which a southerner would call a town or village. Lerwick was altogether too urban and cosmopolitan, and its harbour and repair works were fully used by the Navy. Scalloway, on the other hand, was on the wrong side of the islands for voyages to Norway. But what finally decided us was that the owners of the marine engineering firm in Scalloway, who had already done some very good work on our boats, said they were willing to let our Norwegian engineers work in their workshops together with their own employees, which was just what we needed.

The working head of this firm was Jack Moore. He was (and still is) well known among the Scottish fishing fleets as an ingenious and experienced engineer. He was also the hardest worker I have ever come across — one of those men who might wear a collar and tie and a paddy hat, but who prefer to be up to their elbows, or further, in good black oil, and who might shut the shop at teatime, but who prefer to hammer and weld till midnight. Jack's father, a blacksmith of the old school, could work at his anvil all day long although he was nearly eighty, and was never satisfied till his work was perfect. Jack's brother Bob was fitter, and James Thomson was turner. Both of them had worked there all their lives, and were first-class tradesmen; and all four, through working so long in Shetland, where one can never depend on help in mechanical problems, were very resourceful, and experts at making do. Their workshop was a large shack at the water's edge which contained everything from old horseshoes to the most modern electric welding plant and was so full of machinery and a lifetime's accumulation of useful odds and ends beneath its blackened rafters that it used to remind me of a witch's kitchen, and I would not have been altogether surprised to find a stuffed alligator hanging from the roof or a bunch of charms stowed away among the shelves. In short, it was the best possible kind of workshop for the varied and unexpected jobs we so often had to do.

One result of the move to Scalloway was that we got to know more about Shetlanders and about the strange history of the islands. At Lunna we had had very few neighbours, and had lived in such a cloud of secrecy that we seldom met anyone; and although we were well acquainted with county and burgh officials in Lerwick, they were not typical of Shetland. But Scalloway was a compact village of about a thousand people. They all knew each other, and before long we came to know a lot of them too. If I had lived there I do not think I should have liked the invasion of the village by troops. However, we were not the first to arrive. A coast defence battery, a small R.A.F. detachment and a military hospital were there already; and as the Englishmen and lowland Scots in these units were just as foreign to the local people as our Norwegians, we were received in the most friendly manner. In fact, the British troops who were already there soon had reason to be jealous of some of the handsomer Norwegians, who seemed to possess an irresistible glamour in the eyes of the female sex.

Scalloway in peace-time is the essence of peace. It is the ancient capital of Shetland, and near it is the loch of Tingwall which, as its name suggests, was the site of the Norse parliament in Viking days. But during the eighteenth and nineteenth centuries the town of Lerwick, which was better placed as a port of call for fishing boats, quickly outstripped it in size and absorbed such industrial life as there is in the islands. Lerwick is now the centre of local government, and Scalloway has remained a village, with its character and atmosphere unspoilt by the sordid aspects of commercial life.

The village is clustered on the shores of a bay which is sheltered from the Atlantic by screens of small islands to the westward. Steep hills rise on the west and east of it, and to the north runs a fertile valley of farms and lochs. Its houses are dominated by the ruin of the seventeenth-century castle of the Earls of Zetland, which stands on a rocky point dividing the harbour into two. This castle played an important part in the more recent history of Shetland.

The islands were first colonised by the Vikings in the tenth century. Nothing much is known of the earlier inhabitants, except that they built a lot of massive round fortified towers, some of which are still standing. Both Shetland and Orkney remained a Scandinavian possession till the latter part of the fifteenth century, when James III of Scotland procured them by what now seems rather a shabby trick. For political reasons he married a princess of Denmark, and as the Danes at that moment could not pay all of her dowry in cash they pledged Orkney and Shetland for part of it. The agreement had two important provisions: one, that the laws and customs of the inhabitants should not be interfered with, and the other, that the Danes should redeem the pledge as soon as they could raise the money. However, whenever the Danes did offer the money James and his successors refused to accept it or to give up possession of the islands.

Before this deal was made the people of Shetland were of Norse stock, and lived under a system of udal law which gave every smallholder an absolute right of ownership of his land. But James, disregarding his agreement, leased the estate of Shetland and its revenues to a series of his favourites, and the people came more and more under the oppression of Scottish feudal lords. For over a century Shetland politics were very stormy and distress in the islands increased. The natives tried to maintain their ancient rights against the overwhelming power and the subtle double-crossing of the king's nominees, but it was a losing battle.

The climax of the struggle came in the last years of the sixteenth century, when Mary Queen of Scots gave the islands as heritable property to her illegitimate brother Lord Robert Stuart. Under the udal laws, which had never been repealed, land could not be sold unless a plea of extreme poverty was entered at the land court, and even then the descendants of the original owner retained the right to redeem the sale for many years. Lord Robert therefore adopted a policy of so impoverishing the freeholders of the islands by taxes and fines that they were forced to sell him their lands at prices which, by 'rigging' the land court, he fixed to suit himself. His ill treatment of the peasants became so notorious that on three different occasions he was deprived of his estates by the Crown; but he was a skilful courtier and always managed to get them back, and in 1581 his nephew James VI created him Earl of Orkney and Lord of Zetland. Soon after this he died and was succeeded by his son Patrick, who proved to be even worse than his father. It was Patrick who, in 1600, began the building of Scalloway Castle. Tradition says that its mortar was mixed with white of egg and bound with maidens' hair; but be that as it may, it was certainly paid for by further increases in taxes and built by forced labour.

Earl Patrick's reign of terror was not very long. He introduced a new penal code, in which death or forfeiture of land were the penalties for innumerable offences, including those of leaving the islands without his permission or suing him in any other court but his own. The islanders sank gradually into the depths of despair and poverty; but although they were virtually imprisoned in the islands by the earl somebody managed to transmit their complaints to the king, and four years after the castle was finished troops were sent there to arrest the earl. He was imprisoned and finally executed, and the castle was never lived in again.

The oppression of these early Scottish landlords was never forgotten in the islands; and in the nineteenth century the peasants, whose right to their land by then was only that of crofter tenants, had a reminder of medieval times. It became more profitable for landlords to breed sheep than to lease their land, and, as in the highlands of Scotland, crofters were evicted wholesale from their holdings and forced to emigrate, so that Shetland today is still covered with abandoned cottages and tilled land overgrown with heather and rough pasture. These evictions were perhaps less barbarous, but no less callous, than the Wicked Earl's depredations, and it is not surprising that to this day Shetlanders hate to be thought of as Scotch and are proud of their Norse ancestry, making a cult of the remnants of Norse speech and customs which can still be detected in the islands. In plain fact, Scottish, Dutch and English fishermen throughout the ages, and visitors of other kinds, including garrisons from Cromwell's troops to those of the two world wars, have made the modern Shetlanders a thoroughly mixed race. They are neither Norse nor Scottish, nor indeed anything but Shetlanders. But there are still plenty of Norse surnames among them. Many derive from the custom which survived till quite recent times of giving a boy his father's name with the suffix -son, so that one meets Mansons (Magnus' son), Swansons (Sven's son), Herculesons, Waltersons and so on. Other names of more purely Norse form, such as Ratter, Scollay and Isbister, are found among the Smiths and Scotts of the 'incomers.' The place names throughout the islands and the names of the islands themselves — Unst, Fetlar, Yell, Bressay, Papa Stour, Foula, Out Skerries, Burra, Hildasay — are almost exclusively Norse and have a picturesque outlandish ring.

The modern dialect is as much mixed as the blood. Its general form, and much of the idiom, is Scottish, but it includes hundreds of words of Norse derivation which are peculiar to the islands, and the intonation is more Norse than Scottish. It is very much alive, not only as a common speech but in dialect verse and stories. Most Shetlanders, like most other dialect speakers, can speak B.B.C. English very well, and do so when they are speaking to a stranger; but most newcomers cannot understand the language they speak among themselves. Several of our Norwegians learned to speak Shetland with a Norwegian accent, just as I spoke the west-coast fishermen's dialect of Norwegian with an English accent; and I suppose my mixture was just as odd as theirs.

Modern Shetlanders are misleading to visitors. Many of them, in remote districts, living in a two-roomed cottage perhaps miles from a road and tilling a small poor croft, look primitive and impoverished, but they are seldom either. Strangers sometimes pity them as backward natives, and tell them patronising stories of great cities and the wonders of urban life. This mistaken attitude pleases the Shetlanders, for most of them have travelled the world over in the merchant service, and know all they want to know about London and Glasgow, or for that matter about San Francisco and Singapore; but after seeing the world they have returned to the part of Shetland where they were born, and feel quite justified in pitying the people who live in cities. As for poverty, Shetland has certainly known hard times, but generally speaking there is no serious poverty in the islands now, and many men who go about in the roughest of working clothes and live lives of extreme simplicity have fat bank balances and could well afford to indulge any expensive whim. They are not in the least mean with their money but they do not spend it on show.

Their prosperity nowadays depends mostly on fishing and agriculture, the main product of the latter being the Shetland wool for which the islands are most famous, and the garments which the countrywomen knit from it. Both these trades enjoyed a boom during the war. Old fishing smacks which had been owned in Shetland for thirty or forty years increased enormously in value. Most were chartered by the Navy, which paid a reasonable hire and reconditioned them at great expense when they were returned. And the knitted goods fetched high prices when rationing encouraged people to buy clothes of high quality and factory-made imitations of Shetland patterns went off the market. All Shetland women knit. Before the war it was impossible to make a decent living at it, but during the war a good knitter could make £20 a week and do her housework, and it was not uncommon for a schoolgirl of ten to make £5 a week in her spare time out of class. Nobody should grudge Shetland women this sudden prosperity. It was only a slight compensation for past generations of hard work with very little reward.

Thus when we came to Scalloway we were among people who were hospitable by nature and well disposed by tradition to Norwegians, and who also had the means, after a past of varying degrees of poverty, to indulge their instinct of generosity. They were very kind to us, and we all made friends among them. It is always a blessing to a man serving in the forces to be invited into somebody's house and to be reminded of the happiness and comfort of home life, and it was especially a benefit to the Norwegians, who were so cut off from home, to be able to join in home lives so much like their own. We soon saw that they were going to settle down happily in Scalloway. In the wilds they got bored, and in big towns they did their best to go to the dogs; but Scalloway was a happy medium.

Unfortunately, just as we were beginning to feel we were ready for anything, the political battle for control of the base, which had been waged intermittently all winter between the British and Norwegian authorities in London, came to some sort of crisis, and at the end of the operational season we were told that control of the boats and the Norwegian staff had been handed over to the Norwegian Navy, though control of the operations and the British staff, with the responsibility for providing all kinds of stores, was to remain in Mitchell's hands. It was rather sad to have to hand over our little creation to somebody else, and Mitchell, Rogers and I did not think this new arrangement could possibly succeed. It looked all right on paper, but we were sure such a fine division of command would not survive the strain of working in winter storms. However, as the decision had been made, it was no use saying so; we could only accept it gracefully and try to minimise the degree of its failure.

We had already arranged for the boats to go to various ports on the mainland where the Royal Navy had agreed to refit them. As there was really nothing for me to do in Shetland under the new regime I thought I had better go back to naval service, and at my request I was returned to the Admiralty. But when I reported there I was immediately appointed to supervise the refitting of the boats. So I spent most of the summer travelling from port to port in Scotland, and thus heard of the embarrassing events which were taking place in Shetland without experiencing them myself.

The officer whom the Norwegian Navy appointed to take charge of the boats and crews was a well-known disciplinarian. By that time our crews had come to know us and trust us, and did not want to be under Norwegian command at all; and when the new C.O. started on his very first day by demanding salutes and the scrubbing of decks at dawn the men just refused to have anything to do with him. If they had really been in the Navy their behaviour would have landed them all in gaol; but after a very awkward three months, in which Mitchell was always having to support the Norwegian officer in decisions he knew were unwise and could not be enforced, the Norwegian Navy gave it up and control was handed back to the British. A new Norwegian officer, Lieutenant Leif Hauge, was sent up to Shetland, with much more limited authority, to look after the interests of the crews and to maintain the easy-going kind of discipline we had already established. His position needed a great deal of tact; but the Norwegian authorities' choice of Hauge was as wise as their earlier choice had been foolish. Everyone liked him, and under his good influence the base became happy again.

It turned out that we had made a mistake in sending the boats down to Scotland, because try as I might I could not get the repair firms or the naval overseers to take as much care over the work as our service demanded. Fishing boats in the Navy are used for taking rations round the fleet in Scapa Flow, and as examination vessels at minor harbours, and the repairs they are given are quite adequate for that. In fact most boats of that size, in war or peace, are equipped on the assumption that when a storm is blowing up they will run to port. But our boats, on the other hand, were quite certainly going to be at sea in hurricanes, and would have to ride them out or founder, so that our standards of equipment and repair had to be much higher than anything normally thought necessary. So if there was a damaged plank and I wanted the whole plank renewed, an overseer was apt to say that a three-foot length would do; and if he put in a six-inch block and a two-inch rope in a throat halyard where I wanted something heavier, I found myself up against immutable Admiralty specifications. Often, no doubt, the overseers were right; but I knew what our crews would expect, and I had neither the power nor the wish to send them to sea with a smaller margin of safety than they themselves thought they needed.

So the overseers and I reached an impasse, and I could see that the only way out was for us to do a good lot of the work over again when we got the boats back to the base. In the end this was what we did. It delayed the beginning of operations that winter; but by the time we had finished we knew each of our boats was in perfect condition, and that so far as human forethought could provide against the hazard of nature, we had left nothing to chance; and we never again relied on anyone else to keep our boats in repair.

Another project which had been delayed by the political upset was the building of a slipway in Scalloway on which we could haul up our boats for underwater repairs. There was only one slipway in Shetland, and it was often in use for naval work, so that our boats had to wait their turn. Besides, as it was commercially owned it was awkward to arrange for our Norwegian shipwrights and engineers to work on the boats when they were hauled up. We had intended to get the Admiralty to build us one, but the scheme hung fire; and when the autumn came, and it was obvious that nothing was going to be done till it was too late and winter weather made it impossible, we got permission, and a modest allotment of £750 to build one ourselves. None of us had ever built such a thing before, but we did not think it looked very difficult. The main difficulty we foresaw was to do it within the cost which had been allowed, and which was the most we thought we dared to ask for. So we set about scrounging the ingredients. We heard of a second-hand winch which was lying on top of a hill in Fair Isle. The owner of it said it was not worth his while to get it down the hill and ship it to the mainland, so we could have it if we could fetch it. We took one of the boats there with a large crew on an off day, dismantled it and manhandled the bits down the hillside. We got an engine out of a wrecked fishing boat, and some second-hand rails from Aberdeen. Somebody told me there was a derelict slipway, dating back to the sailing smack days, on the east side of Shetland, and I went to see if there was anything useful left there. I found a very large fairlead embedded in concrete, which was just what we needed to lead the hauling wire from the cradle to the shed where we proposed to install the winch and engine. Nobody seemed to own it, so I took a party of men there and we dug it out. Later, when it was immovably cemented into our slip, I started to get letters and bills from the owners of the ancient slipway, which had not been in use for twenty years, and eventually an elderly gentleman came to see me. He was prepared to be angry, but we reached a very friendly agreement; which was just as well, because a couple of years later when I became engaged to be married and was taken to be introduced to my fiancée's relations I found that he was her great-uncle.

Having collected most of what we needed, we set to work. The first thing we had to do was to enclose a spring called the Lord's Well, which rose mysteriously between high and low watermarks on the site we had chosen, and in times past had been the only perfectly reliable water supply in the village. Then we got a naval petty officer diver to help us in laying the concrete ramp which extended for 170 feet below low water level, and in fixing the rails to it. After watching him for a bit I and all our Norwegian shipwrights had a go at the underwater work. It was an interlude we all enjoyed. An officer in a diving suit was fair game, and the first time I went down the diver suddenly blew me up with air, so that I floated upside down, undignified and helpless. Then he held out what seemed to be a helping hand, but when I clutched it thankfully I found it contained a small but belligerent crab. Between us we finished the job in two months. Personally, I was always on tenterhooks when we hauled up the larger boats on it, and once or twice we did launch them unintentionally when the hauling mechanism gave way. But no damage was ever done, except to my nerves, and when we knew its tricks the slipway worked very well. Ultimately we took up boats of 110 feet in length and 120 tons dead weight, and it increased our efficiency in repair work tenfold. Crown Prince Olav of Norway gave his permission for it to be called the Prince Olav Slipway, and with a plaque upon it to commemorate this honour it is in use by the Shetland fishing fleet to this day.

Encouraged by this little engineering success we also built ourselves a pier. It was made with a home-made pile-driver out of a disused army water tower, and to save time we welded it all together. It is probably the only all-welded pier in existence, and again, when I saw loaded lorries drive out on to it, and seven or eight boats lying alongside it in a gale, I expected it all to disintegrate; but it also is still standing and in daily use by Shetland fishermen.

Another and excellent idea which somebody had put forward during the winter was that we should build a lot of small motor boats, so that when agents had to be landed at places a long way up the fjords all we would have to do would be to launch them in a small boat among the outer islands and let them make their own way in from there. Many of them, particularly those whose job was to observe such things as shipping movements and to report them by radio, and to have as little contact as possible with local people, would also be able to do their jobs more efficiently with a motor boat of their own. Of course the boats had to be built of a type which would not attract particular attention on the coast. Here the Norse history of Shetland was useful to us. Most British dinghies are square-sterned, but all Norwegian ones are double-ended, and to this day look very much like the boats which have been excavated from Viking tombs. Shetlanders have been building these Viking boats since A.D. 900. Through the centuries the type has been refined and perfected under the hard tests of deep-sea fishing, summer and winter, in the open Atlantic, and the modern Shetland boats are second to none in grace and seaworthiness. Our Norwegians all agreed that they would pass without comment anywhere in Norway. So we commissioned two Shetland boat-builders on an outlying island to build us a regular supply of seventeen-foot boats. We installed 1½ h.p. Stuart Turner engines in them, and during the next three winters we exported large numbers of them. It sometimes seemed sad to regard brand new boats and engines as expendable stores; but in fact they were invaluable to the Norwegian organisations in moving the cargoes we sent them, and to individual agents in reaching their destinations safely, and they well repaid their cost. In this, as in everything else, we had to learn by experience. We found that the little engines were extremely reliable, but to begin with we had trouble through seas breaking over the small boats when they were lashed to the decks for the crossing, so that the engines were sometimes submerged and had to be dismantled when they reached the other side. So we made perfectly watertight cases for them. The engines were mounted in a plywood box with a tight lid. The propeller shafts came out of the box through a watertight gland, and the petrol and water pipes were grouped together on a brass plate on the side of the box. A hole was made in the box for the starting handle and closed with a screw cap; when the cap was removed and the handle inserted the hole also acted as an air inlet. The whole box and engine could be removed from the boat or installed again in about ten minutes, and even if the boat did fill with water the engine stayed dry and in running order. I commend the idea to anyone who uses small motor boats.

With the slipway and pier, the boats well armed and in perfect condition, and our offices and stores all organised in the light of the past year's experience, we were ready in September for whatever demands the winter's operations might make.

There only remained one more precaution we could take towards ensuring the safety of the crews and the success of the operations. That was to bring our knowledge of German defences up-to-date. During the winter we had known the strength and position of every German watchpost and patrol vessel, and the shipping regulations for every part of the coast. But during the four summer months when our boats could not cross we could only depend on refugees and on our radio stations in Norway to tell us of any alterations in German dispositions. Refugees by that time were far fewer than they had been the summer before, and the masses of detailed information we needed were too much to expect radio operators to collect and encode and transmit. By the autumn our knowledge was bound to be rusty. Per Blystad, the skipper of the *Olaf*, pointed this out early in the summer, and volunteered to go over at the beginning of August, in a small open boat, to collect the latest information and thus make things safer for the larger boats in September.

We gladly agreed to this suggestion. A very small boat would have a good chance of crossing unseen even in continuous daylight, and Pete was confident he could move about the coast. Mindur Berge, the engineer of Bård Grotle's crew, wanted to go with him.

These two picked out a twenty-six-foot open boat called *Sjö*, in which some refugees had arrived earlier in the year. She was a very undistinguished clinker-built boat with a 4 h.p. semi-diesel engine. Such boats are used in thousands in Norway for fishing with hand-lines and lobster creels, and for transporting farm goods between the islands. They spent most of a happy summer fitting her out with everything they would need for the journey. Pete was a master at making extraordinary things look ordinary. For such a small boat, *Sjö* would have to carry an unusual amount of fuel, water, lubricating oil and food; but he packed it all in old Norwegian oil drums of various brands and sizes, which were just what one might expect to see lying about the floor of such a boat. Although he and Mindur gave the boat and the engine a thorough overhaul, they did not clean her, and during the summer they often went fishing in her so that she smelt of fish and had fishing gear stowed in all the odd corners where a fisherman naturally would stow it. In fact, she was a perfectly sound boat with an excellent engine, with which a summer crossing of two hundred miles could be made without much fear of any mishap from natural causes; but she looked an ill-kept old crock, which nobody would suppose had come from farther away than a neighbouring island. Pete and Mindur, in sweaters and overalls and seaboots, matched the boat. They were both efficient seamen and well trained and ruthless fighters. Pete was a good navigator, and Mindur an excellent engineer. But they managed, without any suspicion of conscious acting, to look the most stupid and unenterprising of longshoremen.

Equipped in this way, they set off in early August. They intended to spend two or three weeks in Norway, going up the coast from somewhere near Haugesund to Stadtland, and to come back by the end of the month. But they never came back. We waited all through September with dwindling hopes for news that they had landed somewhere in Shetland, but finally we had to become resigned to the knowledge that they were lost. It was tragic to have to give them up. Not only were they so useful to us in our work, we liked them both so much. Pete was one of the ablest of the skippers, and perhaps the most intelligent man among the crews. Mindur, whom we called our gentle giant, was everybody's friend, and such a simple, honest and fair-minded person that all the crews were guided by his judgment.

Months later we found out what had happened, but we never discovered exactly how they met their end. They reached the coast safely, and travelled northwards to Stadtland, passing on their way through the sound between the mainland and the island of Målöy. But on their way south again they ran into an unexpected control in this sound and were captured. They were taken to Bergen and kept there in prison for some months. Then they were taken away, and it was thought they were being sent to Germany. But their names never appeared on German records again, and we must suppose that at some unknown place on the way they were executed. This was the death they knew they were risking in their attempt to make life safer for the rest of the crews.

CHAPTER ELEVEN

BIG GAME

IN the autumn of 1942 we made a bold attempt, in conjunction with the Submarine Service, to cripple the German battleship *Tirpitz*. She had been lying for months in a narrow fjord surrounded by steep hills at the head of Trondheimfjord. Her anchorage had proved impregnable to any orthodox attack. The high mountains around it made her an impossible target for aircraft, and it was out of the question to reach her, seventy miles up the winding fjord, with any kind of warship, for the Germans had naturally been lavish with shore batteries, escort vessels and anti-submarine defences.

Since the sinking of the *Bismarck* the *Tirpitz* was the only battleship left in the German Navy, and she was therefore of very little use to them in the open sea. But by keeping her at a point from which she could possibly dash out undetected into the Atlantic, as the *Bismarck* had done, they were keeping British capital ships tied up in the Home Fleet at a time when they were badly needed elsewhere.

In the spring of the year I had thought of a scheme for carrying two aircraft torpedoes underneath a fishing boat, with a release and firing mechanism which could not be detected even if the boat should be searched. I explained the plan to Larsen, and asked him if he thought he could take a boat fitted out in this way through all the German controls into Trondheim, and let off the torpedoes at the *Tirpitz* or any other valuable target he might happen to see. If he had done so it was very doubtful whether he could have escaped. I proposed that the torpedoes should be set so that when they were released they ran on a course at right angles to that of his boat, so that all he would have to do would be to steam past his target and fire them when it was exactly abeam; and we hoped that in the excitement which would follow two underwater explosions inside the fleet anchorage nobody would take any notice of an innocent fishing boat steaming in the wrong direction. No plan was too crazy for Larsen, and he was delighted at the prospect of trying it. So Mitchell forwarded the plans of the mechanism, with the scheme for getting it into Trondheim, to the Admiralty, where it disappeared into the administrative maze and was never heard of again.

Whether this plan was the seed of what became known as Operation Title I do not know, but it seems likely. The first sign we had that something was in the wind was during the summer, when I was sent to Scotland to survey some large Norwegian fishing boats which had just arrived to join our fleet from Iceland. Our headquarters wanted in particular to know the area of clear deck space on each boat, and the lifting power of its winch and derrick. Then they sent for plans of all our larger boats. Mitchell asked what it was all about, but no-one would tell us.

Soon after, Commander Slaydon, R.N., the well-known submarine commander, arrived in Shetland. He was astonished at the secretiveness we had met with, and immediately told us of the vague plans which had so far been made.

The Navy had then just perfected a two-man human torpedo, which they called the Chariot. It was about twenty feet long, and was driven by electric motors. Its crew sat astride it in diving suits, protected by a kind of 'windscreen', behind which were luminous instrument panels and controls. On its nose was a very large detachable warhead. The crew steered it below their target, unscrewed the warhead, set a time fuse, attached the warhead to the bottom of the target with magnets, and then made their escape with the body of the torpedo.

Commander Slaydon told us they were keen to try to reach the *Tirpitz* with two of these machines. The charge which they carried was so big that a successful attack would make it impossible for the Germans to get her back to Germany for repairs, and might very well mean that she would be stuck in Trondheimfjord for the rest of the war. This would free British battleships and aircraft carriers to go to the Mediterranean and the Far East, where they would have a decisive effect on the balance of sea power. The Navy was relying on us to get the two machines, with six men, into Trondheim, and on our organisation as a whole to provide some possible means of getting the men out again after the attack.

After an evening's discussion at Flemington with Commander Slaydon, we all agreed that the job, though difficult, was possible, and we ourselves felt that it was more worth while than anything else we might do in Norway. The outline of the plan we agreed on that evening was as follows:

The two Chariots needed a crew of six men – two to drive each machine, and two 'dressers' to put them into their diving suits. The fishing boat would need four Norwegians to navigate it across the North Sea and through the controls up the fjord. The two Chariots could only be smuggled through the controls by towing them under water; but on the other hand they could not be towed across the sea. We therefore proposed they should be carried on deck to a convenient hide-out among the maze of islands and creeks off Smölen, where the *Nordsjöen* had made her preparations for minelaying. There they should be hoisted overboard and towed up the sixty odd miles of the inner lead to the control point at the mouth of Trondheimfjord, and the fifty miles of fjord which led to the anchorage. At the same time the ship's armament and radio equipment and certain other gear would be jettisoned. The ship and the Norwegian crew would have to be equipped to the last detail as Norwegian, and a hiding place which was absolutely proof against detection must be provided for the six Chariot men and a large quantity of diving gear and stores.

We also agreed that it would be a mistake to use a large boat. The Chariots weighed two tons each, so that two of them could be carried on the deck of any of our boats, and the derrick of any boat could be strengthened to lift them outboard. What was needed therefore was the smallest most inconspicuous boat, since a small boat could probably pass through the controls with a better chance of avoiding suspicion.

The choice of a skipper did not need discussion: Larsen was obviously the man for the job. We got permission to take him into our confidence and told him the plan. Between us we decided that *Arthur* was the most suitable boat. She was a small cutter of a type very common round Trondheim, and she had no distinguishing features. Larsen picked three men for his crew: Björnöy as engineer, Roald Strand as radio operator, and Johann Kalve as deck hand. We also came to the conclusion that Sevrin Roald, the foreman shipwright, would be needed to help in fitting out the boat. These men were only told that something had to be attached to the keel of *Arthur* and something hidden inside her, and they were told not to speak about it to anyone.

As the main control at the entrance to Trondheimfjord was expected to be of the strictest possible kind, it put us on our mettle to hide the Chariots, their crews and gear aboard our fifty-five-foot boat in such a way that no routine search could discover them; and to provide the boat and the Norwegian crew with all the passes they would need. Mitchell, in conjunction with our headquarters and our agents in Trondheim, undertook to provide forged passes, and I was instructed to fit out the boat.

After some discussion, and after consulting the Trondheim agents, we decided that *Arthur*'s ostensible reason for entering Trondheim should be to deliver a cargo of peat from one of the outer islands to the town. Peat was a convenient cargo, not perishable, and bulky in proportion to its weight, so that she could carry a large quantity of it as well as the Chariots. Besides, it was the one thing easily provided in Shetland.

The problem of hiding the illegitimate cargo then resolved itself as follows:

First we arranged chocks to stow the Chariots on deck for the sea passage, and fitted a stronger gooseneck and topping lift to the derrick, which we tested with two one-ton blocks of concrete. Then we beached the boat in a voe outside the village at Scalloway, and fitted two strong eyebolts to her keel about one-third of the boat's length from the stem. Two wires were shackled to the eyes for towing the Chariots, and their free

23. & 24. Submarine chasers *Hessa* (above) and *Vigra* (below), at speed.

25. Ditmar Olsen (left) and Leonard Faeröy on the submarine chaser *Hessa*.

26. Refugees coming ashore at Scalloway from the submarine chaser *Hitra*.

27. Norwegian engineers and shipwrights and local employees of William Moore & Sons pose beside the submarine chaser *Hessa* on the slipway at Scalloway. David Howarth (in centre) holds the base's plaque with its motto "Alt for Norge".

28. Victory parade at Ålesund on 15th May, 1945. The *Hessa's* crew march behind the Norwegian soldiers

29. A recent picture of Lunna House, the first base for 'Bus' operations and the church where Nils Nesse was buried. *Photo: Kieran Murray*

30. Scalloway today showing Prince Olav slipway and the pier, (on the left) where William Moore & Son maintained the 'Bus' boats *Photo: Kieran Murray*

ends were brought inboard and stopped to the main shrouds till they were required.

Arthur had a small cabin aft, then the engine-room, the hold, and a forecastle. To hide the Chariot crews and their gear we built a new bulkhead about two feet forward of the existing bulkhead between the engine-room and the hold. We used old timber and old nails, and carefully dirtied the work so that nobody standing in the hold could see anything amiss with it. The space between the old and new bulkheads was entered through a small door cut from the engine-room side. The door could be bolted from the inside, and was concealed by the electric switchboard in the engine room. It would have been impossible to detect this hiding place except by elaborate measurements or by knocking down the bulkheads.

To make doubly sure that the search at the German control would not discover anything there was the peat. On the sea crossing a petrol-driven generator had to be carried for charging the Chariots' batteries, but this could be jettisoned at the time when the Chariots were hoisted overboard, and enough extra peat could be carried on deck to fill up the space which the generator had occupied. The search would be carried out from an examination vessel in the middle of the fjord, and it would have been well-nigh impossible to get all the peat out of the hold and stow it on deck. The only other way of getting the hold cleared would be to take the *Arthur* ashore to a pier, or to put the peat on the examination vessel, and we thought that unless the examination officers were already so suspicious as to make arrest a certainty they would not take the trouble to do this.

When we had finished this preliminary work on the *Arthur*, Larsen and I and his crew sailed her to a remote sea loch in the north-west of Scotland, where trials with the Chariots were to be conducted.

When we arrived there after a twenty-four-hour passage I began to realise the importance which the Navy attached to the operation. In the sea loch I had been told to report to the small submarine depot ship H.M.S. *Alecto*. But when we entered the loch we suddenly came upon the battleship *Nelson* moored under the very shadow of a steep hill. I remember that she was signalling with a number of lamps from different parts of her enormous bulk, but I knew from experience that battleships are for ever signalling, and we took no notice, but chugged under her bows in search of *Alecto*. When we found her, a signal had already arrived from *Nelson* asking why we chose to ignore her signals, which it appeared had all been directed at us; but the impudence of *Arthur*'s unconcern must have amused the officer of the watch, for I think the message we received was moderately friendly. It turned out that *Nelson* was moored as a replica of *Tirpitz* and was to act as target for our trials. We were delighted at playing a star part in a drama in which *Nelson* was a mere member of the chorus.

We spent a week in practising towing the Chariots and in making night attacks on *Nelson* from different points outside the loch. Everyone was pleased with the results. A series of senior officers came aboard *Arthur* to inspect our preparations, including Admiral Horton, Flag Officer Submarines; and as a mere lieutenant I suffered some embarrassment at the state of my clothes – a disgraceful jacket and cap, no collar and tie, and no shoes except clogs, in which for some foolish reason I forget I had set off in *Arthur* with no idea of the company we were to keep. But luckily the captain of *Alecto*, Commander Fell, was the sort of man who asked me to dine with him in this rig; and he helped to prevent the ultimate embarrassment of an order to report on the quarterdeck of *Nelson*.

At the end of our trials I hitch-hiked by boats and planes back to Shetland to get Lunna ready for the others, for as the whole operation was being kept separate from our ordinary trips we were using Lunna instead of Scalloway as a base for it. Larsen brought *Arthur* with three Chariots and a mass of gear, and Commander Fell and some of his men as passengers. To avoid bad weather they left their course and sailed unchallenged through the Pentland Firth, past the 'gates' of Scapa Flow. They were sure that if they had felt like slipping a Chariot that night they could have stuck the warhead on *King George V*. The Chariot drivers amused themselves with ludicrous dialogues in which they went aboard the flagship and reported to the C.-in-C. that they had inadvertently stuck their warhead on her bottom; and they all hoped that the *Tirpitz* would be no more difficult. Passing Lerwick they were hailed by the naval examination vessel, and to avoid questions Commander Fell and his men hid below decks. He said afterwards that he had been delighted by the hails between Larsen and the examination officer, which, he said, went as follows:

'What ship?'
'Oh, just some old fishing boat.'
'Well, where are you from?'
'Can't remember the name of the place.'   [This was true.]
'Where are you bound?'
'Away up north somewhere.'
'What's that you've got on deck?'
'God knows, they never told me.'

And so on. Larsen could 'stall' for ever if he felt like it, and his half-witted replies were always delivered with an earnest air of helpful co-operation. In the end the examination officer, like many others before and after him, got tired of trying to get any sense out of Larsen and went back to port, and Commander Fell emerged chuckling from the hold.

At Lunna we had about ten days to wait till the moon was in its best phase for the attack, and the time was spent in more practice with the Chariots and in perfecting the plans for getting into and out of the fjord.

While we were in Scotland, Mitchell had been working hard on the problem of getting in, and the agent in Trondheim had completed the scheme for getting out.

We already had plenty of samples of the various German passes used for fishing boats and coasters and their crews, but to make sure what kinds were needed for the control at the entrance to Trondheim we asked the agent there to make inquiries. He confirmed that the boat would probably need a fishing permit, a certified crew list, the usual registration papers, and a certificate stamped and signed by the German harbourmasters at all the ports she had called at in the last three months or so. Each of the crew must have an identity card and a special permit for the defence zone of Trondheim.

All these of course had to be made out under fictitious names for the crew and a borrowed name for the boat. We selected from the *Norwegian Fishing Boat Register* a boat from a place not too near nor too far from Trondheim, which Sevrin Roald knew was similar to *Arthur* in appearance, and we made inquiries in Norway to be sure that it was not requisitioned by the Germans and was still in service. We also ascertained that although the skipper of it was not in the habit of going to Trondheim there was no particular reason why he should not do so. The name and registration number of this boat were painted on *Arthur* and the passes were made out in its name. After the operation its owner had a lot of explaining to do, but managed to convince the Germans that he had nothing to do with what happened.

The fishing pass, registration papers, crew list and crew's passes were easy for the experts to forge, but the certificate showing her past movements was a more tedious job, because of the large number of rubber stamps which had to be made and the numerous signatures on it. We worked out a plausible itinerary for the boat, sailing from port to port for three months and finishing up in the village of Edöy, where there was a small trade in peat; and Mitchell collected from German passes samples of the imprint of the stamp and date stamp used in each port and of the harbourmasters' signatures. These were sent to London, where a set of rubber stamps was cut and the signatures were forged on the forged certificates. All we had to do then was to stamp on suitable dates when the date of sailing of the operation was definitely decided. Finally, all the forged papers had to be dirtied. Passes on fishing boats are always stained with oil, and creased and frayed at the edges, and I do not know of any way of making them like that quickly except by carrying them in a dirty trouser pocket for a time. So this was duly done. When they were finished I do not think Scotland Yard could have detected the forgery. Certainly they were masterpieces wasted on the examination officer in Trondheimfjord.

Meanwhile the finishing touches were put to the boat and its equipment. Everything British was removed. New electric light fittings and wires which had been installed were taken out again and replaced with used Norwegian ones, and every oil drum and tool was checked over to see that it was of Norwegian make. The crew were fitted out with Norwegian clothes. The anti-aircraft armament for the sea passage was fitted on mountings which could be removed completely and thrown overboard before entering the fjord, and the radio transmitter and receiver, with their batteries and aerial, were also installed so that they could be taken out again without trace. The Chariots themselves were mounted on chocks on deck, the chocks being only nailed down so that they could be pulled up. The petrol generator for charging the Chariots' batteries was secured in the hold, and its exhaust pipe was led through the existing hole where the winch drive passed through the deck. With some difficulty we got enough sacks with no markings on them to hold the peat. We had a stroke of luck when a refugee boat came into Scalloway just before the *Arthur* was due to sail. From her we got current Norwegian magazines and perishable food — black bread, butter in Norwegian wrappings and so forth — which we were able to add to the German ersatz coffee and Norwegian tinned foods which we always kept in stock.

I think that nothing whatever was left undone to ensure *Arthur* a safe passage through the controls. But we could not foresee exactly what would happen, and in the end, of course, the courage and cunning of Larsen and his crew would be by far the most important factor in winning through.

Apart from the scheme for getting into Trondheim, elaborate plans had been made for getting the ten men out again after the operation. These escape plans were left in the hands of our principal agent in Trondheim, and to explain them he came over to England and thence to Shetland. He travelled — I do not know why — as a Lutheran pastor. The British crew under Commander Fell had been greatly amused at the whole of their contact with the adventure-story atmosphere in which we were accustomed to live, and when I brought them from Lunna to Flemington to meet him it was a pleasure to see their interest in and respect for the clerical figure fresh from enemy country.

His preparations were also as thorough as they could be. After the attack the British crews of the Chariots were to land within a certain stretch of the south shore of the fjord and make their way a short distance inland to a road which ran parallel to the shore. If possible this road would be patrolled by members of the agent's organisation who would have a car ready to take the men straight to the Swedish frontier, a hundred and twenty miles away, before dawn, and before the time fuses of the war heads had exploded on the *Tirpitz* and put the whole district in an uproar.

If this rendezvous failed the crews were to make for a certain conspicuous hill, where they could hide in thick woods during the day after the attack, meeting the agent's party on the bare summit of the hill the following evening. By that time, it must be assumed, escape from the area by car would be impossible, and the agent's men would therefore guide the crews across country on foot by two agreed routes to Sweden.

As for the *Arthur*, it was obviously impossible to get her out of the fjord by the way she got in, and the four Norwegians and two British sailors who would be left on board her when the Chariots set off for the attack would have to scuttle her and get ashore. After some discussion of ingenious means of scuttling without making a noise it was agreed that the simplest way was the best, and we provided them with two large augers. They could bore a few large holes in her bottom with these, and also disconnect and open the engine seacocks, which would fill her with water quite quickly. Some of the party maintained that she would not sink even when she was full of water, and it was an impossible point to prove without dry-docking and measuring her. In the end we put some extra ballast in her, which satisfied the doubters; but this was one question we did not positively answer before she sailed. It was not of very great importance if she should float gunwales under.

After scuttling the ship the six men were to row ashore to a second rendezvous, where cars would be waiting for them; and if that meeting failed they were to join the four men from the Chariots on the hilltop the following night.

Finally, if both these plans failed, or if the landing had to be made somewhere else in the fjord, the agent had investigated a number of cross-country routes to the Swedish border which could be undertaken by small parties. In case they had to walk to Sweden all hands were provided with rucksacks, rations and suitable clothes, and maps of the routes were printed on silk.

While all these preparations were still in train, Commander Fell and the Chariot crews continued practice at Lunna, particularly in making runs by compass at night in waters which were only familiar to them from charts which they had memorised. I was seldom out with them, but I remember one night when we slipped a Chariot from *Arthur* in conditions like those they expected in Trondheimfjord. It was a clear frosty night and the aurora was brilliant, hanging across half the sky like a curtain of which the folds were gently swaying as if a breeze stirred them, and reflecting a wan light from the cold calm sea. The dressers silently pushed and pulled the crew of the Chariot into their close-fitting diving dresses, and helped them to put on their leaden boots and oxygen gear. With their masks in place, black and shiny, the two men who a few moments before had been very human seemed like Wellsian monsters as they climbed clumsily over the rail and down into the water. In the water their agility returned. One submerged, to bring up the Chariot towing beneath our keel, and in a few moments it broke surface with a faint hiss of compressed air. They both swam alongside it, and in the light of the aurora we could see them making adjustments to its trim. Then they mounted astride it, and with a faint hum and the swish of the propeller the black shape gathered way, curved into the lines of light reflected from the north, and gradually sank from view till nothing but the moving heads of the two men could be seen, with a wake flowing from each. Then the water closed over their heads, the wakes vanished and the hardly perceptible sibilant noise of their movement was cut off. The aurora flickered and danced and the sea flowed silently as if they had never been there.

After several delays the day came when the *Arthur* was due to sail. It was a beautiful morning at the end of October. H.M.S. *Alecto* had come up to Lunna and was anchored in the outer harbour. *Arthur* was lying at the pier. The last detail was ready, and a high-level reconnaissance by a Spitfire the night before had shown that the *Tirpitz* was in her usual place, and that the submarine nets round her had not been moved. I said my goodbyes to Larsen, Björnöy, Kalve and Strand and the British crew and went up to the house by myself. These partings were always deliberately casual, but personally I often felt an emotion which I took care to conceal. This time I was more deeply moved than usual as I stood at the window and watched *Arthur* start on her journey. *Alecto* was not a big ship but she made *Arthur* seem very small, so that her fifty-five-foot hull looked like a toy as she chugged out of the harbour for the last time, cleaving the blue water into a sun-speckled wake. *Alecto* saluted her with a blast on her siren which echoed from the hills, and she answered in a smaller voice, but proudly. I was proud of her too: so small a ship, and ahead so great an adventure.

For the first twenty-four hours after *Arthur* left Lunna she met a strong easterly wind and the sea was rough. A small fishing boat in a steep head sea is perhaps the most uncomfortable form of transport there is, and very few people who are not used to it could stand the quick lift to the crest of a wave, the hovering moment on top when gravity is suspended, and the sickening crash as the bluff bows fall into the trough. All the British crew were seasick, but they managed between them to stand watch and watch with the Norwegians, and during the crossing Larsen, who was tired out with the preparations for the trip, slept for a solid ten hours. As usual the crossing was uneventful. They saw no sign of human life, and in spite of the weather it was a very happy party.

In the evening of the day after they sailed they closed the coast to fix their position. There was a slight haze, which was welcome as a shelter in case of air patrols, but they sighted snow-clad mountains above it, and identified peaks about sixty miles south of Smölen, where they intended to enter the inner lead. The entrance they were to use had been well lit in peace-time, but now of course all the lights which had shown to seaward were extinguished, and it would be impossible to find the way in in the dark. On the other hand, it was within sight of a German-manned lighthouse, which would make it dangerous to enter in broad daylight. So they reduced speed to reach it in the first light of the following dawn; and next morning, after a peaceful night in more moderate weather, they steamed safely into the sound and made their way into the maze of shallow channels and low islands off the west coast of Smölen, where they dropped anchor in a little bay to hoist out the Chariots.

They had all been worried about the Chariots on the journey, as *Arthur* had been taking it green, and heavy seas had fallen on them from time to time. But after they had had breakfast they took off the tarpaulins which covered the Chariots and found no damage had been done. On the other hand, when they dug out the motor generator from the peat in the hold they found it had shifted and broken its exhaust pipe. They started it, with difficulty, and found it made a most alarming noise; and while they were still wondering whether the noise would attract any attention, it fell over on its side and refused to go any more. The bolts which held it to its base had broken. The Chariot crews tested their batteries and decided they had held their charge well enough to be used as they were, so the generator was thrown overboard.

To guard as far as possible against surprises while they worked with the Chariots, they had posted a look-out; and as soon as the Chariots were uncovered he reported a plane approaching. They hastily covered them up, and tried to look unconcerned as the plane approached them, passed over very low, then turned and passed over again.

For the whole morning their work was interrupted so often by aircraft that they had to postpone hoisting out the Chariots. Once a Chariot was hoisted on the derrick it could not be lowered in a hurry, and would be very conspicuous from the air.

They were also delayed by two fishermen who appeared in a rowing boat and asked all kinds of embarrassing questions about the gear they could see on deck, and the state of the fishing industry in the port from which *Arthur* was supposed to have come. However, none of our skippers could resist a chance of getting useful information about the Germans counter measures to the pinpricks we inflicted on them, and Larsen reported afterwards: 'After giving them a number of vague answers, I asked them a lot of questions about the prohibited area seventeen miles west of Smölen. They told me that in the spring of 1942 there had been a boat from England which had landed some people there. The Germans had found out that a landing had been made in this area, and had immediately declared it a prohibited area. It was patrolled by planes and any fishing boats found in it were fired on. It is very hard to get away from Norwegians who talk.'

This seemed to offer an explanation of the unusual number of low-flying aircraft, and as the *Arthur* had passed through the area by night and was now well clear of it there was nothing to worry about. On the contrary, it was satisfactory to think that a much earlier operation of ours was still occupying German planes in perfectly useless patrols.

After midday the activity of the planes seemed to be dying down, and the Chariots were hoisted overboard. The water was not deep enough to let them hang down vertically on their wires, which was their natural position when they were not being towed, so they had to be moored temporarily with a rope round their tails, about three fathoms down. They were plainly visible in the clear water.

As soon as they had been sunk another fisherman arrived: a particularly garrulous old gentleman, who refused to be put off with vague answers but sat in his boat staring down at the Chariots and speculating aloud about their use in fishing. The British crew went below when he appeared, and the Norwegians told him that the Chariots were a new invention for sweeping mines – a fabrication which became more and more involved till they had to pretend they had a German crew aboard, sleeping in the cabin. He was so inquisitive that they were rather mistrustful of him, but after hearing that he lived all by himself in a hut on a neighbouring islet they gave him some coffee and butter and at last got rid of him, thinking that although he would be sure to gossip his news would not spread for a day or two.

It was dark by the time they had finished the preparations. Our intention had been that they should leave Smölen that evening for the journey of sixty miles up the inner lead to the mouth of Trondheimfjord, and should pass through the control the following morning. But the weather was worsening again, and there would be a considerable sea in the wide lead; so they decided not to risk starting their tow in darkness and a rising sea, but to wait till the weather improved. It would mean being late at their rendezvous with the escape organisation, but provision had been made for a day's delay; and besides, their escape was a minor consideration.

Next day the weather was better, and Larsen took a typical decision. We had always assumed that the journey up the busy lead would be best made in darkness; but at midday he thought things looked good and set off in broad daylight. In making plans we always tried to play for safety; but as *Arthur* had to go through the control and up the fjord itself in daylight, there was no real reason why she should not go up the lead in daylight too – it was only prolonging the risk, not increasing it.

During the morning they listened to the last of a series of radio messages we had been sending them, giving them the reports of the frequent reconnaissance flights which R.A.F. Spitfires were making for them over the *Tirpitz*. Nothing had happened in Trondheimfjord to cause them to change their plans, so they dismantled the radio and brought it on deck. At two o'clock they raised anchor. As soon as they reached deep water they threw the radio and its batteries and aerial overboard and streamed the Chariots on their towing wires; and they rearranged the peat in the hold so that it seemed to be full to the hatches. Then at their full speed, which with the Chariots in tow was between five and six knots, they set course up the lead. There were many merchant ships passing up and down it, but they were able to give them a wide berth and thus to avoid crossing their wash and running a risk of damaging the Chariots.

None of the six British crew had seen Norway before, and whenever there was no shipping too near they came up on deck and watched the snow-covered mountains and dark wooded valleys past which they were steaming, and looked with interest at the groups of small painted wooden houses. It was a beautiful scene, most peaceful by nature, but now full of human menace.

In the late evening they came to an island off the mouth of the fjord where the agent had told us of a reliable man, the shopkeeper, who could give the latest news about the control. They dropped anchor off the island in ten fathoms, so that the Chariots could hang straight down without touching the bottom, and Larsen went ashore in the dinghy and found the shop. As Larsen and the shopkeeper had never met before, the agent had arranged a password. Larsen was to ask, 'Do you need any peat?' The shopkeeper had been told that when a stranger came in and asked this question he was to answer no, and mention the name of the agent. After a little conversation Larsen put his question. 'Yes,' the shopkeeper replied with enthusiasm. 'I could certainly do with some. In fact I'll take all you've got.'

For a moment Larsen saw disaster looming, and pictured himself having to sell his precious cargo to avoid suspicion. But on consideration he felt sure he had not come to the wrong shop, so he prompted the man.

'Well, I can't give you much,' he said, 'because of course the cargo belongs to So-and-so really' – naming the agent.

'You mean Rolf So-and-so from Hitra?' the shopkeeper replied. 'What does he want with a cargo of peat?'

'No,' said Larsen, convinced in spite of the ludicrous password that he had the right man but that he had forgotten the code. 'I mean Odd So-and-so from Trondheim.'

Then recognition dawned in the shopkeeper's eyes. 'Oh, of course,' he said, 'how stupid of me. You're the man Odd told me was coming from England.'

They both burst out laughing, and the shopkeeper took Larsen into the back of the shop, where he told him every detail of the control on the fjord. It did not seem there would be any difficulty we had not foreseen. In fact, when the shopkeeper saw the bundle of passes Larsen had been provided with, his only criticism was that there might be too many. He advised Larsen only to produce his fishing permit to begin with, and thought that the others might not be asked for. He told Larsen the exact route through the minefields which guarded the mouth of the fjord, and the exact position patrolled by the examination vessel.

Larsen, who had prepared every detail of the operation with meticulous care now found himself in urgent need of bootlaces, so he tried to take the opportunity to buy some; but they were 'in short supply,' and he had to make do with string.

During the trip up the lead the engine had been running badly, and in spite of Björnöy's efforts it got more and more sluggish, till by the time they stopped in the evening it did not look as though it would carry them for the fifty miles farther up the fjord to the *Tirpitz*. So while Larsen was ashore the rest of the crew took the head off its single cylinder to see what was wrong. They were alarmed to find that the piston was cracked half across its top, and the edges of the crack had started to burn away, leaving an open hole straight down into the crankcase. Obviously they had only just stopped it in time, and would have to do something about it before they could move at all. It was a defect which normally an engineer would not try to repair, but during the night Björnöy made a copper patch to fit the domed top of the piston. They had to call again on the shopkeeper to try to borrow a tap to thread the holes they drilled in the piston top. His son took them to a farmer who had a workshop and woke him up in the middle of the night. He lent them the tap, and by seven in the morning they had bolted on the patch and reassembled the engine. It worked all right, but it was only a makeshift repair and could not be expected to last very long. It was an added worry all through the next day to know that at any moment the patch might come off and smash the cylinder head or the piston.

When daylight came they found the water was still very clear, and although the Chariots were now hanging down on the full length of their wire they were still plainly visible from the deck. When the boat was under way her wash hid them, but there was a risk that they might be seen when she had to stop alongside the examination vessel. Still, there was nothing to be done about it except to hope that the Germans would not look down.

At ten o'clock in the morning they started on the climax of their adventure. They were all elated by the knowledge that the moment had come to put our months of preparation and their courage to the test, and that the next few hours might bring either capture or death, or the opportunity to do a deed of world-wide importance. As they steamed the last few miles to the mouth of the fjord they systematically removed the last traces of British use from the boat. The remaining British food and the guns were stowed in the double bulkhead, where all the diving gear and the rucksacks and provisions for the escape were already hidden. Finally the six Englishmen crept into the dark narrow space, the secret door in the engine-room was shut on them and the switchboard closed over it. Once inside they were in pitch blackness, and could only guess what was happening from the sound of the engine and the footfalls on the deck overhead. The Norwegians prepared themselves for their part of innocent fishermen.

As they passed through the minefields they steamed very close to an armed trawler which was patrolling them. No notice was taken of them, which seemed to show that they looked all right from the outside. As they entered the fjord, below the massive forts which guarded it, they saw the examination vessel. There was only one. It was moving very slowly in the middle of the fjord.

Two other boats were ahead of them, and they watched them go alongside the examination vessel, wait there a few minutes, and then carry on towards Trondheim. When their turn came Larsen went forward on deck with the passes in his pocket, and Björnöy took the wheel. Strand and Kalve stood by to heave lines aboard the German boat.

There were several German sailors standing at the rail watching them. Björnöy had to take the way off the boat gradually, to make sure that the Chariots did not overrun their wires and break surface ahead, and as they gently approached and the boat's wash died away there was a minute of suspense when the Germans, had they looked down at the water, could certainly have seen the Chariots. But they did not. Lines were thrown and the two boats touched. When they were lying close together there was less chance of the Chariots being seen, but as the examination vessel was longer than the *Arthur* they would still be visible from the bows. A German naval lieutenant jumped aboard.

Larsen took his fishing permit and the consignment note for the peat out of his pocket and offered them to the officer; but he stood and looked round the deck and then made for the after cabin. Larsen followed him down, leaving his crew standing on deck under the silent gaze of the German sailors.

In the cabin the officer sat down at the table and opened a portfolio of papers. Larsen sat down opposite to him and handed him the fishing permit.

'Your crew list, please,' said the German.

Larsen gave him the crew list and registration papers and the printed notice saying that contact with England was punishable by death, all of which were pinned together. The German examined the fishing permit and registration papers carefully back and front. He did not say much, but when he spoke it was in a mixture of Norwegian and German, and Larsen, who had been speaking a mixture of Norwegian and English for a long time, found it difficult to avoid using English words. The German noticed the forged signature on the registration documents.

'Ah,' he said, 'this is an old friend of mine. I used to know him well in Bremen, but I did not know he was in Ålesund.'

Larsen took a quick look at the document, upside down, to make sure that the Ålesund stamp was on it, and that this was not a subtle trap.

'Yes,' he said, without any sign of interest. The thing he feared most was friendly conversation.

The German only glanced at the crew list and the document which had been prepared with such pains to show all the ports which the boat had called at for three months. But he noticed that the boat had been in Kristiansund and asked if they liked the place.

'All right,' said Larsen.

The German looked over all the passes again, as if to make sure that nothing was missing. Then he looked in his dispatch case and brought out the all-important pass to proceed to Trondheim. He filled in the name, number and tonnage of the boat.

'Cargo?' he said.

'Peat,' Larsen answered. But the German did not understand the Norwegian word for peat, and repeated it.

'Peat? What is that?'

Larsen resisted an impulse to use the English word, and did not know what it was in German. He explained that it was stuff for burning. They dug it up in the islands, and were taking it to the town to sell.

'Dig it up? Oh, yes, I understand now. How do you spell it?'

He wrote the word on the pass.

'Any radio on board?'

'No.'

'Any photograph apparatus?'

'No.'

'Passengers?'

'No, none.'

'And a crew of four?'

'Yes.'

'Your name?'

Larsen gave his assumed name, and it was entered on the pass.

'And the crew is controlled, yes,' said the German. 'And registration papers produced. Very good.'

He looked through the pass again. Then he signed it.

He had been down in the cabin for about a quarter of an hour, and to the crew on deck, who were half expecting at any moment an outcry or an exchange of shots from below, the time had seemed endless. The Englishmen in the double bulkhead knew from the slow running of the engine that they were still alongside the examination vessel, and that some discussion much longer than we had expected must be going on.

When at last the German officer emerged from the cabin hatch he looked down into the engine-room and forecastle and into the wheelhouse. He did not have the hold opened to look at the peat, but handed Larsen the pass and climbed back aboard his own boat.

'Carry on,' he said.

The German sailors cast off the mooring lines, and Björnöy put the engine in gear. The crew held their breath for a minute longer, till their wake obscured the water and the Chariots were towing again securely under the keel. Then in the highest of spirits they went down to the engine-room to let the British crew out and to tell them that the worst of the job was over.

Going along the fjord everyone's excitement grew. The fjord was full of shipping, and aircraft were flying in and out all the time. Once a German destroyer passed them, outward bound. Yet nobody took any notice of them, and they realised that now they had been admitted to these strictly controlled waters they were far less likely to be interfered with than anywhere else on the coast. There was nothing now between them and the *Tirpitz* except fifty miles of fjord and the torpedo nets, which the Chariot crews knew would not cause them any trouble.

The first part of the fjord runs nearly south-east, but about half-way to the place where the *Tirpitz* was lying it turns to the north-east. All the afternoon they cruised up the south-easterly part. The sea was calm and the weather fine, and the Chariot crews stayed on deck except when anything passed too close. But by-and-by they noticed that the clouds were moving quickly from the north-east, and when they passed the mouth of a valley cold gusts of wind blew down it. They began to think that when they turned the corner into the north-easterly part they would have a rough passage, as they would be meeting a head wind and sea blowing down over twenty miles of open water.

The change came abruptly soon after dark. Within a few minutes of rounding the bend in the fjord they found themselves pitching into a steep short sea which gave the boat an unnaturally lively motion. In a moment, as they rose to a crest they felt the tug of the towing wires on the keel. The bows fell into the trough, and when they rose again the sharp tug was repeated. Then something hit the propeller.

At once the boat's motion eased, and they knew that the Chariots were gone.

In despair they cruised on up the fjord at slow speed. One of the divers put on his gear to go down in the slender hope that one of the Chariots might still be there, but the sea got so bad that Larsen persuaded him to wait till they reached calmer water at the head of the fjord.

When at last they reached the lee of the hills beyond the town the diver went overboard. Their worst fears were confirmed. Both the wires were hanging from the keel, and on the end of each was the towing lug from the nose of the Chariot, which had been torn off by the boat's pitching. It was the bitterest disappointment. They were within five miles of the *Tirpitz*, which was easy range for a Chariot. Nobody knew they were there, and the way to her was wide open. But their weapons were sunk beyond retrieving, and there was nothing whatever they could do.

As they steamed slowly on they discussed how they should get out of the dangerous place they had got into with such difficulty. It was not going to be possible to land on the stretch of shore where the agent's party might have met them. The wind was blowing on to it, and the sea would be breaking heavily. If they had been in two parties, four on the Chariots and six in the boat, the six could have got ashore in the dinghy with a wetting. But with ten men aboard two trips would have to be made in the dinghy, and after beaching it for the first trip it would be impossible to launch it through the breakers for the second. They would have to fall back on the next alternative means of escape: to land much farther north in the fjord, where there was shelter, and to walk over to Sweden without help.

They started to throw the peat overboard, as we knew from experiment that it held air and stayed buoyant for a long time, so that to leave it on board would delay the sinking of the boat. As they approached the place where they had decided to land they bored four or five holes in the hull just above the waterline. They launched the dinghy, and a first party of five went ashore. One brought the dinghy back. Then Larsen took *Arthur* half a mile out into the fjord and they opened the seacocks. The water flooded the engine-room, and when it had risen till it stopped the engine the rest of them abandoned *Arthur* and left her to drift and sink.

By two in the morning all the men had met on the shore, and they walked up to a wood nearby, where they had some food and made plans. They decided that as soon as they got away from the immediate neighbourhood of the *Tirpitz* they would split up into two parties of five, which would be less conspicuous than ten men in a body. It was only about sixty miles to the Swedish frontier as the crow flies, but the first part of the journey would be through a thickly populated farming district full of lakes, and the latter part through mountains, so that it would be a much longer distance on foot.

Before dawn they had a short sleep in a wood. They were not quite sure where they were, but soon after they started they came to the shore of a large lake. This seemed a convenient place to separate, so Larsen, Kalve and three of the Englishmen skirted the lake to the southward, and Björnöy, Strand and the other three to the northward.

Larsen's party soon found they were much farther south than they had thought; for as they reached the crest of a hill during the morning they saw an arm of the fjord below them, and less than a mile away was a large warship at anchor. It was the *Scharnhorst*, and they were very close – too close to be comfortable – to the main anchorage. The *Tirpitz* was hidden by a shoulder of the hill, at about the same distance.

This at least fixed their position, but now that they were only armed with a revolver each they would have preferred to be as far from the *Tirpitz* as possible. So they set a compass course to the eastward and walked all day, keeping to the woods as much as they could, and making many detours to avoid houses and open country. The Norwegians, of course, were in the civilian clothes they had used to get through the control, but the British were wearing submarine jackets over naval battle dress, which, though it was not immediately noticeable as a uniform, was unusual enough to make chance encounters unadvisable. None of them spoke Norwegian. Although their use of uniform was sure to make the escape more difficult, it was expected to give them the protection of prisoner-of-war conventions if they were captured. The Norwegians, if they had allowed themselves to be taken, could not expect anything but execution.

Larsen was used to escaping in comfort, and for three days they walked by day and fed and slept well in farmhouses by night. Each evening he and Kalve went into a farm, leaving the Englishmen outside, and sounded the farmer's politics; and when he had proved to be a 'good Norwegian' they told him they were helping three Englishmen who had crashed in a plane. Each of the farmers and their families took all five men in for the night though they were risking a concentration camp by doing it.

Larsen was so confident that he sometimes did things which in anyone else would have been called foolish, but as he always got away with it nobody blamed him; and in one of these farms, where the two sons of the house had been unusually helpful and friendly, Larsen and Kalve gave them their revolvers. With thirty miles to go and frontier guards to consider this was hardly a wise action; but the very foolishness of it is somehow attractive.

By the fourth day they had reached the foothills of the high land which separates Norway from Sweden, and farms were scarcer. But there were plenty of cowherds' huts, which at that time of the year were empty, and they spent the fourth night in one of them. As the land rose higher they were more and more hampered by snow, and they were all getting footsore and tired.

The next day they made slower progress. There was a road running in the right direction, but the nearer they got to Sweden the more suspect they

117

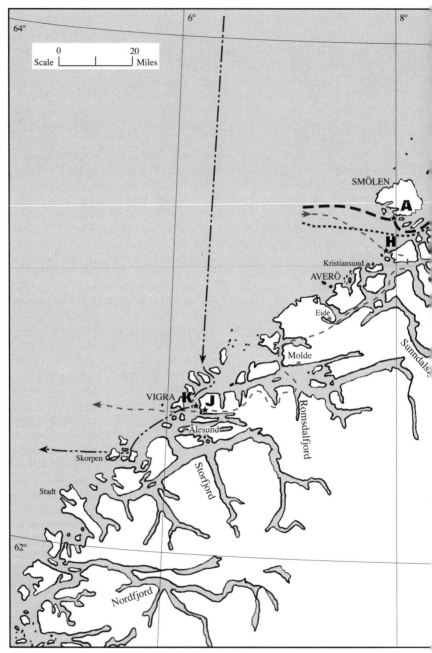

The Möre district of Norway showing routes of several of the main operations.

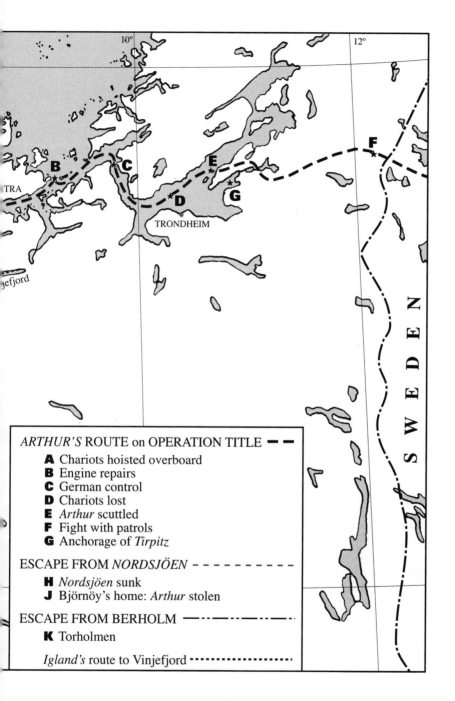

ARTHUR'S ROUTE on OPERATION TITLE ▬ ▬
A Chariots hoisted overboard
B Engine repairs
C German control
D Chariots lost
E *Arthur* scuttled
F Fight with patrols
G Anchorage of *Tirpitz*

ESCAPE FROM *NORDSJÖEN* ‐ ‐ ‐ ‐ ‐ ‐ ‐ ‐ ‐
H *Nordsjöen* sunk
J Björnöy's home: *Arthur* stolen

ESCAPE FROM BERHOLM ▬ ‐‐ ▬ ‐‐ ▬
K Torholmen

Igland's route to Vinjefjord ▪▪▪▪▪▪▪▪▪▪▪▪▪▪▪▪▪

119

would be as refugees, and any policeman or soldier they met at that stage would have tried to arrest them on sight. So whenever the road led past houses they struck off into the mountains, which meant a struggle through snow-laden forests of fir and across streams running in deep gulleys.

When night fell they were tired out, wet through and cold, and one of the Englishmen, Able Seaman Robert Evans, was suffering severely from sore feet. It was probably frostbite. They were less than ten miles from the border, but they could certainly not follow the road all the way, and they felt they could not manage to cross the mountains, where each step in the snow was an effort, without a night's rest. So Larsen tried his story again at a farm. But this time it failed. The farmer would not let them in, and directed them to another farm where, he said, they used to take in tourists. They tried the second farm, but by mistake went to the wrong one and were refused again. When they did get to the right one it was only to meet with the same answer.

This was most unusual, and it looked as though there must be some strong German influence in the place; or perhaps as refugees were common on that route the local people had been particularly threatened by the Germans to stop them giving help. At all events it seemed suspicious, so they carried on up the road, discussing whether they should stop somewhere for the night or try to reach the frontier at once. It was extremely dark. Soon they came to a sharp bend in the road, and were plodding wearily round it when they heard the word 'Halt.' They were face to face with two armed policemen.

They stopped, in the pitch darkness, at arm's length from the two men. They could just see that one was in uniform and one in plain clothes. The man in uniform had a sub-machine gun, and the other was holding what seemed to be a revolver.

'Keep on moving,' said the man in plain clothes, pointing in the direction they were going.

'Where to?' said Larsen.

'Never mind where to. Just keep on,' the man ordered. He added to the one in uniform, 'Got your safety catch off?'

'Where do you want us to go?' Larsen asked again. He and one of the Englishmen were in front, Kalve and the two others close behind them.

'Move on or we shoot. Drop those sticks and put your hands up.'

Larsen dropped a stick he was carrying and began to raise his hands. Then he realised that Kalve and he were unarmed, and that the three Englishmen could not understand what was being said and were waiting to see if he was going to talk them out of this situation.

'Draw your gun,' he said in English to the man beside him. At the same moment Kalve behind him told the other two Englishmen to shoot.

They and the police all opened fire at point-blank range. Everyone scattered and ran.

A few minutes later Larsen and two of the Englishmen met at the far side of a field, where a river ran parallel to the road. One of them had seen Kalve farther up the river bank, running. The other said that the third of the Englishmen, A.B. Evans, had been hit and fallen in the road.

None of them knew if he was killed or wounded, but they decided reluctantly that there was nothing they could do to help him. His feet were already bad, and he had been walking with difficulty. Now the whole district would be on the alert, and if he was only wounded it would be quite impossible to get him alive across the frontier, ten miles across the open snow-covered hills. It was a case in which the only hope of life was to be captured.

The three walked on through the night, and before dawn they came to a stone which marked the Swedish border, and walked into a frontier post. Kalve arrived a little later. Björnöy and his party crossed without trouble farther north. They suffered from cold, and Björnöy lost several toes through frostbite, but all the men came through alive, and after some delays in Sweden the four Norwegians were flown back to England and rejoined us in Shetland. Larsen was awarded the Conspicuous Gallantry Medal for his part in what everyone thought a most daring expedition which deserved success.

It was some time before we heard the sad news of what happened to Evans. He had been wounded and was captured. The Germans put him in hospital and he recovered his health. Then they executed him. This action was considered to be contrary to international law, as he was a member of the armed forces, carrying out a legitimate operation of war in uniform, and it was among the crimes with which Admiral Dönitz, who was then commanding in Norway, was charged at the Nuremberg trial.

CHAPTER TWELVE

SUCCESS AND TRAGEDIES

WHILE we had been making preparations at Lunna for the attack on the *Tirpitz*, the main base at Scalloway was getting under way with ordinary operations. We had made a late start that season because of the unsatisfactory way the summer refit had been carried out in Scotland, and in September and October only half the boats were in operational trim. But in October, four big new boats which had escaped to Iceland when the war in Norway ended were sent down to Scotland and handed over to us. They were the *Bergholm*, *Brattholm*, *Andholmen* and *Sandöy* – all of the highest class of modern Arctic whalers, strong and sound and fit for any weather. One by one we armed and equipped them, and they all played their part in the voyages of that winter.

The first dozen trips to Norway, in September, October and November, were successful and free of trouble – good routine trips to land agents and dump stores at convenient points. It would be tedious to describe them all. The fact that we were able to regard trips as a matter of routine was partly due to the comfortable way all the essentials of the base had fitted into Scalloway. We occupied buildings all over the village. At the west end of the harbour was Moore's engineering shop, with our pier and slipway alongside it. Two condemned houses, a disused coal store, an old weaving shed and a herring-curing station housed our shipwrights' workshops, marine stores, engine spare parts and radio workshop, as well as a mess for the British sergeants. At the end of the village there was also an old net factory which we had converted into barracks, and which, with four Nissen huts, accommodated the crews when they were ashore. Farther along the main street we had rented a house for the office and cipher staff and the intelligence records and chart room. A little later on we acquired a range of wooden huts towards the back of the village to accommodate all our British staff and an officers' mess; and later still, when we found ourselves with several Norwegian officers attached to us we got a small empty hotel for them. Next along the street was the road transport workshop, and at the eastern end the armoury and about half a dozen stores for 'export goods'. Everything was close at hand, and it was much easier to keep things running smoothly than it had been the year before, when half the base was in Lerwick and half at Lunna.

The stores of export goods were quite highly organised. The weapons and explosives which we sent to Norway were packed in a number of ingenious containers designed to make distribution easier within the country. Some were in crates identical with those of well-known Norwegian firms and stamped with their usual markings, others in fish barrels and others in five-gallon paint drums which were fitted with a tube extending from the bung to the bottom which was filled with paint, so that if any inquisitive person removed the bung and dipped in a stick he would only find paint and not the Sten guns which surrounded the tube. With a large variety of containers and an even larger variety of contents, there was a lot of work in packing cargoes. The goods required by different organisations varied; some needed explosives, others arms or uniforms or camping equipment or iron rations; and each had preferences as to containers, depending on the general trade of their district.

B.Q.M.S. Almond was in charge of the stores. It was a good thing he was a very efficient quartermaster, because in the course of time the variety of his stores grew far beyond most quartermasters' worst nightmares.

Apart from the usual quartermaster's stores, and the weapons and explosives which were sent to Norway, he had to deal with the stock of a ship's chandler: sextants, barometers, canvas and cordage, paints and marline-spikes and anchors, and all those sweetly tarry-smelling goods which attract some men to chandlers' windows as hats in hat shops are said to attract some women. Apart from our daily rations, he had to be able to provision any number of boats for a month at a moment's notice, or to procure tons of tinned food for some embryonic army which had been forced to take to the hills. Worst of all, perhaps, were the peculiar demands which agents made on his stores at the last moment before they sailed. They were all fitted out in London, but it was only natural that before they left us, and so cut their last link with the friendly world, they should think of all kinds of things which they would insist they must have. It was against our main principle not to give them all that they wanted, provided it was somewhere near the bounds of reason. Most of them deserved all we could do for them, and much more; though a few, finding themselves for the moment the object of everyone's solicitude, became arrogant and demanded things at which we had to draw the line. From time to time 'Q' had to find, in a hurry (and in Shetland, which itself is remote from any source of supplies), every kind of camping equipment from tents to tin-openers; every kind of clothing from an Arctic explorer's furs to a frogman's diving suit, or from a white snow-camouflage overall to a Norwegian-cut lounge suit; every kind of weapon from a knuckle-duster to a six-pounder. He became quite familiar with the parts of portable radio transmitters and motor generators. Eskimo kayaks were included among his stores. On several occasions agents broke or lost their false teeth just before they left and 'Q' had to get them new ones; others suddenly thought that they had better not leave land without corn plasters, or laxatives, or a new pair of glasses. Many mentioned that they needed a few bottles of whisky, which 'Q' sometimes procured for them, and one or two demanded that he should provide female company for their last night ashore, at which he put his foot down. It was always enjoyable to watch him writing down a long list of apparently impossible requests, with an expression of increasing gloom and exasperation – enjoyable because one knew that he was really enjoying it too, and that the more outrageous the things which were asked for the more pleased he would be when he produced them, and so added to the tradition that you couldn't beat 'Q.'

In the autumn of that year Mitchell left us for some more important job. From a selfish point of view I was sorry; but the base had got through its initial difficulties and was working smoothly, thanks to the foundations he had laid. The relations between ourselves and the Norwegian authorities had reached a fairly stable state, and we had quite got over the feeling, so common among people who run outlying stations of a large organisation, that headquarters were liable at any moment to let us down; indeed, we regarded our superiors with an unusual respect and affection. So if Mitchell had to leave us, I could not deny that the time had come for him to do so. Rogers was the obvious person to take Mitchell's place as C.O. of the base. He was better than I was at getting on with senior officers in the neighbouring services, and was a much better disciplinarian; whereas I was needed as a technician, and was in closer communion with the Norwegian fishermen. It did not make much difference to either of us which was nominally in command of the other. A little later on Captain Martin de Bertodano joined us to bring the number of British officers up to three again, and to take over Rogers' job of running the British shore staff. He turned out to be very good at this job, and, which was almost more important, an excellent companion.

That autumn the Crown Prince of Norway came to visit us. There were the usual inspections of our boats and shore establishment – not specially tidied up for the occasion, for illustrious people often came to see us, and by then we had made a habit of presenting ourselves to them as we really were, as a working unit and not as a parade-ground one. I myself, having been a flag lieutenant for a short time, knew that some admirals, at least, rather despised the special spit-and-polish which they cast before them like a shadow on their journeys to junior ships and shore stations, and would prefer to be made welcome with a drink and see things as they normally were. (For anyone less than royalty, Mitchell used to encourage me to be discovered in dungarees in some dirty part of a ship's bilges, whence he would hail me to be introduced to the celebrity.) Prince Olav decorated a number of the crew men, and we had a luncheon party at Flemington and a supper party for all hands in the barracks. The luncheon was served by some of our British drivers, and on the whole they did very well; but the man with the dish of roast beef arrived before the man with the plates, and the royal guest being served first, and being absorbed in conversation, got his helping of beef to within an inch of the tablecloth before anyone noticed there was nothing to put it on. That put a pleasant end to formality, and the party went with a swing. In the evening everyone sat down to a Norwegian *kveldsmat* – a delectable meal which has no English equivalent – and afterwards the Crown Prince wandered round the barracks with an earthenware mug of rum punch which someone had thrust upon him, talking in the most amicable way to everyone who buttonholed him. All the Norwegian fishermen seemed to address him with the intimate and informal 'thou,' and fired questions at him about politics and the war. He seemed really to enjoy their company, and answered serious questions seriously and foolish ones with repartee which made everyone laugh. That of course was the certain way to win the affection and respect of the Norwegians, who would be very ready to despise an aloof and more conventionally dignified ruler. He was so skilful at the business of royalty that his visit raised everyone's morale to new heights. We had always felt ourselves that we were doing something worth while, and his interest and approval was an official confirmation of our private belief.

Although everything seemed to be going so smoothly, and the boats were crossing regularly to and fro, we were not so foolish as to think that our troubles were over. There was seldom a day when all the boats were safely in port, and we knew all the time that we were only having a run of good luck, and that tragedy might strike us again at any moment.

It came, suddenly, one early morning in December. Bård Grotle was at sea in *Aksel*, on his way home from a landing in the far north, and we were expecting a radio signal from him reporting what he had done and when he would be back. But when the signal came there were only five groups in the cipher. The first four gave a position about 200 miles north of the base. The last group deciphered to the words, 'SEND HELP.' There was no indication of what was wrong, only that last desperate group of four figures.

Two hundred miles was over twenty-four hours' steaming for the fishing boats, so none of them could reach the spot till the next morning. But there were some Norwegian naval M.T.B.'s in Lerwick, so the first thing we did was to get one of them to make for the position *Aksel* had given. Then we asked the R.A.F. to send aircraft. The M.T.B. and a Catalina both arrived in the area that afternoon, but they saw nothing before darkness fell. There was a wind of about thirty-five knots from the west and a moderate sea on top of a heavy swell. It was not weather to trouble the fishing boats, but the M.T.B. was damaged by it and had to return during the night. Meanwhile one fishing boat had left for the area, and we moved another up to the northern tip of Shetland, with orders to report by telephone from there.

The next morning at first light another Catalina left the seaplane base in Shetland, prepared to search all day. The fishing boat should have been approaching the area during the early morning.

At dusk the Catalina returned and its crew reported that they had found them. They first saw them in the afternoon. *Aksel* was floating gunwales awash and the crew were in their dinghy and a rubber float. Before dark *Aksel* went down. The men in the dinghy had waved. But the Catalina had not been able to find the fishing boat to direct it to the spot, and the sea was much too rough for it to come down and take off again.

The weather was worsening. With a more exact position to guide them, we dispatched the second fishing boat, but the seas were too high for more M.T.B.'s to sail. The C.-in-C. Home Fleet, who was at Scapa Flow, had been following our news, and when he heard that the men had been located and were in such a desperate situation he sent a destroyer. By the next morning the destroyer and the two fishing boats were all as near the spot as the accuracy of their navigation allowed, and the R.A.F. sent up several aircraft to co-operate with them. But it was all of no avail. They searched the whole area, not only that day but for three days longer; but nothing more was ever seen of *Aksel* or her crew.

Of course we never knew what had sunk her. It did not seem likely that the weather alone would have done her any damage. She had been through far worse many times, and though we remembered that once in a storm she had sprung some of her trenail fastenings, that damage had all been repaired. There was nothing in the signal to suggest an air attack, which was the most likely kind of trouble; but of course the signal might have been sent at the height of a fight against a bomber, when the briefest signal would have the best chance of getting through; or it might have been sent at the last moment before rising water reached the transmitter, and time was too short to encode and transmit any more than the five essential groups.

It was a bitter blow that Bård and his crew, of all people, should be lost. Bård himself had such an outstanding and yet simple character that we all felt we knew him very well, and cherished him as a kind of mascot. Both he and his boat and most of his crew had been with us from the very beginning, sailing regularly to Norway and back without any fuss, and without worrying at all about Germans. We remembered the time they had stayed for four days in Traena having a party while we worried more and more about them; and the time (it was just a year ago) when they had brought Christmas trees for us all from the enemy coast; and the time Bård had saved up and placed an order, on one trip, for an accordion from a firm in Oslo, and called to collect it next time he was in the neighbourhood.

And Bård's awful old hats, and the way he would stay in bed till dinner-time; everything we remembered of him was unmilitary, perhaps exasperating, but certainly endearing. And so strong was his own conviction that the *Aksel* would always come back that we had all unconsciously learned to share it. We could hardly believe she was sunk, and he dead. Every one of the men half believed he had sailed his dinghy to Norway and would come back again. This possibility was discussed endlessly, and for months there were rumours that he had been seen there and was only waiting for a chance to escape. In the face of the obvious evidence, I almost believed it myself. I tried not to admit the truth to my mind, and so to postpone the distress of imagining that moment of terror (I see it so clearly) when, in the inhuman cold and darkness of the wastes of sea, Bård at last understood that his luck had failed him, and lost hope, and knew that he was drowning.

At almost the same time we lost a second boat and its crew, though we did not know about it till some weeks later; and the next month we lost a third. While we were searching for the *Aksel*, the *Sandöy* was up in the Traena district with a load of explosives. Her crew were comparatively new. Most of them had been neighbours living in a small island off Ålesund. They had come to Shetland together as refugees and joined us together, so we told them they could choose a skipper among themselves, and gave them a boat to man. They had done about half a dozen trips before they left for Traena.

The *Sandöy* became so much overdue that two or three weeks after the loss of the *Aksel* we had to give up hope of seeing her again. Weeks later we began to hear stories from people who lived on the outer islands south of Traena of a fight which they had seen between aircraft and a ship hull down on the horizon. No other Allied ship had been within hundreds of miles of the place at that time, so it was certain that *Sandöy* had been attacked on her way north. No survivors or bodies or wreckage were ever washed ashore, so far as we could hear, so we thought she must have been blown to bits by a direct hit with a bomb, which might have detonated part of her cargo.

The third loss was the *Feie*, one of the Hardanger cutters we had kept in reserve. Ole Grotle, who used to write such chatty logs and had been sailing successfully for two years, had taken her over, and was due to sail almost straight across the North Sea to the islands south of Bergen. The *Feie* left Shetland and disappeared. The weather was fine, but she never reached Norway. It was the only time we lost a boat and never had any news at all of what had happened. Somewhere on the short twenty-four hour crossing she met with some fate so sudden that her crew could not send a signal to ask for our help.

It would not have been surprising if the loss of three boats and of twenty-four men out of the sixty or so who were sailing regularly had made the others nervous; and if we had seen any signs of unwillingness among them to carry on, I think we should have suggested to headquarters that the trade was becoming too dangerous to be worth while. But the crews which survived did not falter at all. Orders for operations continued to flow in from London, and there was never any lack of volunteers to carry them out. New recruits were sent to us to fill the gaps, and every few days a boat would leave Scalloway, returning after a trip of four to ten days to report another cargo or passenger ashore. So the link was maintained between Norway and the Allied world; till in March even more trouble beset us.

CHAPTER THIRTEEN

MAN-HUNT IN LAPLAND

IN March yet another boat was lost. Plans had been made at headquarters
to send four men and a cargo to the very north of Norway as a nucleus for
the organisation of sabotage of German fuel and ammunition depots. The
northern part of Norway, from Lofoten to the Finnish frontier, formed a
long narrow corridor between the no-man's-land of ocean on one side and
neutral Sweden on the other, through which most of the German supplies
to the north Russian front had to pass. It was also, of course, the German
base for attacks on convoys to Archangel. Hitherto nothing had been done
to organise resistance in the district because of the difficulty of getting
there – it was about nine hundred miles from Shetland – but there were
known to be plenty of Norwegians still living there who would be very
willing to train as saboteurs, and the landing of this first party of organisers
and instructors was regarded as a matter of some importance.

The point for the landing was to be among the islands off the town of
Tromsö, in latitude 70° N., longitude 19° E., about 350 miles beyond the
Arctic Circle and 150 miles short of North Cape. From our point of view
March was late in the year for such a journey. It was the equinox, and we
had lost the protection of the polar night; but on the other hand there was
less risk of bad storms in March than in midwinter. A more important
consideration was that in midwinter the landing party would have found it
difficult to get their work started, or even perhaps to keep alive. On the
whole it did not look an unusually dangerous job for our crew. The danger
would be prolonged, as the crossing would take five days each way, and
for the whole journey they would be within the range of German fighter
planes, and far beyond any possible source of help.

The boat chosen for the trip was *Brattholm*, one of the four we had got
from Iceland. She was a fine strong seventy-five-footer with the usual
single-cylinder engine, as well suited as any boat of such a size could be
to fend for herself for eighteen hundred miles. The crew were comparative
new-comers to the base. There were five of them, under a skipper called
Sverre Kverhellen. The four passengers were accompanied by a man who
had worked for the post office in the district, and whose job was to help to
establish their first contacts and then to return with the boat. Thus eleven
men left Scalloway. One of the passengers was a sergeant, Jan Baalsrud,
and it was from him we heard the story, months later; for he was the only
survivor.

The day they sailed was the 24th of March. Five hours out from

Scalloway the engine stopped and it took them a long time to find the cause – a fragment of metal in the fuel system which moved with the motion of the boat and intermittently blocked the pipes. After this trouble they had no more delays, and pushed on at about seven knots in good weather for three days on a north-north-easterly course. On the second day out they sighted three German planes and two unidentified ships – one of the four occasions in four years when our crews saw other ships at sea. One of the planes circled the boat for a time and they cleared away the guns, but eventually it flew away.

On the 27th the skipper altered course slightly to the eastward to pass north of the Lofoten Islands and approached the coast obliquely.

Five days out from base they made an accurate landfall and identified the ice-bound peaks of the island on which they were to land. The passengers had made careful preparations to prevent the cargo being captured. The maps and papers they had with them were stowed in an accessible place with a bottle of petrol and a box of matches beside them, and among the tons of high explosive in the hold they set a priming charge and two fuses, one of five minutes and one (for a last emergency) of thirty seconds. It would have meant suicide to light the short one. During the last few miles before they entered the sounds between the islands they primed some hand grenades and overhauled and loaded their personal arms.

But at the mouth of the sound they intended to sail into they saw a patrol boat. Our information about patrols on this extreme northern coast was naturally not so thorough as it was farther south, and we had not known that a boat was stationed there. It was lying so close to the landing-place they had meant to use that they had to change their plans and choose a point farther north. The post office man suggested a little enclosed bay called Toftefjord in a small island just north of Tromsö, and the skipper altered course and took the boat safely in there. It was an ideal hiding-place. It was surrounded by hills, and an islet in its narrow entrance screened it from the sea.

They had expected Toftefjord to be uninhabited, but there turned out to be a small house on the western shore. The skipper and one of the passengers put on civilian clothes and rowed ashore to see who lived there. There was only a woman and two children in the house. The man of the house was away fishing, and his wife said she did not expect him back for some weeks. The passenger told the woman their boat was held up with engine trouble, and as there was no telephone in the place and it was miles to the nearest neighbours there seemed to be nothing to worry about.

The man from the post office knew of a merchant who had a shop on the far side of the island. He did not know him by sight, but he was reputed to be trustworthy, and it was decided that three of them should take the motor dinghy and go to see him, in order to get as much local information out of him as they could, without, if it could be avoided, involving him in their plans.

When they got to the shop the merchant was in, and by way of opening the conversation they told him also that they had engine trouble, and made some inquiries about spare parts. But as they talked they began to have a vague suspicion that something was wrong, and that this was not the man they had expected to find; and then the man told them he had only just bought the business. Its previous owner had died a couple of months previously.

This was a piece of bad luck, but it was the kind of thing which was bound to happen in opening up such a remote district, because the news available in England about individuals would often be rather out of date. However, they had not told the new merchant who they were, and the chances were that he was quite as sound as his predecessor; so they did not worry, but cut short the conversation as quickly as they could without giving grounds for suspicion and returned to the boat.

As a second attempt to get fresh information about the district they decided to try two fishermen who lived a few miles away, and who were also noted in intelligence reports as being reliable. Three of the party set off again in the motor dinghy. They found the men, and when they sounded them in conversation they got a good impression of their politics; so they told them half the truth, saying that they had come from the south of Norway with food and weapons which had to be stored for future use. The fishermen gladly fell in with the idea, and suggested a hiding-place for the cargo. It was arranged that one of them should come to Toftefjord at four o'clock that afternoon to pilot *Brattholm* to the best place for landing the stores; and then the three men went back to the boat to get everything ready.

All through that afternoon, as they waited for the pilot to arrive, they heard the sounds of aircraft out at sea and bursts of machine-gun fire. They supposed training flights must be going on. The landing-party went below to get some sleep in preparation for the night's work, leaving some of the *Brattholm*'s crew on deck. At four o'clock a shout from the deck awoke them, 'The Germans are here.'

All of them rushed on deck. A German warship was entering the fjord, past the small island in its mouth, a few hundred yards away.

Brattholm's heavy machine guns were dismounted to preserve her camouflage. The German ship was already blocking the only exit from the bay, and everyone realised in a moment that the planes and the shooting they had heard were not practice but a patrol drawn round the spot which was shepherding all fishing boats back to harbour. There was no escape for *Brattholm*; and had they reached the open sea, there were eight hundred miles of hostile ocean between them and any help. The only thing to do was to blow up their ship and cargo, and to try to blow up the German with her.

All their papers were collected at once and burned. The German ship opened fire. The crew of *Brattholm* took the first dinghy and made for the shore, while two of the agents lit the five-minute fuse and put their radio transmitters on top of it. The third agent fired at the Germans with a Sten gun in the hope of delaying them a moment till everything was ready. The fourth got the second dinghy ready and held it on the far side of *Brattholm*, where the Germans could not see it. As soon as the fuses were lit all the remaining men jumped down into the dinghy. They stayed hidden alongside *Brattholm* for several minutes while the fuse burned. While they lay there they could see the crew in the other dinghy. Two of them were standing with their hands up. Three were wading ashore. One was lying on the shore, apparently dead.

When three minutes had passed they rowed for land, trying to keep in the shelter of *Brattholm*, but the Germans saw them and opened fire on them with machine guns. At the same time two rowing boats were lowered from the German ship and set out for the shore.

The German ship approached *Brattholm* and made to lie alongside. Just as the ships were about to touch the fuse ignited. But unluckily only the primer exploded. *Brattholm* caught fire, and the Germans, seeing that a trap had been laid for them, put their ship full speed astern. All the time they maintained their fire against the dinghy. None of the men in it was hit, but the boat was riddled with holes and began to sink.

Then the cargo exploded. *Brattholm* vanished in a flash. The blast threw some of the men out of the dinghy, and in a few seconds it sank. If the explosion had come when it was intended it would have destroyed the German ship.

The men began to swim, still under fire, the hundred yards which still separated them from the shore. It was very cold, and ice was floating in the water, but they all reached the land. As they staggered across the beach one was shot in the head and killed instantly. The others, of whom Sergeant Baalsrud was one, reached the momentary shelter of some rocks.

So *Brattholm* met an honourable end, and of the eleven men who made for the shores of Toftefjord only Baalsrud lived to tell of it. Later on he heard how the Germans had discovered them. The merchant they had been to see had thought there was something queer about them, and could not make up his mind whether they were pro-British Norwegians involved in some illegal activity or Quisling *agents-provocateurs* sent to test him; so in order to play safe he reported the visit to the Norwegian magistrate. This man was bound by his office to pass on such reports to the Germans, but for some reason he put off doing so for ten hours – perhaps to give the men a chance to get away. As soon as he told the Germans they sent their most powerful available vessel from Tromsö to Toftefjord and patrolled the coast with aircraft. Baalsrud heard that after the fight the merchant was very repentant for what he had done, and that his life was made a burden by threats of revenge from other Norwegians.

So the misfortune of the death of the previous owner of the shop, which led the party to make contact with a man who suffered from indecision, was the cause of the disaster.

Baalsrud's own report of his escape is not properly a part of the story of our base, because he was one of our passengers and not one of our crews. But it was a great story of physical endurance, and I shall translate his own words.

Toftefjord, where the fight took place, is in the outermost island north of the town of Tromsö. A series of sounds and islands lie between it and the mainland. The town is on a small island in the innermost sound, and at that time it was the most important naval and military centre in north Norway. The inner sound was therefore heavily guarded, and the surrounding country was well garrisoned.

The islands are steep and rocky, with sparse vegetation, and in April they are thickly covered with snow just beginning to thaw. The mainland is cut up by a series of fjords, and the tongues of land between them are Alpine in character, with precipitous mountains, always covered by snow and glaciers, rising straight from the seashore to heights up to six thousand feet. The branch valleys from the fjords, and the main valleys at their heads, are fairly well populated; but inland is a barren wilderness of high fells, ice-bound in winter and covered with lakes and bogs in summer, and seldom visited by anyone except the Lapps who tend wandering herds of reindeer. Among these desolate hills is the Swedish frontier.

Baalsrud's only chance of escape was to reach Sweden. It was not very far — about seventy miles as the crow flies. But the Germans knew he was still at large, there were the sounds to cross, and the whole journey lay among icy mounatins and trackless hills. It took him two months. This is his story*:

'When I reached land after swimming from the dinghy I was exhausted, but I managed to crawl up the beach and shelter behind a rock. While I was swimming I had lost one of my rubber seaboots. As I struggled up one of the men was shot in the back of the head and killed outright. I shouted to the others to follow me, but there was no answer. The German patrol which had been landed spotted me and opened fire at about fifty yards' range. With one foot bare and nearly frozen I ran a little way into cover. I had no chance of getting away from them as I was too worn

* As Baalsrud's report assumes that a reader would have a knowledge of the country and the German defences, I have made slight alterations to avoid obscurity, and to preserve the continuity of the narrative the alterations are not indicated.

out, and to get any farther I would have to cross their course. So in the cover of the rocks I drew my pistol and aimed. But it misfired. I tried again, but it had jammed. I pulled out the magazine and took out the first two cartridges. Then it worked. I shot the first German, a lieutenant, twice, and he threw his arms up and fell. I hit the second one too, but did not kill him. The other two made off. If they had taken cover on the spot instead of running away I would not have had a chance of getting away.

'Now I had to climb the long steep hillside to try to get out of sight of Toftefjord and over to the other side of the island. When I was half-way up I felt a sharp pain in my foot. A bullet had taken off most of my big toe. Because of the frost and snow it did not bleed much, but this wound made it difficult to run. At last I got over the top of the hill and into cover again. When I looked back I saw that the Germans had put ashore what I thought to be between seventy-five and a hundred men. I could see most of our people, but none of them were moving. I thought they were all dead, but it turned out later that I was mistaken.

'I was in a desperate situation myself, with the Germans after me, and without knowing my way around in the district. On the other side of the island there was less snow, and I ran here and there trying to mislead the Germans. Eventually I got down to the sea again and went on along the beach. There I left no tracks, but I knew the Germans would get me sooner or later, alive or dead, if I could not find some way of deceiving them.

'Between that island and the next there is a small holm. I swam out to it. I stayed there about a couple of hours, running to and fro to try to keep warm. It began to get dark. The Germans were using electric torches and signalling to each other, so I could easily follow their movements. I do not think they had thought of the possibility that I might have swum away from the island. It was terribly cold after dark, and obviously I had to get away from the holm if I was not to freeze. The only thing I could do was to swim over to the next island, which was nearly three hundred yards away. I don't know how I managed it, but in the end I got there, with cramp all over my body.

'I rested for a little while, then set off along the shore looking for a house. Soon I met two girls of about fourteen. They were scared of me at first, but when I told them I was a Norwegian seaman they took me to a house where one of them lived. There I met five other people: two elderly women, a girl of about twenty, a boy and a child. Three of them were the people from Toftefjord. When the shooting had started they had left their house, but they had seen most of what had happened.

'I sent the two girls out at once to keep watch. The women took my clothes to dry them, and gave me dry underclothes, new socks and a rubber boot to replace the one I had lost. They dressed the wound in my foot and rubbed my legs till I got the feeling back in them.

'Half an hour later the eldest son of the house came in from fishing. I discussed with him the possible routes I might take to get farther south. We knew that sooner or later the Germans would search all the houses round there, so we agreed that I should sleep a few hours, and that then he would take me to the next island, Ringvassöy. In the meantime we sent the younger brother over to Toftefjord to try to find out what had happened to my companions. Twice while he was away the 'sentries' reported boats approaching. Both times I had to jump into my wet clothes and hide a little way away from the house, but luckily both boats went past. I told the people exactly what to say if they were questioned by the Germans.

'A couple of hours later the boy came back from Toftefjord and told us the warship had just left the place, apparently to patrol round the island, but that German soldiers were still ashore looking for me. He had not seen any of our people. *Brattholm* had vanished. On a nearby island he had found some bits of ship's planking and the remains of an oil drum. He had seen an ammunition belt hanging in a tree.

'After the boy got back the eldest son and I went in a rowing boat across to Ringvassöy.

'There was a possibility I might get a lift that same night to the mainland with the husband of the district midwife on Ringvassöy, so we went to his house on the west side of the island, but unfortunately he had left some hours before. The midwife had some patients upstairs. She was willing to hide me till the next evening, but I did not think it right to stay in a house where there were sick people. I had a good meal and then set off, walking south to make them think I was keeping to the west side of the island; but instead I crossed over to the other side and walked on along the beach till the early morning, when I found another house and went in. The people welcomed me in a very friendly way. I was tired out, and as soon as I had explained what they should do if anything happened, I went to bed.

'I slept all that day (the 31st of March) and was ready to start again in the evening. Before I left I got some more local information, and told these people the same story I had told the others. But I did not tell them what houses I had been to or where I was going.

'At seven o'clock that evening I began the climb over the mountains to get down to the south end of the island, opposite the mainland. The mountains there are steep and dangerous, but it was not very dark, and I thought I could manage it at night. When I had been going some hours it began to snow, and finally with the snow and the darkness it became impossible to see anything, and I had to turn back.

'I did not want to go back to the house, so I took shelter in a cowshed. Early the next morning the snow stopped, and I started again. This was the 1st of April. It was misty, and there was a strong penetrating wind, but after

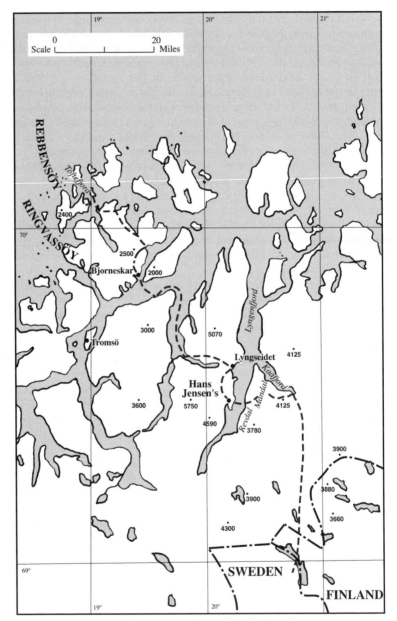

Baalsrud's escape route from Toftefjord to Sweden.
(Approximate height of the main peaks in feet)

thirteen hours I got through to the sea again and went into a farm. The people were rather suspicious of me at first because I would not tell them where I had come from. I explained to them why I could not say anything, and showed them my uniform and my damaged foot, and convinced them that I was all right. I decided on a way of retreat, then went to bed and slept till the next day.

'On the 2nd of April I rested, and also talked with the people who lived in the house. They were a man and wife and their thirteen-year-old daughter. My feet were beginning to pain me a good deal.

'At seven in the evening on the second I set off again on my march along the coast towards the south. The mountains often fall steeply to the sea here, so several times I had to go a long way inland to get through. I reached the next houses at six o'clock in the morning and went to one of them. The man who lived there was very nervous, because he had already heard rumours about me. He had also heard that the police were hunting round and looking for radio transmitters. He refused to keep me in the house for long, but I got some food and rested for a couple of hours. By then I had decided to make for a place called Björneskar at the south end of Ringvassöy. It was impossible to get there by the direct way along the coast in daylight, because it is thickly populated; so I had to go over the mountains again. The snow was deep, and the rubber boots were uncomfortable, and my feet were painful. The weather was bad, still windy and foggy.

'A little before eleven o'clock in the evening I got to Björneskar after a walk of twenty-eight hours. I was now in one of the best guarded areas in this part of Norway, on the shore of Tromsöysund. There were three patrol boats stationed in the neighbourhood, and strong German forces on land.

'It would be an annoying situation if the civilians here would not help me. People I had met before had told me that Erik Björneskar was a highly respected and trustworthy man. So I took the chance of visiting him, and found him in his kitchen with his wife and his two boys. Here I told the whole story from beginning to end as well as I could without mentioning the names of any of the people who had already helped me. I did bluff a little when I said that I had come to him because we had had good reports of him in England. He was astonished and said, "Did they actually get through to England?" Then I knew that he had helped refugees already, and I said that I did not know whether they were in Sweden or in England, but that their reports must have reached my headquarters. After this there was no longer a question of whether he would help me, but only of how he could best get me safely out of my difficulties. He had been in Tromsö that same day, and had heard about the excitement in Toftefjord. People were saying that a fishing boat with saboteurs from England had gone in there, and that the merchant there had been suspicious of them and had reported them to the police. The Germans had surprised the saboteurs and sunk their boat. The crew were captured, and most of them shot on the spot. When the Germans got back to Tromsö people saw three prisoners being brought ashore. Two of them were seriously wounded, and the third was an older man, who I knew must have been the leader of our party. Two were shot the next day, but the third was still alive and in hospital.

'When I heard that one, and perhaps more, of our party were alive and in German hands, I knew I must give a warning to our contacts in Tromsö. It was impossible for me to go into the town myself. I therefore got Erik to go in for me, but warned him to be very careful, because it was quite likely that the two main contacts would already have been arrested, or that the Germans would be shadowing them. Erik thought it was unwise for me to stay in his house while he was away, because the telephone and telegraph office was in the same building. He suggested he should row me over to the mainland that same evening and find somewhere there where I could lie low and rest. I agreed with him, and we decided to start at two a.m., when it would be darkest. In the meantime he went to see his father, who lived near by and was nearly eighty, and they found a pair of skis and ski boots for me. Unfortunately the boots were so small that I could only get one pair of socks on, but anyhow they were better than seaboots. It was dark and foggy when we started. I was too tired to row, and that was just as well, because otherwise they would never have believed my story that I was in the navy. In spite of the searchlights and patrol boats we got safely across to the mainland. They showed me a house which I could go to without danger.

'There I found a married couple with a young daughter. They also had an adopted son, but I did not see him. It was not at all easy to convince the man of the house that I was all right, but I succeeded in the end and they let me go to bed. I slept and rested there till midnight the next night. The man had decided to take me that night in a motor boat across the mouth of the fjord. This would be farther away from the heavily defended area round Tromsö, and would also give a better route over less thickly populated country to the southward. He owned a fishing boat together with his adopted son and one of the neighbours, and without saying anything about me he told the neighbour to come to join him at ten o'clock to set some nets. We started at midnight. I told them to keep near the land so that I could jump overboard and swim ashore if the patrol boats stopped us, but we got through without any mishap, and they put me ashore.

'From this point there was a road which ran up the shore of the fjord and then crossed over a narrow neck of land called Lyngseidet to the next fjord, Lyngenfjord. I intended to follow the road on my skis to the head of Lyngenfjord. By then I had sufficient food with me and was well fitted out with clothes, so that I could sleep in fishing huts and byres and would not need to have any contact with the local people. I carried on up the road in the darkness and reached Lyngseidet, but there one of my ski bindings came loose and I wasted some time repairing it. The time was half-past five, and I was hoping to get past that area, which was well populated, before people started waking up.

'But just as I reached a small village, a whole flock of Germans came out of a school. They must have been billeted there and have been on their way to breakfast. They filled the whole road and I had to ski on through the crowd. Luckily they cannot have been fully awake, otherwise they could not have failed to take some notice of me in full Norwegian uniform, with naval badges and the word Norway in English on my shoulders.

'Immediately I passed them the road went steeply downhill for several hundred yards. I suddenly saw three Germans at the foot of the hill. They were looking at the papers of some civilians. The road was blocked. But just in front of me a footpath led off to the right. Trying to look natural, I turned off along this path and got away. But the distance between the mountainside and the sea was so small that there was no chance of getting past them without being seen. From the map I remembered that there was a summer track leading up the mountains and running parallel to Lyngenfjord, and I knew it was passable on skis. I therefore climbed high up the mountain side and began to cross the slopes above the fjord. The weather was fine and cold, and I kept the fjord in sight all the time.

'During the afternoon such a gale blew up that I could hardly keep my feet. The only thing I could do then was to get down to the fjord again. The drifting snow became so thick that I could only see a yard or two. It was very steep, and suddenly I fell. I do not know how far I fell. When I came to myself again I found I had lost both my ski sticks and one ski, and the other ski was broken in three places. I had also lost the clothes I was carrying in a rucksack, and worst of all, my food. I had also received a hard blow on my head and lost my sense of direction. I tried to dig myself down in the snow, but I was too cold, especially in the feet, so I had to keep on walking and hoping for the best. I sank deep in the snow at every step.

'The next day, the 6th of April, the weather was just as bad. Several times I tried to dig myself in, but it was too cold. That evening I began to hear voices speaking to me. The only thing I remember of the next two days is the nightmares I had, in which I met all my dead companions.

'In the evening of the 8th I reached a house, and opened the door and fell inside. The man in the house belonged to an illegal organisation in the district, and he knew at once who I was and where I came from, so I was in safe hands. He massaged me and made me swallow hot milk and brandy, and I woke to a kind of half-consciousness. My eyes were hurting, and I found I was snow-blind. He put ointment and bandages on my feet, and then got me up into the loft, where he made a very comfortable bed for me. I slept there nearly four days.

'Early on the morning of the 12th I awoke fully, and found that I was still nearly blind and could not stand on my feet at all. The owner of the house called himself Hans Jensen, but this I learned later was his 'cover name.' He told me that immediately after I fell in his door he went out to see where I had come from. The weather had been fine that last day, so he could easily follow my tracks. He said I had come down from the mountains, and had been going round in circles in a little wood less than a kilometre from the house. For the last twenty-four hours I had not been more than a few kilometres from the house, and sometimes I had passed within a few yards of it

'Jensen told me what he had heard in Tromsö and other places about the disaster in Toftefjord and the fate of the prisoners. It confirmed the stories I had heard before, but now I heard that the last prisoner had been shot — three days after he was captured. Two Tromsö men had been arrested. Later I learned that they were our two main contacts.

'The Germans and the police had been round everywhere in Lyngenfjord, searching the houses for radio transmitters and arresting the families of people who had fled to Sweden. They were patrolling Ulsfjord and Lyngenfjord with fast motor boats. Jensen therefore thought it would be best to move me to a safer place as soon as I was well enough.

'On the other side of Lyngenfjord there was a burnt-out farm, of which only one small hut remained. As nobody lived there, and it was four or five miles from the nearest neighbour, it seemed to be an ideal hiding-place. The same evening Jensen and two other men took me across to this hut. The place is called Revdalen. There they installed me quite comfortably, with food and a stove within reach. The intention was that they should come back within two days to see how I was getting on. In the meantime they would try to find out what could be done next, get hold of a doctor and inquire whether it was possible to transport me over to Sweden if I could not use my legs again. We agreed that as long as I was ill it was best for me to know as little as possible about their organisation.

'I stayed in the hut for two days, and on the 15th of April they came back. I felt much better by then and could move my toes a little. They told me it was very difficult to get a doctor, so one man had gone into Tromsö to find out how one treated frostbitten limbs. Although I was still in great pain, it looked as though my feet would get all right again, so we decided to wait a few days before we did anything more to them. The men left me then and promised to come back in two or three days.

'A few hours later I began to feel a violent pain in my feet. I could not sleep, and it got worse and worse. In the morning the skin had begun to peel off, and some septic matter was coming out. It smelt horrible. The pain increased and my toes began to go black. It hurt so much that I could not lie still in bed, and sleep was out of the question. On the third day I ran out of food. At the same time a gale blew up again, and I knew it would be difficult for Jensen to row across the fjord in such weather. I lay there four days more, seven days altogether, becoming more or less unconscious. On the 22nd I had given up all hope and thought something must have happened to the men who had helped me, but a little after two in the morning Jensen came in with two men I had not seen before. They had tried several times to row across the fjord, but had always had to turn back.

'As soon as they saw my feet they saw it was gangrene, and that the only chance I had was to get over to Sweden as quickly as possible. They had already been in touch with the organisation in the next valley, Mandal, and thought they could get a Lapp from there who could take me over the border. They went home again and promised to arrange either transport or a doctor. Three days later four men came with a sledge. They were to haul me up to the top of the mountain range between Lyngenfjord and Mandal, where we should meet people from Mandal who would take me a stage farther on the journey. They put me in an old Norwegian army sleeping-bag with two blankets and bound me to the sledge. The mountainside was so steep that they could not possibly haul me up: they had to lift the sledge up foot by foot. I had the choice of having the pressure of blood either in my head or my feet, and it was equally hard to bear either way. I therefore fainted very often, and have no idea how many hours it took to get up to the top. However, eventually we reached the meeting-place and waited there for two hours, but nobody came. Three of the men went out to search in different directions, but came back without having seen anything. I was now in a difficult situation. I could not stand being carried down again, and the men could not stay up there. There was therefore no alternative but for them to leave me there and hope they would be able to find me later. They promised to send a message at once to Mandal that I was ready and waiting at the agreed meeting-place.

'The reason why the men from Mandal did not meet us, I learned later, was that the police had been there for the past two days making a house-to-house search, and that nobody had been allowed to leave home.

'The second day I spent on the top of the mountain a snowstorm blew up, and it continued for five days. I lay the whole time under the open sky with nothing to eat or drink. I had to keep moving as best I could inside the sleeping-bag to avoid freezing, and because of this I got big sores all over my body.

'On the evening of the seventh day Jensen came back and dug me out of the snow. He had been sure I would be frozen to death. He said the folk from Mandal had been out looking for me but could not find me under the snow. They would probably be coming again that evening or the next morning, and he put up a stick with a flag on it beside me so that they could find me more easily. On the 2nd of May, just before five in the morning, four men arrived from Mandal. They meant to haul me across to Sweden that same day, and we started off, but after six hours the weather got bad again and they turned back and took me to the mountains on the other side of Mandal. They hoped to move me from there the next evening, so there was no point in taking me down into the valley. They built a snow wall round me, gave me the food they had with them and went down again to organise transport. It would take them at least four hours to get down, and probably longer to get back again so I could not expect them before the evening. It had already come to the time of year when it is light nearly all night, and fairly warm during the day. When the sun shone the snow melted so that I got wet through, and when evening came the sleeping bag froze to ice.

'The next evening two men came with food and medicine, and brought the news that a Lapp was coming to fetch me, either the next evening or the one after. Four nights in succession they came up from the valley to be on the spot and help me when the Lapp arrived, but he did not turn up. Eventually they got in touch with him again. He did not dare to make the journey, because the Germans had sent three ski patrols to the frontier. The men from Mandal decided then that four of them should make another attempt to haul me over. It was very difficult for them to arrange this, because although it was only about twenty miles to the frontier they might have to go some distance into Sweden before any house could be found. This would mean being away from home for four or five days, and as they all had their regular work to do such a long absence would cause suspicion. On the other hand, the Lapps had no settled home and could move about without causing comment. They also had reindeer for pulling sledges.

'On the evening of the 9th of May four men came up the mountain again to make the attempt, but as soon as we were ready to start the weather began to change again. A thick mist came down and it began to snow, so we had to give it up once more.

'In this way I lay up on the mountain for nineteen days, and grew weaker and weaker. All the time the men from Mandal did all they could for me, and it was not their fault that I could not get any farther. Nearly all my toes rotted off.

'On the 22nd of May they carried me down into the valley again. While I had been lying up in the mountains some German soldiers had arrived in Mandal, so the organisation had fitted out a cave to hide me in. I was put on a soft bed where it was dry and warm, and they gave me enough food. I lay there for four days and dozed most of the time. In the meantime they had arranged a new means of transport with the organisation in the next valley beyond Mandal, Kaafjord. It was decided that we should meet their party at an agreed place in the mountains two nights later. The next evening eight men came from Mandal and carried me up to the meeting-place. We arrived there after thirteen hours' climbing. Just before they left me, two new men arrived to act as interpreters between me and a Lapp who was coming from Kaafjord. These two stayed with me till the next morning, when they also had to go down. In the evening two more came and stayed through the night. Soon after midnight a man arrived from Kaafjord and told us the Lapp was ill and could not help me.

'An hour later a local Lapp passed by on his way from the frontier where he had his herd of reindeer. The men told him of all the difficulties we were having, and when he had heard the whole story he offered to take charge of me.

'We started the next evening with his reindeer sledge, and two days later we reached the frontier of Finland. We crossed the northern corner of Finland and entered Sweden by the winter road across the lake of Kilpisjarvi. Just before we left Norway we were sighted by one of the enemy ski patrols. They opened fire to halt us, but they were two or three kilometres away and did not have a chance of catching us.'

As soon as the Swedish Red Cross heard that Baalsrud had arrived in the country they sent a plane fitted with floats, which landed on an ice-free stretch of river and picked him up. He lay unconscious for a week in hospital and spent two more months in bed. He had lost all the toes on his right foot, and only the little toe and part of two others remained on the left, but medical treatment saved his feet, and in the autumn he flew back to England and reported for duty.

CHAPTER FOURTEEN

THE LOSS OF THE *BERGHOLM*

ON 17th March Larsen left Scalloway to carry out the last trip of the season to Traena. By the end of the month, when he was due back, it would be too light up there to visit the district again till September. He had one of the big new boats from Iceland, the *Bergholm*, a seventy-five-footer which he had taken over after he got back from the *Tirpitz* affair, in which he had scuttled his old favourite the *Arthur*. One of the three men who had been with him on that occasion, Johann Kalve, was still in his crew, but his engineer, Björnöy, was still in hospital in Sweden with frostbitten feet, and Strand, the wireless operator, had lost his life in the *Feie* when she disappeared. Larsen's present crew was of seven men: engineers Faröy and Vika, deckhands and gunners Klausen, Enoksen, Noreiger and Kalve, and radio operator Hansen. He had three passengers on their way to the Mosjön army, and four tons of cargo.

Bergholm was faster than the smaller boats, and they made good time to Traena in fine weather, arriving off the islands in three and a half days. Larsen sighted the coast and fixed his position in daylight, and when darkness fell he closed in and felt his way in among the skerries. He reached one of the sounds between the islands, where the rocks rose steeply from the water, and laid the *Bergholm* alongside them. One of the passengers jumped ashore and climbed over the steep hills to some houses on the other side of the island.

When he came back he brought with him a man who had volunteered to come with them to another very small island where a single family lived who he thought could take charge of the passengers and cargo until the small local boats were able to ferry them across to the mainland. Larsen took *Bergholm* through the sounds to this little island and moored her to the quay there. The owner of the island had a boathouse on the quay, in which were two dinghies and a lot of nets. They woke him up, and found he was quite willing to keep the cargo in the boathouse and to take care of the passengers. Most of the rest of the night was spent in taking out the boats and nets, packing in the cargo, and arranging the boats and nets on top of it.

By the time this was finished it was too late to put to sea again that morning, and as it was a good place to lie, sheltered from observation on all sides but one, Larsen stayed there till the following evening. All day, from the island, they watched a German patrol boat steaming up and down its beat near by, and there were several alarms when it seemed to be approaching a point from which its crew could have seen the *Bergholm*. Had it done so they would have had to fight their way out, so they cleared away the guns and started the engine. It was only an armed Norwegian Arctic whaler, and they could probably have sunk it, but the after-effects of a fight on the passengers who had been landed and the local people who had helped them would have been disastrous, and Traena would have been finished as a landing-place. So it was lucky that its beat seemed to stop just short of the point from which the quay would have been visible, and that each time discovery seemed imminent it turned back on its tracks. As darkness approached it steamed off towards the mainland, and at eight in the evening *Bergholm* left for home. It was still very fine and clear.

At two o'clock the next afternoon they were steaming on their homeward course, parallel to the coast and about seventy-five miles off it, when a twin-engined plane approached them from astern and flew round them, very low and about three hundred yards away. As they expected the plane to attack at a moment's notice, and as they were much farther offshore than an innocent fishing boat had any right to be, they dropped their camouflage and manned the guns. But it did not attack; it flew off towards the coast.

The crew of the plane had certainly seen their guns, and it seemed sure that when it reached the coast and their position was reported, a real attack would be made. Larsen altered course to the westward; but after a bit he reflected that in such perfectly clear weather, at eight knots, he had no chance whatever of evading a search, so he returned to the course he had set for Shetland. The crew tested all their weapons and brought all the ammunition on deck. They had a single .5 Colt machine gun mounted forward and a twin one aft, two twin Lewis guns amidship, and two unmounted Brens.

Larsen never had much use for radio, and he did not try to send us a signal. Perhaps he reasoned, in his usual logical way, that it could not be any help. He was three hundred and fifty miles from Shetland, which was too far for fighter planes to be sent to protect him. Even if we had known what was happening we could not have done anything at all. There were five hours to go till dusk, and if they were to survive till then it must be through their own efforts.

About six o'clock the attack came. Two twin-engined sea planes approached the boat from the port beam and circled it at a height of two hundred feet. Then, diving to mast height, they flew across her bows, firing with cannon. *Bergholm* returned the fire with all her guns. Not much damage was done to the boat, but for a few seconds the decks were swept with cannon shell splinters, and Klausen, on the port Lewis mounting, received so many wounds that Larsen sent him below.

The planes stood off and circled for about five minutes. Perhaps the fire put up by *Bergholm* was more than they had expected, and they were discussing it on their short-wave radio. After a time they swooped again, both attacking from the starboard side. As they approached, Larsen at the wheel tried to turn the boat to bring all the guns to bear. Another storm of shells and splinters hit her. The Colt and Lewis tracers were seen hitting the planes. Enoksen, at the twin Colt, staggered away from his guns with his face and hands hidden with blood. When they went to help him they found he was riddled with shell splinters from head to foot, and he could not see, so he also had to be sent below. Kalve, at the bow Colt, was hit in one hand and one foot. As the planes roared by he swung his gun round and aimed it with his remaining hand, then jammed his other elbow on to the trigger. Faröy and Vika, the two engineers, were firing the two Bren guns. Hansen had gone below to try to send a radio signal to us, but the aerial was shot away. By then the boat was badly damaged, but she was still under way, and they knew they had damaged the planes. Suddenly as they watched for the next attack, one plane broke away and flew off low towards the coast.

The other one went on circling round, then dived again. Faröy and Noreiger had taken over the Colts. Enoksen was trying to get up the ladder again from the cabin, but he was hit again and fell back down the hatch. Faröy was also wounded, but was able to stay at the gun.

On its next attack the plane dropped a stick of six bombs. None of them fell near the boat, but its cannon fire was still accurate, and Faröy was wounded again and could not do any more.

Then there was nobody left to man the Lewis guns or Brens. Noreiger was still at one Colt, and Vika took over the other. Larsen was still at the wheel in what remained of the wheelhouse, manoeuvring the boat to meet each attack.

In the next run another stick of bombs came down, and the last of them fell a few feet from the stern. It shook the boat badly. Noreiger and Vika both shot accurately, and Larsen saw strikes on the plane. But as it receded once more Vika fell, and when Larsen ran to help him he found his foot was shot off above the ankle. Five of the eight men aboard were out of action. Hansen had come up from below and reported that the radio was dead and the boat was leaking. Larsen, wondering how to dispose his remaining men to meet the next attack, looked up at the plane. It was disappearing to the eastward, smoking.

The whole fight had lasted just over half an hour. This short time had wrought a terrible difference on *Bergholm* and her crew; but dusk was falling, and they could be sure that the night would give them respite. Larsen, Noreiger and Hansen, who were not wounded, first went to attend to the other five men. Vika was the most seriously hurt. Someone had already put a tourniquet on his leg, but they knew he was dying, and they thought he knew it too. He was conscious, and sometimes smiled, but he did not speak or complain. Faröy, Enoksen and Klausen were in great pain from the number of steel splinters in their hands and heads and bodies, and they could not move. Enoksen, however, was not blinded, as they had thought at first, it was only blood which had run into his eyes, and the shock of a shell which exploded in front of his face, which had made him unable to see. Kalve, who only had one leg and one hand out of action, was able to move and to give some help with the work that had to be done. They disinfected the men's wounds and bandaged them, then turned their attention to the boat.

The engine was still running, and with the wheel lashed she was holding nearly to her course; but the water in the bilges was rising, and the two pumps on the engine could not hold it in check. Kalve and Noreiger manned the hand pump, but still the water rose, and in spite of all they could do, at about eight o'clock it reached the air intakes of the engine, and the engine stopped.

In the meantime Larsen had inspected the rest of the boat. The decks were full of holes and covered with blood and empty cartridge cases. The masts were still standing, but a lot of the rigging was shot away, and wire and rope were swinging from side to side as the boat rolled. The wheelhouse, in which Larsen had stood unscratched through the whole engagement, was literally shot to pieces. The windows were all gone and the inside was littered with broken glass. All the doors were shot away, and the wooden walls and roof were smashed by exploding shells, so that nothing but the broken framework remained.

Most important of all was the lifeboat, which was stowed on top of a deckhouse on the port side of the wheelhouse. Most of its gunwale was split off, and it had seven shell holes in its bottom. Larsen and Noreiger set to work to patch the holes with canvas and sheets cut from bully beef tins. Hansen collected food and water and navigating instruments, and the lifeboat's mast and sail and oars. By midnight they had made the boat tight enough to be kept afloat, and they launched it and stowed the essential stores aboard. Larsen tore up his marked charts and ciphers and threw them overboard. Then came a grievous struggle to get the wounded men up the steep companionway from the cabin and into the boat without hurting them too much. At last they got Vika laid in the bows, on the floor of the boat, and Enoksen and Faröy amidships. Klausen and Kalve had to sit up in the stern, as the boat was only sixteen feet long and there was no room for them to lie down. The three who were not wounded arranged to take turns at rowing, two at a time, each rowing for four hours and resting for two. At one in the morning they abandoned the *Bergholm*. It was dead calm.

The first thing they had to do was to get as far away as possible before dawn, when the Germans would very likely send out a plane to see what had happened to the wreck. She might still be floating; a wooden ship will often float with gunwales awash. If so, there was a chance that the Germans, seeing no life aboard, would assume that they had all been killed; but it was more likely that they would see that the lifeboat was gone, and would make a search for it.

But apart from getting away from the scene of the fight, Larsen had to decide where to make for. They were seventy-five miles from the nearest point on the Norwegian coast, and three hundred and fifty miles from Shetland. After thinking it over, he decided that it was very unlikely that they could reach Shetland in the lifeboat. It was heavily laden, and with most of its top plank on each side shot away it had very little freeboard, so that a very moderate sea would have swamped it. Besides, with the best of luck it would take them say ten days to get there, and none of the wounded men could be expected to survive so long in an open boat. On the other hand, he did not like to take the shortest route to Norway, partly because he thought it was what the Germans would expect him to do, and partly because it led to a part of the coast, near Trondheim, where he had no friends he could rely on, and he thought that even if they got there safely it would be difficult to get away again.

So he made up his mind to steer for Ålesund, where he had stolen the *Arthur* after he had been shipwrecked the year before, and where he knew that Björnöy's father, who had helped them on that occasion, was in touch with Knut and Karl-Johan, who operated the radio station. It was a hundred and fifty miles away, twice as far as the Trondheim coast; but Larsen was a seaman by nature, and the prospect of rowing so far in a leaky boat did not worry him, provided that it gave some small hope of getting the wounded crew alive to Shetland.

The two men rowing took one oar each, sharing the midship thwart. The third unwounded man, taking his two hours off from the oars, could not lie down because there was no room, and was occupied with helping the wounded men to shift their positions and to take food and water. Kalve was able to bail with his undamaged hand, and he did so continuously. At four o'clock on the first morning Vika asked for water and aspirins. They had no aspirins, but Larsen gave him the water and he seemed satisfied. When he went to him an hour later he had died. They wanted to bury his body in Norway, but later on their journey they wrapped it in a blanket and lifted it overboard. They remained stubbornly sure that they would reach safety in the end.

At dawn on the first morning, when they had been rowing for six hours, it was still calm and crystal clear. They saw a plane searching the place where the *Bergholm* had been. It flew in increasing circles, and they realised that its crew must have found the wreck, seen that the lifeboat was gone, and started to look for them. Planes remained in sight for the whole of the day, quartering the ocean in which a boat seems dreadfully conspicuous and vulnerable. Whenever the planes approached the rowers shipped their oars, in case the flash of sunlight on the wet blades should show them up. Often the planes came so close that the men in the boat were certain they had been seen, and nerved themselves to a fresh attack like those of the day before; but each time the plane sheered off, and after a day of suspense at last the darkness fell and covered them. They rowed all night.

On the second day a light breeze came, and as there was no plane in sight they hoisted the sail, and for a time they made good progress. But at dusk it fell calm again, and they rowed for the third night.

The third day was sunny and calm again, and they rowed all day without seeing anything.

During the fourth night they saw a light ahead. They made towards it, and saw it was a fishing boat. They hailed her and drew alongside. Larsen climbed stiffly aboard. He told the fishermen that he and his men had been torpedoed in a merchant ship, and he asked them if they had enough fuel to get to Shetland. The fishermen were friendly and sympathetic, but they said they were only allowed to carry enough fuel to get to the fishing grounds and back, in order to stop them sailing across to the other side. They came from Kristiansund, and were willing to take Larsen and his crew back there with them and to help them to escape; but Larsen was doubtful whether it would be possible to escape from there, so he thanked them but refused the offer. He also refused food, saying they had plenty in the lifeboat. The fishermen gave him his exact position, which was thirty-five miles offshore, and he returned to the boat and started to row again.

At dawn on the next day, their fourth in the boat, they could see land, but it was still a long way off. As they struggled on towards it they saw a lot of fishing boats coming out towards them. This was an unwelcome sight, for it meant that by the evening, when the boats got back to port, the approach of a shipwrecked crew would be common knowledge. But it could not be helped, and when the boats reached them they hailed the first, and Larsen asked again if they had enough fuel to get to Shetland. This time the skipper tried to persuade them against going to Shetland, and after some hedging he came out into the open and said that if they would come back with him he would use his influence to help them; he thought it would only mean a month or two in prison, and then they could join the merchant service for the Germans. Luckily, before the conversation had reached this stage, his crew had given the men in the boat some cooked fish and coffee. It was the first hot food they had had for four days, and they felt much better for it; and they thanked the skipper politely, and went on their way. It turned out later that they had hit on the only local quisling.

When he got home that evening he reported them to the Germans, and was seen the next day walking in Ålesund with a German officer.

After leaving the fishing boat they rowed at the best speed they could make. They were sure he meant to report them, but they did not think he would lose a day's fishing to do it; so their only hope was to get into hiding on the coast before he could reach home. As they neared the coast a tidal stream against them slowed their progress, and they had a hard struggle to make any headway against it; but about three in the afternoon, very thankfully, they reached the first of the islands, and ran the boat in among some rocks, and waited for darkness.

There were still about ten miles to go, among the islands, to the place where Björnöy lived. They set off at eight, and got there soon after midnight. They were very tired, and some of the wounded men were very ill.

Larsen went ashore and knocked at the door of a man called Nils Sorviknes, who had helped him when he had been there before. It was some time before he could get an answer, and he leaned against the doorpost in the last stages of exhaustion. But at last the door opened, and Sorviknes, astonished to see him again, took him inside. Larsen told him what had happened, and told him he had six men waiting in the lifeboat. He asked what chance there was of getting a boat to go to Shetland. Sorviknes said he would talk to Björnöy, but that it was too late to do anything that night; and when Larsen told him the name of the fishing boat they had spoken to, Sorviknes knew it at once as belonging to a quisling, and was sure that by then the Germans would have been told that they were in the district. So the first essential was to hide them before dawn. He thought for a while, then advised Larsen to go to a man called Lars Torholmen, who lived with his wife and two sisters in the only house on a very small island a couple of miles away. He gave him a letter to Torholmen, and told him to lie low there till he got further instructions.

Back in the lifeboat, Larsen took to the oars for the last time and rowed to the small island. He went ashore again, and woke Torholmen, who took him in without any hesitation. As soon as he gave him the letter from Sorviknes and explained about the wounded men in the boat, Torholmen and his two sisters came down to the shore and between them they carried the wounded men to the house. The mother and the sisters put them to bed and fed them and washed their wounds. It was beginning to get light, and the boat had to be disposed of before daybreak. There was no time to take it out and sink it, so Larsen and Torholmen rowed it round to the other side of the island and hid it in a boathouse. It was a compromising thing to keep on the island, but there was nothing better they could do. As the sun rose they got back to the house, and Larsen was also put to bed. They all slept for the whole of the day.

They stayed with Torholmen for a week, living in two rooms at the top of the house, and being well looked after by the three ladies. With good food and rest their strength began to return, but some of the wounded men were still in great pain from the shell splinters in their bodies.

Björnöy, on whom they were relying to find them a boat to get away, was skipper of a local ferry, and Nils Sorviknes was one of his crew. So they knew that Sorviknes would be able to tell Björnöy about them during the ferry's morning run to Ålesund on the day they arrived. But the story Larsen had been able to tell Sorviknes was incomplete, so one of Torholmen's sisters invented some errands in Ålesund, and went as a passenger on the boat to give him more details. She also asked him whether he knew of a doctor who could be trusted to come to Torholmen to see the wounded men, as she was worried by signs of sepsis and gangrene.

On their second day with Torholmen, which was a Sunday, Björnöy came to see Larsen and to tell him what he was doing. The problem of getting them away had been made much more difficult and dangerous by their meeting with the quisling skipper. As they had expected, he had reported their arrival to the Germans and a tremendous search was going on. Within an hour of their arrival at Torholmen's house the Germans had started an air search of the whole of that part of Norway, and had sent two armed trawlers to the part of the coast the quisling had thought they were making for. They had also dispatched a ferry steamer to land parties of soldiers on each of the string of large islands which ran north from Ålesund; and they had evidently seen or photographed the registration number which was painted on the *Bergholm* at the time, for they sent a detachment of thirty men to the village which the number denoted. Advertisements offering rewards for their capture were printed in the papers, and everybody in the district was talking about them. The little island where they were hiding was in the very middle of the area which was being searched, and Björnöy thought that until the excitement had died down it would be foolish to risk the slightest move which might draw attention to the place. He did not think it was safe even to bring a doctor out to the island. He offered to take the wounded men to the doctor, in a rowing boat by night, but it would be a dangerous journey, partly over land, where the men would have to be carried and the whole party would be at the mercy of anyone who happened to see them. Larsen and Björnöy agreed that in any case the doctor could not do much unless the men went to a hospital to have the splinters extracted, and they decided to give up the idea unless any of them got much worse.

Björnöy was against using a local boat to escape to Shetland if it could be avoided. The Germans were obviously very anxious to capture the *Bergholm*'s crew. If a local boat disappeared they would be sure to guess that the crew had escaped in it, and their punishment of the owners would be severe and might even lead to discovery of the whole organisation to which Björnöy belonged. Although this might be risked as a last resort, he had first got in touch with Karl-Johan, and had a radio message sent to England to ask us to send a boat over to fetch them.

This signal, of course, was the first news we had had in Shetland of what had happened to the *Bergholm*. Knowing that she had been attacked confirmed us all in our opinion that the use of fishing boats was getting too dangerous to be worth while. By the time we received it, it was the beginning of April. The nights were already very short, and to send a fishing boat into a district already so thoroughly on the alert would be very risky. A naval M.T.B., on the other hand, would not only have a much better chance of doing the job, but also of fighting its way out if it was spotted. The Navy was very willing to send one; but unluckily the weather by then was very bad, and until it moderated it was impossible for these fast light craft to leave harbour. Every one of the fishing boat crews which survived at the base was ready and eager to go, and the fishing boats could easily have weathered the gale. But Rogers would not let them. It was natural that everyone's first reaction was to set off at once on a rescue expedition; but when he weighed it up he concluded that it was wrong to take so great a risk of losing a second crew, and that so far as we could tell it was probably safer for the *Bergholm* crew themselves to stay in hiding till an M.T.B. could go, than to embark on a fishing boat which might so very easily be lost on the voyage home. It was hard for him to decide to leave the crew in their dangerous position, but he was certainly right; and the decision was transmitted to Ålesund, and ultimately to the men on the island.

Meanwhile the search continued around and over their hiding-place. From the windows of the house they could see aircraft quartering the district, and every day Torholmen brought them news of what the Germans were doing. The search lasted for nearly a week. Then a rumour spread in Ålesund that a fishing boat had been stolen. Larsen heard it and was pleased, because even though the Germans would not be able to trace it to its source and prove that it was true, they would certainly not be able to prove that it was not, and as time went on they would probably be more inclined to believe it. It would at least offer them a plausible explanation of the disappearance of the boatload of men. He never knew whether it was a spontaneous rumour, or whether it had been started by some friend as a means of bringing the search to an end. At all events it seemed to help. The intensity of the search gradually died down, and after about ten days the Germans seemed to have given it up as a bad job. Why they missed the little island where the men were hiding remains a mystery. Perhaps it was because it was so small, or because it was so close to the headquarters town of Ålesund, or perhaps they hardly expected that men who had rowed a hundred and fifty miles would row a farther ten among the islands.

As soon as it began to seem that the Germans were convinced the crew had escaped from the district, Björnöy proceeded with his plans for getting them away. He had asked through Karl-Johan that the rescue boat should be sent to the island of Skorpen, a dozen miles farther south, where we had already landed and picked up many agents. Johann Skorpen, the fisherman who lived there, was well used to hiding people and would look after the crew somewhere on his island till the boat could come.

Moving them down there would be the most difficult job. There was a control point on the way at which papers had to be produced, but boats were not usually searched there; and if Björnöy could find a boat with a plausible reason for going through this control, he thought it would be better to risk this than to bring one of our boats too close to Ålesund.

The movement was deputed to Sverre Roald, another member of the organisation, who lived in the island of Vigra, close at hand, and was a neighbour and relation of our foreman shipwright Sevrin Roald. After the men had been a week with Torholmen, Roald came one night to tell them what he had arranged. The next night he came again, and they embarked in his little motor boat. But by then the calm spell which had lasted throughout their journey in the lifeboat had given place to strong southerly winds, and after trying to stem the short seas between the islands they had to give it up and go back to Torholmen.

The next night the wind had dropped a little, and they tried again. This time they reached the island of Vigra in safety, where Roald transferred them to another boat: the small decked fishing boat which was to take them through the control to Skorpen.

There is an important radio station in Vigra, which was guarded by German sentries. The fishing boat was lying within a hundred yards of the station buildings, within sight of the sentries. The trip to Skorpen had to be postponed through bad weather, and the men stayed on board the boat for five days. It was an inconvenient position to be in, because they could not go on deck in daylight but had to stay confined in the little cabin of the boat. But on the other hand it was reasonably safe, because the Germans would not expect the seven men they were looking for to be hiding in a boat under constant watch. Sverre Roald had to be careful in his visits, but he managed to see them every night, bringing them food and the latest news of how things were going. At last they were able to get away. They passed the control quite easily and safely, and reached Skorpen, where Roald handed them over to Johann Skorpen and went back to Vigra. Skorpen installed them in a cowshed on the opposite side of the island to his house, and brought them a primus stove and some food and coffee.

Skorpen was not worried at having them there, because his house and island had been searched only a week before and he did not think the Germans would bother him again for some time. Some M.T.B.s manned by the Norwegian Navy had attacked a convoy in that district, and it seemed that the Germans had not seen the boats leaving the coast and believed they had been sunk and that the crews were hiding. They had been searching for them round Skorpen, just as they had been searching for the *Bergholm* crew round Ålesund, and a party of soldiers had been landed in each island. Luckily Skorpen had seen them coming, and had retreated to the hills, taking with him his radio set, since it was forbidden to possess such a thing, and leaving his wife, who would be less suspect than himself, to deal with the search party. The officer in charge of the party had opened her door and said, 'Where are you hiding them?' It must have alarmed the lady, whose house had harboured so many different agents and refugees; but she pretended not to be able to understand the German officer's Norwegian. This universal means of avoiding difficult questions must have been very annoying for Germans who were perhaps not very sure whether they were really able to make themselves understood or not. It was very effective. The party searched the house and found an old pair of headphones from a disused crystal set, which they took away with apparent satisfaction.

As this search had been made so recently, and as the *Bergholm* crew were now out of the immediate area where the Germans had supposed them to be, they settled down with a feeling of comparative security to wait for the boat from Shetland.

Our headquarters had arranged with Karl-Johan that they should send a code message in the B.B.C. Norwegian news bulletin on the night before the rescue boat was due to arrive at Skorpen. Karl-Johan had warned Skorpen to expect this message, and Skorpen listened every evening on the radio which he had retrieved from the hilltop. When Roald got home and sent a message to Karl-Johan that the men had safely arrived at the rendezvous, a signal was sent to our headquarters and passed on to us in Shetland. The weather was still bad, and although the naval M.T.B.s were ready to sail we had to wait another week before they could leave the harbour. As soon as the wind subsided the code message was broadcast by the B.B.C. and an M.T.B. left Shetland. Skorpen heard the message, and when the boat entered the sound of Skorpen the next evening the seven men were waiting on the shore. Afterwards Larsen said, 'We were glad to be on our way.'

CHAPTER FIFTEEN

EPILOGUE

UNTIL Larsen and his crew were safely back in Shetland none of us had much heart to talk about plans for the future. But when the M.T.B. had returned and the wounded men were on the way to recovery, we began to discuss what we should do next. We found we had all independently come to the conclusion that the days of the fishing boats were over. During the winter we had lost five of them, half the number we usually kept in commission, and 42 men out of about 100 who sailed regularly. That could not go on. The crews were still willing to sail, and they all knew that success must be paid for by the loss of lives; but we were no longer achieving success. When plans were made to send in an agent or a cargo, there must be a certain minimum probability that they would arrive in safety, and now the probability had fallen below the level at which the planning was worth while. We could all see the reasons why things had become so difficult. One was that our efforts had been sufficient to worry the Germans thoroughly, and make them suspicious of any fishing boat which was conceivably big enough to cross the North Sea. We had also managed to goad them into building up an enormous and costly system of patrols. But the principal reason, the effect of which was increasing all the time, was that there was such a shortage of fuel in Norway that the large boats which were still there and had not been requisitioned by the Germans were one by one being forced to give up fishing, so that our boats were becoming more and more conspicuous on the coast.

Meanwhile, the naval M.T.B.s which were stationed in Lerwick had been making their hit-and-run raids with very few casualties. Their open attacks on convoys called for less finesse than our secret meetings; but we and our crews were sure that if we had boats with anything like their speed and fire-power we could adapt them to do our job in comparative safety. The two problems we had to answer were how to get such boats, and how to reorganise ourselves to run warships instead of fishing boats.

Of course one way out of the difficulty was for the whole job to be handed over to the Navy, but I am sure none of us ever considered that for a moment. We took it for granted that if we had the boats we could do the job better, and I suppose the naval authorities thought so too, because although they were very helpful when we consulted them they never suggested taking the job over. And, in fact, we did have an accumulation of experience in our base which it would have been a pity to waste. Between us all, we knew the Norwegian coast extremely well, not only geographically (though we had already lent pilots to destroyers going into the leads) but also socially: we knew the politics and personalities of hundreds of people who lived in strategic places, and they knew us. Besides that, we knew all about the whims of agents, and our base organisation – cipher offices, stores, repair shops and so on – were well suited to their specialised jobs. And our independence of the three services was a great asset, because we were not bound by their regulations and yet could call on any of them for help, which they always gave us.

So it never crossed our minds that the Navy might take over our job and our problems, and we were determined that by the autumn, somehow or other, we would re-equip ourselves so that we could keep communications open next winter. The search for new boats went on all through the summer, and sometimes we got depressed and began to be afraid that we would have to close down the base, and that contact with the home forces in Norway would have to be restricted to the air and an occasional naval operation.

Our first thoughts, of course, were of Coastal Forces craft, M.L.s or M.T.B.s; but we soon found that Coastal Forces had no boats which could combine speed, range and seaworthiness in the degree we needed. Both Fairmile M.L.s and D Class M.T.B.s, the largest and most powerful craft of Coastal Forces except for one or two steam gunboats, had been stationed in Shetland, and we had seen for ourselves how the weather beat them. They had been tied up in harbour for week after week in winter when our fishing boats had been sailing without any trouble, and when they had been at sea in weather our crews regarded as moderate they had come back with frames broken and hulls leaking. Besides, neither type had the range to reach more than a small proportion of the Norwegian coast, and as they used petrol it would be dangerous to carry large supplies of extra fuel. The smaller Harbour Defence M.L.s had better range and were said to be seaworthy, but their speed was only eleven knots, which was not much of an improvement on the fishing boats.

I went to the Admiralty and searched through the files of the Small Vessels Pool. What we were looking for was something very unusual: a boat small enough to be piloted in narrow channels in the dark and laid alongside fishermen's jetties, able to weather any storm whatever, with a speed of at least fifteen knots and a range of fifteen hundred miles. We considered fishery cruisers and icebreakers and whalecatchers and several large motor yachts. One or two seemed possible as a last resort, but none really came up to our standards. We even thought of getting a boat built, though it would have taken a long time, and I argued that if we did so we might as well make it look like a fishing boat so as to take advantage of such value as still lay in camouflage. Our headquarters commissioned a well-known naval architect to design a boat for us, and he and I between us produced plans of a sixteen-knot fishing boat armed with concealed Oerlikons and a six-pounder. It was fun to design, but perhaps it was just as well that it was never built.

We had already foreseen that we would not be able to wander about the ocean in a minor war vessel without even telling the Navy, as we had in fishing boats, and that whatever boat we used would have to carry naval recognition signals and other codes. These were only issued to officers, and as none of our skippers were commissioned I had made a private bargain with Larsen that if I could find a boat he would take me with him in it in something like the capacity of an admiral in his flagship: he would sail the boat, and I would provide the necessary gold braid.

Most of the summer passed in frustration. From time to time our headquarters told us they were trying America, which was even then regarded as the source of all bounty; but nothing happened until suddenly, in August, someone touched the right spring. Admiral Nimitz, who was Commander-in-Chief of the American naval forces in Europe, was told of our troubles, and he immediately sent a request to America for three U.S. Navy submarine chasers to be sent over for us. Then the whole weighty efficiency of the American Navy came to our aid, and everything happened with bewildering speed. Within a week, to help our base in Shetland, things were moving in Florida. Three submarine chasers were detached from their base in Miami, sailed to New York and loaded on merchant ships. Within three weeks of the first request they arrived at various ports in this country and assembled in the Clyde.

We knew nothing about their capabilities, except that Admiral Nimitz said they were just the thing for the job. I went down to the American base at Roseneath on the Clyde and awaited their arrival with the utmost interest. When I saw them coming into the Gareloch, looking like young destroyers, I was as excited as a schoolboy.

They were certainly a change from fishing boats. Not only were they bigger – a hundred and ten feet in length – and nearly four times as fast – for they cruised at seventeen knots and had a top speed of twenty-two; but they were equipped with every possible gadget and comfort for the crew – central heating, an oil-fired galley, refrigerators, ice-water fountains, wine lockers, hot and cold showers, electric toasting machines, typewriters, and so on. Even fur-lined coats and boots were provided, and various peculiar hats, to add to our motley uniform. The main engines were two twelve-hundred h.p. diesels of revolutionary design, and were the only ones of their kind in Europe (they were supercharged two-stroke engines with vertical crankshafts and four banks of four cylinders each, driving electrically-controlled variable pitch propellers). Everything possible was electric. There were forty-two different electric motors in each boat, and each boat had two generators, either of which was enough to light the village of Scalloway.

Needless to say, therefore, my second reaction after the first excitement was to wonder whether we could possibly run such complicated mechanisms in our little base, with our half-civilian crews of fishermen and our maintenance squad of fishing-boat shipwrights and mechanics. But nobody outside the base expressed any doubts, so of course we kept our misgivings to ourselves; and as things turned out we need not have worried.

The Americans were very helpful in handing over the boats. Their complete crews, three officers and twenty-three men to each boat, had been sent over with them. They did not know till they reached Roseneath that they were to part with their ships, and being the first sub-chaser crews to be sent to Europe they had left home in an atmosphere of heroics, believing they were some kind of suicide squad. But when they got over their disappointment at such an anti-climax, they did everything they could to teach us to run the boats. Our fishing-boat crews were combined into three crews of twenty-two men each, one under Larsen, another under Salen (these two being promoted sub-lieutenant), and the third under a Lieutenant Eidsheim, who had joined us as Hauge's second-in-command. The crews were sent down to Roseneath when the boats arrived, and Hauge and I met them in Glasgow. I had been wondering what the Americans would think of us, because the men hardly knew enough drill to be able to march in step, and had the most rudimentary ideas of naval etiquette. They had a tendency, when they did have to march, to march out of step on purpose, just to show they were a cut above the ordinary navy. When the sixty-odd men scrambled out of the train we found the holiday atmosphere of their journey had been too much for them, and the majority were very cheerful and quite incapable. Luckily it was dark by the time we got to Roseneath, and not many people saw our march from the quayside to the barracks. It was like Piccadilly on Cup Final night.

But next morning, when the crews saw the new boats for the first time, everything was very different. They were desperately keen to prove that they could handle them, and I was surprised to find how quickly they picked up information which was not only entirely new to them but delivered in a foreign tongue. We spent a week with the Americans, finishing with a trip to Londonderry, where the anti-submarine armament which we did not need was removed. Then, with one American officer and three engineers, we set off up the west coast of Scotland and set course from Cape Wrath to Scalloway. It was a great day when the ships arrived there.

We had a busy time at the base for the next month. Our slipway had to be lengthened to take the new boats, and we made a lot of additions to the boats themselves. Each of them already had a Bofors gun forward, and we mounted two twin Oerlikons on power-operated turrets, a two-pounder, and two Colts on the upper bridge. We fitted echo sounders, electric logs and radar, and built davits to carry two of our motor dinghies on each sub-chaser. At the same time the crews were doing gunnery practice, and the engineers were scratching their heads over the instruction books of the big diesels.

By the end of September we thought we were ready to start; and as soon as we did all our difficulties ended. We found the engines ran like clocks, and the boats could stand up to any weather we put them through. Sometimes we gave them an awful battering, and in several gales in the first few months waves made a clean sweep of their foredecks. But we replaced the essential fittings with stronger ones, and as for the inessential ones, we just plugged the holes in the decks and did without, until everything which wind and water could sweep away was gone, and what was left had been thoroughly tested. The variable pitch propellers were a great help to seaworthiness. Most fast boats either cannot run slow, or become unmanageable at low speeds; but by setting the propellers of the sub-chasers at a low pitch one could run the engines at a normal speed and yet keep the speed of the boat in a head sea within safe limits, or even heave-to. Their speed and armament, combined with our knowledge of the Norwegian coast, made operations easy. Certainly accurate pilotage was still needed to enter the intricate unlit leads at night; but the danger of any trouble with Germans was very small compared with our earlier experiences. Even in daylight, at sea, the boats enjoyed a security we had almost forgotten. They were quite often inspected by enemy aircraft, but were never attacked, and as usual the seas were absolutely empty of shipping. That winter we completed thirty-four operations, and the next, the last winter of the war, we did eighty, without any casualties. The only warlike incident was an attack on one of the boats at night by a British aircraft, which mistook it for a submarine and dropped depth-charges.

Work with the sub-chasers was so successful and so uneventful that it almost took on the nature of a naval patrol, and a detailed chronicle of it would make dull reading. We carried on making regular crossings from Shetland to all our old haunts in Norway up to the end of the war; and perhaps the oddest thing about our base was that in spite of the fact that we ran quite formidable war vessels over great stretches of ocean, we remained till the end quite independent of the Navy and the other armed forces. The naval authorities under the Commander-in-Chief, Home Fleet, and the Admiral Commanding the area, whose headquarters were at Scapa Flow, were always very helpful to us, lending us guns and such things and passing our private cipher signals through their radio channels, and giving us advice when ever we asked for it; but they never suggested that they should have any authority over us or over what we did in their ocean. I think one might say they regarded our efforts with amused admiration.

As Allied strategy never called for an invasion of Norway, our work and that of the forces in Norway which we supplied always remained a side-show and never reached the climax which we expected would come before the end. At the end, we wondered whether it had all been worth while. It was a question we could not answer. Perhaps nobody could. But certainly it helped to win the war in some small ways. Without the contact which our boats afforded between the Norwegian people and the part of the world not dominated by Germany, the unhappiness of Norwegians would have been deeper. Everyone in Norway knew that the route to and from Shetland was always kept open, and this knowledge helped to maintain their hope of ultimate freedom and their wish to fight for it. The arms which we transported, nearly four hundred tons in all, were used in many acts of sabotage, some under direction from London and others arranged spontaneously by the organisations in Norway; and these arms also had a psychological effect both on the Norwegians and the Germans, making the Norwegians self-confident and the Germans nervous; for both sides knew that a large and ever-growing proportion of the men of the country were armed and trained and that it was only a matter of time before they would rise and fall upon the occupying forces without mercy. There must have been many German soldiers in small isolated garrisons to whom the capitulation of Germany appeared as a release from this inevitable fate.

The radio operators we landed were sufficient to provide the Allied High Command with thorough information of everything the Germans did in Norway. By the end of the war there were sixty radio transmitters in the country.

As a sideline we picked up three hundred and fifty refugees, most of whom were in trouble with the Gestapo; a work of mercy which would have justified much of our effort.

Finally, the size of the forces the Germans thought it necessary to maintain in Norway gives some measure of the danger in their eyes of the guerrilla forces we supplied. Throughout the invasion of Europe, and even of Germany itself, ten divisions of German troops were held in Norway. Our base of a hundred men was an essential link in a chain which bound down 284,000 German soldiers.

During the night before Germany capitulated, armed Norwegian troops appeared in every town in the country and accepted the surrender of this enormous garrison. In Bergen, for example, three thousand men were under arms, wearing uniforms and carrying Sten guns sent in our fishing boats and sub-chasers from the stores in Scalloway. The next day we sailed the three sub-chasers for the last time, two to Bergen and one to Ålesund. They arrived openly at last and were received with great rejoicing.

Whether it was all worth while upon a broader view is an even more difficult question. In writing a book on a kind of warfare which was picturesque and adventurous and sometimes even enjoyable, I have been anxious not to lead any members of a younger generation to think that these are, or ever can be, the qualities of warfare itself. Our adventures were not created by the war, but by the adventurous spirit of the men who sailed our boats. Adventure can always be found by the adventurous, in war or peace, and enjoyment by the joyous. For a very few war may increase the opportunity for adventure; but for nearly all ordinary people it brings no gain, but only pain and sorrow, whether the war is won or lost. The drowning of Bård and his crew, the dreadful end of the *Blia*, the execution of Mindur and Pete: these were the effects of war upon us. And to ascribe glory to the violent death of any young man loving life is only to add further folly to the failure of human wisdom which is the cause of war.

AFTERWORD

THE WATERS BEYOND

ORIGINALLY published in 1951, *The Shetland Bus* has scarcely ever been out of print, but this is the first edition to be actually published in Shetland. The text is unaltered from the original, but the edition contains much that is new: a Foreword by His Excellency Mr Kjell Colding, Norway's ambassador to Great Britain; additional contemporary photographs, hitherto unpublished; fine modern photographs of 'Bus' locations; and stills from the film of the book. Readers might be interested, too, to know a little more about the context of the book, both before and after it was first published. Apart from anything else, it was very nearly never published at all.

If this Afterword is couched in personal terms, I trust I might be forgiven: to refer often to 'my father' will seem clumsy, yet to use just his name seems unduly impersonal.

The Shetland Bus operation powerfully influenced his life, not least because – as the improbable consequence of a firing exercise off Foula in one of the US Navy's sub-chasers – he fell in love and married. After the war he and my mother stayed on in Scalloway. He began building fishing boats, writing this book in his spare time, and when it was finished (after five years) he sent the manuscript to a literary agent in London, who returned it with the comment that no one would want to read of such an obscure wartime adventure. He put the manuscript in a drawer, where it remained for another year until he met 'a learned and charming man', Dr Mortimer Manson, editor and proprietor of *The Shetland News*. Well aware of the Shetland Bus, Manson suggested that my father should write a book about it. 'I have', he answered. Manson borrowed the manuscript, read it and telephoned the very next day to say it must be published. I was told in later years that his only real criticism was the working title: 'What's it supposed to mean? *"The Waters Beyond?"* Beyond what?'

'Well, beyond Lunna Voe, and beyond Scalloway. I used to watch the boats go out to the waters beyond, and of course I never knew if they would come back safely. So the thought of "the waters beyond" meant quite a lot to me.'

'I'm afraid it won't mean anything at all to anyone else. The title must tell readers what the book is about. Everyone called the operation the Shetland Bus, so why not call the book that?'

'All right', said my father - adding decades later, 'I've never been much good at titles.'

He was always eager to acknowledge his debt to Dr Manson, for without that encouragement and advice the book might have lain unremarked for ever. Instead *The Shetland Bus* became the first of his 24 books; and the rest, as they say, is history.

Except that it isn't – or at least, there is more to the saga than is told in this book. Some of it was not told because it was unknown at the time or developed later, and some because he chose not to tell it. One of the small points unknown at the time was included in some (though mysteriously not all) later editions of the book: a German reader who had been on the occupying naval staff in Trondheim wrote to say that when *Arthur* was scuttled after the attempted attack on *Tirpitz*, she drifted into shallow waters before sinking. Her masts remained visible and the wreck was salvaged for inspection. This revealed the secrets of her construction, and the Germans were able to deduce roughly the kind of attack that had been intended. Since the great battleship was eventually sunk anyway (on 12th November 1944, by bombers), the knowledge did them little good.

A more significant element which my father chose not to tell in detail was the conduct of the operation after the US sub-chasers were introduced. Readers who wish to learn more about that aspect should consult a more recent book, *The Waves are Free: Shetland/Norway Links 1940 to 1945* by James W. Irvine, which contains much information difficult to find elsewhere.

In his autobiography, my father discussed the nature of history and the writing of history. 'Surely', he said, 'history, whatever else it is, should be a record of human experience.' *The Shetland Bus* certainly fulfils that criterion. Nevertheless it does contain a few errors of fact, and there are two which, though not serious, have been repeated by other writers, and so are worth correcting. The first is about the sub-chasers, and the second about Larsen's decorations.

The US Navy's gift was not from Admiral Nimitz: he masterminded the Pacific War, and was never directly involved in European naval theatres. Rather, these 'young destroyers', which so transformed the nature of the operation, came from Admiral Harold R. Stark. Stark was Commander-in-Chief, US Naval Forces Europe, from April 1942 until the war's end, and afterwards wrote an attractive compliment:

The dangerous tasks these hardy Norwegians performed (for the most part unsung) all during the war in their small craft, plying between the British Isles and Norway, constitute a splendid page in their country's generations of brave men who have gone down to the sea in ships. I am proud to add my tribute to them. They were a great bunch.

So they were, and few people would argue with the verdict that Leif Larsen was the greatest of them all. My father profoundly admired his courage and modesty, and correctly records his unparalleled range of British decorations; yet he cites the wrong reason for Larsen's lack of a VC, saying that he could not receive Britain's highest military accolade because he was a foreigner. But several foreigners have received the VC, and it appears that the only reason Larsen did not (for he certainly deserved it) was that the Bus operation came under the aegis of the secret Special Operations Executive rather than the regular forces.

Most of my father's books were to do with history, and in his autobiography he remarked, 'people naturally began to think I was a historian. But I am not, and I would rather confess it than wait to be found out.' He meant he was not a trained historian: he graduated in physics. As a 'confession' it was a bit late (his autobiography was his 22nd book, written when he was 74 years old) and it was somewhat out of place: even if he occasionally got a minor fact wrong, many people, professional historians among them, have wished that more history was written in his seemingly effortless style.

Some people have asked why he received no official British recognition for his part in running the Bus. The question embarrassed him: in his opinion he had not deserved any, and he would say the Norwegians were all far braver than him – all he had had to do was run the show, send them out as well prepared as possible, worry when they were away, rejoice when they returned and mourn if they did not. 'Of all the jobs I ever heard of in war', he wrote:

that would have been my first choice: boats, Norway, individuality and independence, yet with the status of a naval officer – a job that was unique and had no precedent, either in peace or war, yet was certainly useful, if anything in war can be said to be useful.

He was very fond of Norway, and would have been quite content simply to know he had helped in its wartime needs. However, for the same reason, it meant a great deal to him when Norway's wartime monarch King Haakon awarded him the Cross of Freedom and granted him a knighthood, First Class, in the Order of St Olav: the highest honours that Norway could confer upon a non-Norwegian. He never mentioned these in writing, not even in his autobiography, because like Larsen he was a man of great modesty of character. I record them in this edition as matters of fact; but I am glad Norway saw fit to confer them.

There are other Shetland Bus developments which are so closely related that they should not be overlooked here. One is outlined in Chapter 13, 'Man-Hunt in Lapland', describing the astounding escape of Jan Baalsrud across occupied Norway after *Brattholm*'s betrayal.

This escape, and the selfless help given to Baalsrud by hundreds of Norwegians, became the subject of my father's fourth book. Its title, *We*

Die Alone, was a translation of one of Pascal's 'Thoughts', *On mourra seul*. The philosopher's point was simply that whoever we are and whatever we do, when we die, we die alone: that each death is individual and solitary, the most private and singular of all experiences. This universal spiritual truth was heightened in Baalsrud's case by the fact that when his death was most probable – buried alive for weeks in the snow on the high plateaux of northern Norway – he was physically just about as alone as anyone could be. Thus, to call the book *We Die Alone* was doubly apt and really rather clever, and got past the original hardback publishers; but Collins, its paperback publishers, decided it was another dodgy title, and without consultation changed it to *Escape Alone* — 'which', said my father, 'I thought undistinguished and boring. Billy Collins himself explained that you could not give your aged aunt a Christmas present called *We Die Alone*. "But it's not a book for aged aunts," I told him, too late.'

Further direct Shetland Bus developments came when both these books were filmed. Early in 1991 a nationwide poll in Norway voted *The Shetland Bus* the best Norwegian film ever made. I cannot judge; but I suppose they should know. Certainly it was widely described as 'the most authentic war film ever made', not least because of the unusually (perhaps uniquely) high proportion of the cast who played themselves. The part of Leif Larsen, for example, was played by Larsen himself, and because in real life he always *was* himself, treating kings and commoners exactly the same, he was just as good at acting the role in peacetime as he had been at doing it in wartime. Oddly enough, one of the few people who did not play themselves was my father: he did a screen-test like everyone else, and was told he did not look the part. Instead he was chosen to play a minister and seemed perfectly convincing, while a fine professional actor, Michael Aldridge, made an equally convincing David Howarth.

Obviously, these developments of the theme of the Shetland Bus were of great importance in my father's working life, but by themselves they do not demonstrate Shetland's importance in his inner life. The islands were his home for eleven years, and long before his death he said exactly what he hoped might happen to his remains. By the time he died on 2nd July 1991 he had not lived in Shetland for nearly forty years; he had travelled the world, writing books about Africa, Saudi Arabia, Panama, Greenland and Tibet, as well as several of history's most famous battles on land and sea; and after everything, all that he wanted was for his ashes to be taken back and buried at sea in Lunna Voe, the place where his part in the Shetland Bus really began.

In a bitter-sweet experience on 'a day between two weathers' – one of those blissful unpredictable blue calm sparkling days so treasured in Shetland – I carried out his request with family and friends, using a fishing boat and (as an RNR officer myself, of the same rank that he had held during the bulk of the war) in uniform and in accordance with naval ceremony. But the saga of the Shetland Bus did not end there.

Jan Baalsrud had already died, on 30th December 1988, just twelve days after his 70th birthday. In a rare gesture of honour, King Olav V (son and successor of the wartime King Haakon) sent an inscribed wreath of flowers to the funeral. The following summer in the far north of Norway, Jan's ashes were buried by his daughter and brother in the same grave as one of the men who helped him survive more than half a lifetime before; and the 'Baalsrud March', an invigorating 80-mile trek along his escape route, has taken place in every subsequent summer, as a tribute to all his helpers.

With that 'March' the saga of the Shetland Bus continues; and that is not all. Leif Larsen too had died, at the age of 84, on 12 October 1990: a national hero with many Norwegian honours as well as his incomparable series of British decorations, but unchanged to the last, as modest as he had ever been. And on 8th May 1995, the fiftieth anniversary of VE Day, a statue to his memory and that of all the Busmen was unveiled in Bergen harbour by HRH Crown Prince Haakon.

The Royal Norwegian Navy kindly invited me, my wife and our sons to attend. Naturally we travelled by sea, over waters which the Bus had helped make peaceful. Four of the original vessels (two fishing boats, a small motor yacht and *Hitra*, one of the sub-chasers) were clustered round the quay. *Hitra* was the first sub-chaser to reach Norway, in November 1943, and the only one that still survived. After total restoration she had begun a new career, visiting Shetland often and touring the Norwegian coast each summer, for the interest and instruction of old and young. Seeing all this and meeting the Larsen family (Leif's widow, daughters, sons-in-law and grandchildren) and many veteran soldiers and sailors, my sons began to understand that the Shetland Bus was not simply an old family story, but one of significance abroad, and that VE Day was a great prize for the whole of Europe.

Thus the saga of the Shetland Bus still continues today, in young Shetlanders, in young Norwegians, in my sons, and in others who have started their own voyages across 'the waters beyond'. With its message of hope, courage, endurance and the indomitable desire for freedom, the Bus sails on into a new generation.

Stephen Howarth
Shelton, Nottinghamshire
1998

INDEX